כהן גרוס על החגים

FROM SINAI CAME TORAH

VOLUME I: ESSAYS ON THE JEWISH FESTIVALS BY RABBI RONALD H. GROSS

© 2018 by Rabbi Ronald Gross

908-377-1008

✥ Dedication ✥

This Sefer is dedicated to my wonderful and very special grandchildren

May Hashem bless each and every one of you and grant you all lives with much ברכה והצלחה

May your grandmother and I always merit to receive much continued נחת from all of you.

From Sinai Came Torah: Table of Contents

Rosh HaShanah

1. TO LIVE IN THE HOUSE OF G-D 20
2. ONE MAN'S ATTEMPT DOES MAKE A DIFFERENCE 26
3. ENTHUSIASTIC DETERMINATION 31
4. IF I AM NOT FOR MYSELF, WHO WILL BE FOR ME 39
5. TO BE HUMBLE AND PROUD 44
6. TO BE STIRRED TOWARD OPTIMISM 52
7. STRIVING TODAY FOR A BETTER TOMORROW 58
8. THE SOUNDS OF THE SHOFAR: LAUGHTER AND TEARS 66

Yom Kippur

9. JUDAISM IN ACTION 75
10. FROM CONFUSION TO UNDERSTANDING 81
11. FROM DARKNESS TO SALVATION 86
12. REMEMBERING THE PAST, LIVING THE PRESENT, STRIVING FOR THE FUTURE 96
13. LIVING THROUGH OUR ACTIONS 102
14. LINKING THE PAST TO THE FUTURE 111
15. NOT DYING IN VAIN 118
16. THE WE OF THE JEW, THE I OF THE WORLD 125
17. *ANI YEHUDI* – I AM A JEW 131
18. YOM KIPPURIM—A DAY LIKE PURIM 140

Succos

19. THE UNITY OF ISRAEL 150
20. THE UNIVERSAL SUCCAH 158
21. THE SYNTHESIS OF THE ANCIENT AND THE MODERN 166
22. THE *PITOM* AND THE *OKETZ*: A LESSON IN JEWISH DISTINCTIVENESS 172

Shemini Atzeres - Simchas Torah

23. SACRED TASKS, DIVINE BLESSINGS 180
24. BLESSINGS, NOT CURSES 187
25. THE THREE KEYS TO LIFE 191

Chanukah

26. A BEACON OF LIGHT IN A WORLD OF DARKNESS 196
27. FACING THE ENEMY WITHIN AND WITHOUT 203

Purim
28. ALWAYS REMEMBER – NEVER FORGET 208
29. FASTING AND FEASTING 213

Pesach
30. FREEDOM AND TENACITY 217
31. DAYEINU: APPRECIATING WHAT G-D HAS GIVEN US 225
32. TRANSFORMING BITTERNESS AND SORROW INTO HAPPINESS AND JOY .. 234
33. DEMONSTRATING OUR UNIQUENESS 243
34. WHO KNOWS FOUR: HOW, WHEN, AND WHY 252
35. THE DAWN OF A NEW TOMORROW 261
36. WHY BOTHER WITH TRADITIONS? 269
37. TO BE TEMPTED, OR TO BE THREATENED 280
38. SILENT GRATITUDE VS. EXUBERANT SHIRAH 287
39. UNCOMPLETED SONGS; UNFINISHED TASKS 298
40. IGNITING THE FLAME OF ETERNITY 303

Yom HaShoah
41. DEATH NEED NOT BE FINAL 309

Yom Yerushalayim
42. G-D'S GIFTS AND ISRAEL'S RESPONSIBILITY 315
43. THE MOST BEAUTIFUL WAKE-UP CALL 322

Shavuos
44. SHAVUOS: OUR ULTIMATE FREEDOM 331
45. WHO IS A JEW? 337
46. YIZKOR: OUR UNIQUE MEMORIAL DAY 343
47. TRANSFORMING A DESERT INTO A PARADISE 349

Tisha B'Av
48. A DAY TO MOURN; A TIME TO HOPE 353
INDEX 362

Introduction

After receiving *semicha* from the Rabbi Isaac Elchanan Theological Seminary of Yeshiva University in June of 1971, I became the Jewish chaplain at the Fort Benning army base in Georgia. I served there from 1971 to 1973 as the rabbi of the Jewish community on the base. Towards the conclusion of my tour of duty and with the help of Hashem, I published my first book, *To Illuminate a Darkened Society*. It was based on the sermons, speeches, classes, and writings which I presented to my congregation.

In September, 1973, I was fortunate to be chosen as the Rabbi of Congregation Sinai Torath Chaim in Hillside, New Jersey. For the next five years, I gave weekly sermons, discourses on the Torah portions and the Yom Tovim, and occasional lectures and speeches. Upon my leaving the rabbinate, all these talks and speeches were filed away. They became part of my historic memory for almost 40 years.

Last year, my beloved son-in-law, Rabbi Yaakov Kibel, completed and published a Sefer on the public lectures and speeches of his late father. He began encouraging me to put my past talks into book form. After much contemplation and deliberation, I decided to follow through on this project.

I am publishing these talks mostly for my wonderful family. In particular, these essays are dedicated to my beloved and adorable grandchildren. At present, they range in age from 21 to 3 years old. I hope that this will serve them as a *Mesorah*, a heritage to them from their grandfather. I pray that they will find these words useful and instructive. I hope that they will have as much pride in my efforts as I have in each and every one of them.

This project will hopefully be a three-part endeavor. The first volume consists of *Divrei Torah*, ideas and discourses on the Yom Tovim. The second volume will be based on the weekly Torah portions. The third book will consist of the occasional speeches that I have given both during my years in the rabbinate and the 39 years since. They will be based on the life cycle of the Jew, from the cradle to the grave and everything in between.

Most of the *Drashos* in this volume were dated; they were delivered in the 1970s. Events and specific actions of that era are not really applicable today. I therefore modified and rewrote many of these essays so as to be contemporary and timely. Some, however, by their very nature and content were kept intact. This was done so that the reader will get the flavor of the times and the very specific and important problems and messages of that period.

I have chosen to begin this trilogy with the section on the Yom Tovim. This was based on two *Pesukim* found in Parshas Emor (Vayikra 23:2-3). The Parshah discusses many Halachos and different aspects of the *Chagim*, The Torah says (23:2):

דַּבֵּר אֶל בְּנֵי יִשְׂרָאֵל וְאָמַרְתָּ אֲלֵהֶם מוֹעֲדֵי יְקֹוָק אֲשֶׁר תִּקְרְאוּ אֹתָם מִקְרָאֵי קֹדֶשׁ אֵלֶּה הֵם מוֹעֲדָי:

Tell the Jewish people: The festivals of G-d that you are to designate as a holy convocation . . .

The Gemara in Rosh HaShanah interprets the word אֹתָם as if it were read אַתֶּם, meaning, "you." This means that you, the Jewish people, represented by Beis Din on earth, will designate when Yom Tov will occur. This Halacha is buttressed by a Midrash in which the *Malachim* ask Hashem, "When will Rosh HaShanah occur? Hashem responds, "Let us go down to the בית דין של מטה, the earthly court, to see what they have decreed."

My Rosh Yeshivah, the Rav, HaRav Yosef Dov Soloveitchik *zt"l*, explains that this demonstrates in no uncertain terms that Hashem has given over to man something of Himself, a part of His divine powers. Even on Rosh HaShanah when Hashem judges כל העולם כולו, all of mankind, we puny human beings are given the right to decide when this day will occur. The Rav says that this demonstrates that man can create *Kedusha*, holiness. It is for man to build and develop that sanctity. This is done through our Mitzvos and *Ma'asim Tovim*.

This is not, however, the same with Shabbos. That day is determined solely by Hashem. The Torah says in the subsequent verse (23:3):

שֵׁשֶׁת יָמִים תֵּעָשֶׂה מְלָאכָה וּבַיּוֹם הַשְּׁבִיעִי שַׁבַּת שַׁבָּתוֹן מִקְרָא קֹדֶשׁ כָּל מְלָאכָה לֹא תַעֲשׂוּ שַׁבָּת הִוא לַיקֹוָק בְּכֹל מוֹשְׁבֹתֵיכֶם:

For a six-day period, labor may be done, but the seventh day is a day of complete rest, a holy convocation; you are to do no work. It is a Sabbath for Hashem in all your settled places.

Shabbos occurs every seventh day. On that day, Hashem rested, and thus we are to do the same.

HaRav Yaakov Kamenetzky *zt"l* in his *Emes L'Yaakov* says that Hashem, and He alone transformed the seventh day of the week, the Shabbos, into a *Yom Kadosh*, a holy and sanctified day. It is as if Hashem said, "I have sanctified the Shabbos; now I give to you, the Jewish people, the power and the permission to make the Yom Tovim sacrosanct." As Shabbos has its very own special *Kedusha*, so too should the Yom Tovim be infused with its own holiness and sanctity.

On Shabbos during the *Shemoneh Esrei*, the silent *Amidah* we say:

ברוך אתה ה' מקדש השבת.

Hashem alone transforms the seventh day of the week into *Shabbos Kodesh*, a day of holiness. He then passes this *Kedusha* to us. We then, in turn, infuse Divine venerability into the *Regalim*. Thus, on Yom Tov we say:

ברוך אתה ה' מקדש ישראל והזמנים.

This idea of man's aiding, assisting, and transforming the world from one of emptiness and darkness to completeness and illumination and our adding *Kedusha* to the world is the theme of many of the *Drashos*. It is about how and what we do to make this world a better place. We come with an optimistic and positive view of the future.

Hashem produced *Kedusha*, holiness. He then gave some of it to us. The rest is up to Klal Yisrael to make ourselves into an *Am Nivchar* and an *Am Kadosh*, a chosen and a holy nation. Hopefully, by our actions, by our *Ma'asim Tovim*, we will be able to, at the very least, ignite the eternal flame of destiny. This will, *im yirtzeh Hashem*, eventually illuminate all of mankind and make the world a better and safer place for all

The title of this book is very special to me. Most of the chapters are based on the sermons given at my shul, Sinai Torath Chaim. I spent five wonderful and glorious years at that synagogue with my congregants who were all very kind, considerate, and very supportive. We developed a truly outstanding relationship. I therefore chose to commemorate those years by naming the title of my book after the basis and origin of my talks: מסיני תצא תורה – *From Sinai Came Torah*.

Ronald H. Gross
August 27, 2018

צבי הירש גרוס
ט"ז אלול תשע"ח

Acknowledgements

There are a number people to whom I owe a huge debt of gratitude and who I wish to acknowledge and give thanks.

I must first be מכיר טוב to *HaKadosh Baruch Hu* for the constant and abiding love which He has shown me over all these years. He has given me the opportunity to be able to write and deliver my sermons and speeches. I believe with all my heart and soul that if we but put our trust and faith in Hashem, at the end of the day, we cannot fail. All that occurs, both the good and the perceived bad, is all *bashert*. It is all predestined, from Hashem.

I would like to acknowledge my exceptional and marvelous children, Frumie and Hillel Drebin, Aryeh and Goldie Gross, and Dena and Yaakov Kibel. Besides being so caring and concerned for all our needs, they have always been there for both Rivkie and myself in every situation. In the Mitzvah of כיבוד אב ואם they have no parallel. They have always gone לפנים משורת הדין, over and above the call of duty.

All my children have been my inspiration and motivation to carry on and complete this project. They each have given me ideas and suggestions which I have incorporated into this book. I want to wish them and their fantastic children, our darling grandchildren, good health, mazel, and beracha in all their endeavors. May they all continue to serve Hashem and their respective communities in the truly regal and beautiful manner in which they lead their lives and in their total commitment to ה' יתברך.

I would like to especially single out and thank from the bottom of my heart my very dear son-in-law, Rabbi Yaakov Dovid Kibel. He gave me the idea and the impetus to explore this project. He has also served continuously as my editor-in-chief. He personally read, reviewed, and critiqued each and every chapter. He assisted me in transforming these *derashos* from the spoken word to the written text.

He constantly gave his input and offered countless suggestions and מאמרי חז"ל to enhance and make the book readable and up-to-date. His masterful comprehension of the English language and his encyclopedic knowledge of both the תורה שבכתב and the תורה שבעל פה and the various מפרשים have contributed greatly to this book. He may have remained in the background and behind the scenes. However, without his help and assistance, this project would never have gotten off the ground. It never would have seen the light of day, and it certainly would not have come to fruition.

In addition, I wish also to acknowledge his *Aishes Chayil,* my youngest daughter Dena, for allowing Yaakov to spend so much time in order to help me with my "labor of love." In addition, I want to sincerely thank Dena for her yeoman's work in proofreading each and every chapter. She too gave several valuable and constructive suggestions.

I wish both of them continued success in their professional lives and in their truly great commitment to *HaKadosh Baruch Hu* and *Klal Yisrael.*

Finally, אחרונה אחרונה חביבה, to my beloved wife Rivkie. She has, for all these years, been my rock and my anchor both in good times and during challenging situations. She alone, more than any other person in the world, helped me develop into a better and more compassionate and caring person.

Her love, commitment, and her total loyalty to her family, both immediate and extended, is remarkable and truly inspirational. Her giving of herself to her many friends is legendary. It serves as a shining example that we can all emulate.

Rivkie served for almost two decades as the college guidance and seminary advisor at the Bruriah girls high school division of the Jewish Educational Center. In that capacity, she endeared herself to all the girls with whom she came in contact. Her advice was always most intuitive. She spent countless hours getting to know the students, their needs, and their capabilities.

My wife geared her advice to the girls in a non-judgmental manner; indeed, it was given with compassion and love. She instinctively knew what each girl needed and what the proper vehicle was for them to get the maximum growth and development both spiritually and intellectually.

Rivkie created a warm and unique bond with many of her students. Many of the girls continue to call upon her for help and advice in making life decisions. She always says that Bruriah was great for her. That may be true. However, in actuality, she was great for Bruriah.

My *Eishes Chayil* has also listened to each and every one of these *Drashos* both while we served in the rabbinate and in the years since. She has always given her very intuitive, thoughtful, and insightful suggestions. If I have produced a book which is instructive and readable, she deserves a tremendous amount of credit.

In addition, I am forever grateful to her for being such an incredible, loving, and wonderful wife. Her entire raison d'être is her devotion and dedication to my well-being and to the welfare of our children and our grandchildren. She is not only the perfect partner in my life, she is also my best friend and the person whom I most want to spend every waking minute with.

The Gemara in Kesuvos (63a) quotes the great and legendary Rabbi Akiva. When talking to his *Talmidim* about his beloved wife Rachel, he said, "שלי ושלכם שלה הוא" "Whatever learning that is mine and the learning that is yours all belongs to her. She deserves all the credit for all of our knowledge."

To you, Rivkie, I can truly say, "To you I owe everything." May Hashem bless you with good health, happiness, and continued *nachas* from our wonderful and remarkable family. May *HaKadosh Baruch Hu* grant us the *zechus*, the merit, to share many more years together with *gezunt,* good health. May we be blessed to grow old together and continue to be there for each other.

In Memoriam:

To the two men who have had the most profound impact on my life:

My dear, beloved, and very special father, Moses P. Gross

אבי מורי, ר' משה פסח ניסן בן ר' צבי הירש הכהן עליו השלום

    My father was a man of great principles and impeccable integrity. His love and concern for his fellow man was only surpassed by his affection and dedication to his family. He was a devoted and loving son to his widowed mother. He also took care of his elderly aunt who never married and thought of my father as the child she never had. His love for my mother and caring for all her needs became the hallmark of his life. They were each completely dedicated to one another heart and soul. In addition, he always had הכרת הטוב to his older sister and brother-in-law for helping him grow and develop and provide him with a דרך הישר during his formative college years.

    His commitments to תפילה בציבור, לימוד התורה, and all other aspects of Yiddishkeit was uncompromising and unalterable. He lived his relatively short life helping others. He assisted the poor, the needy, and the downtrodden. He performed many private acts of Tzedakah, giving of his own money or arranging for interest free loans, as well as personally guaranteeing those loans. These חסדים only became known to us during the Shivah and beyond by individuals who were the recipients of his kindness and concern.

He made constant visits to the hospitals to see his ailing friends and cater to all their needs, bringing them joy and *chizuk* when they were quite ill. His emotional support to the families was a great source of solace and comfort. They always knew that when they needed a shoulder to cry on, a hand to hold, and a good and solid עצה, they could always count on Moe Gross.

He often went to multiple shuls on Yom Tovim in addition to his own minyan in order to *duchen* for those who did not have a kohen. He was very proud that he was a descendant of Aharon HaKohen; this, in fact, was his modus operandi. Like his illustrious ancestor, he was a true אוהב שלום ורודף שלום.

My father worked tirelessly for a number of Jewish institutions in his Borough Park community. His great love was Yeshiva Toras Emes Kamenetz, where he was an officer and board member for over 30 years.

My father also served as a gabbai in his weekday shul, Congregation Bnai Yehudah, for over two decades. In that capacity he was kind, fair, and just. He carried out his duties very admirably and compassionately.

He taught me to help and assist any and every Jew who needed a helping hand. He taught me never to turn down anyone who needs help and assistance, regardless of his religious observance or affiliation. He taught me to be fair and open-minded to each and every person. Mostly, he taught me to never straddle the fence when action is required. He used to say, "Whoever straddles the fence is bound to fall off."

It was my great pleasure to have worked together with my father in business for 12 years. Most importantly and much more significantly, it was my great privilege and honor to have had him as a father and as a mentor. He epitomized everything a father should be. He truly represented the Mishnah in פרקי אבות:

על שלשה דברים העולם עומד על התורה ועל העבודה ועל גמילות חסדים.
The world rests on three things: on Torah, on devotion (prayer), and acts and deeds of lovingkindness.

That was my father. As someone said to me during the Shiva, "With his passing, the Orthodox community of Boro Park will never be the same." 28 years after his *petirah*, indeed, it has not been the same.

My wonderful and very special father-in-law, Rabbi Samuel L. Fink
מורי חמי, הרב יהושע בן ר' ראובן זצ"ל

Rabbi Fink was an outstanding rabbi, a teacher par excellence, and an enormous *Talmid Chacham*. He devoted himself heart and soul to the Jewish community for over 60 years. He served as a congregational rabbi in Utica and Syracuse, New York, in Passaic, New Jersey, and for over 50 years in Brooklyn, New York at the Young Israel of Bedford Bay. He taught Torah and helped thousands of Jews come closer to real, genuine, and authentic Yiddishkeit. In additional to his rabbinical capacity, he taught Talmud for over 40 years at Yeshiva University. His care and concern for the students was legendary. To this day, many credit him for helping mold their lives as Torah-true Jewish adults. He was a leader of men, a teacher's teacher and a rabbi's Rabbi.

In his capacity as a shul Rav, he impacted the lives of hundreds of his congregants. With his outstanding sermons, his erudite lectures, his brilliant teaching of Chumash and Gemara, and his overall love for each congregant, he made a tremendous impact on all his *ba'alei batim*.

Many who had not previously been religious were influenced by him to commit to a life of Torah-true Judaism. Not only did they become *Shomer Shabbos,* but their children, grandchildren, and even great grandchildren have remained *frum* and have built lives dedicated to authentic Judaism.

I firmly believe that the Mishnah in Tractate Sanhedrin (4:5) truly encapsulates my father-in-law and his manifold contributions to *Yahadus*. The Mishna says:

וכל המקיים נפש אחת מישראל מעלה עליו הכתוב כאילו קיים עולם מלא.

He who saves the life of one Jew is considered as if he saved an entire world.

For his heroic acts of saving hundreds and hundreds of families and now generations of Jews, he is, I am sure on the highest rung and plateau of עולם הבא.

He served with distinction as the president of the National Council of Young Israel Rabbis. For many years he was at the helm and was the heart and soul and the very conscience of the Vaad HaRabanim of Flatbush, earning him the respect and admiration of *Gedolim* such as Rav Moshe Feinstein zt"l, Rav Aharon Kotler zt"l, and Rav Yisrael Belsky zt"l.

First and foremost, however, he loved and cherished his family. He was totally devoted to them. He served as a role model par excellence. On numerous occasions, he declined leadership roles in the American rabbinate. He did so because he wanted to help and lead his family during some very difficult and trying times. His dedication and devotion to my late mother-in-law was so very special and beautiful. When she became ill, his only thought was to help and be a source of strength and support to her.

He was the rock and source of strength to his children. He was responsible for their growth and development into great *Talmidei Chachamim* and leaders in the Jewish community. Mostly, he instilled in them a love and comradery for each other, teaching them to always be there for one another. This has made the family a loving and caring unit to this day. The affection, the respect, and the support which they exhibit towards each other has not weakened at all with the passage of time; moreover, it continues to strengthen each year. It truly serves as an inspiration to us all.

On a most personal level, he treated me as a beloved son. He demonstrated care, concern, and a great deal of love. He helped me develop as a rabbi. Much more importantly, he helped me become a better husband, father, and grandfather.

There is hardly a day that goes by that I do not think of these two giants of men. I love them so much, and I continuously miss their presence and their counsel. I am however, profoundly grateful to them for helping me become a more productive human being and a devoted and dedicated Jew.

יהי זכרם ברוך. May their memories forever be a blessing and an inspiration to us all.

ROSH HASHANAH

1. To Live in the House of G-d
Rosh HaShanah 5778 (2017)
בככסה ליום חגנו

There is a very interesting and instructive phrase which is recited on Shabbos at the Ma'ariv and Shacharis services as well as in the Kiddush of Shabbos morning:

וְשָׁמְרוּ בְנֵי יִשְׂרָאֵל אֶת הַשַׁבָּת לַעֲשׂוֹת אֶת הַשַׁבָּת לְדֹרֹתָם בְּרִית עוֹלָם: בֵּינִי וּבֵין בְּנֵי יִשְׂרָאֵל אוֹת הִוא לְעֹלָם כִּי שֵׁשֶׁת יָמִים עָשָׂה ה' אֶת הַשָׁמַיִם וְאֶת הָאָרֶץ וּבַיּוֹם הַשְׁבִיעִי שָׁבַת וַיִּנָּפַשׁ:

And the children of Israel shall keep the Sabbath to make the Sabbath an eternal covenant for the generations; between Me and the children of Israel it is a sign forever that in six days Hashem created the heavens and the earth and on the seventh day He rested and was refreshed.

Shabbos, therefore, is a memorial for בריאת העולם. Hashem created the world and rested on the seventh day. That is the theme and the modus operandi of Shabbos.

On the Shalosh Regalim we say:

אֵלֶּה מוֹעֲדֵי ה' מִקְרָאֵי קֹדֶשׁ אֲשֶׁר תִּקְרְאוּ אֹתָם בְּמוֹעֲדָם: וַיְדַבֵּר מֹשֶׁה אֶת מֹעֲדֵי ה' אֶל בְּנֵי יִשְׂרָאֵל:

These are the appointed festivals of G-d, holy convocations which you are to proclaim in their appointed times. And Moshe declared to the children of Israel the appointed festivals.

On Yom Kippur, just prior to the Shemoneh Esrei at Ma'ariv we say:

כִּי בַיּוֹם הַזֶּה יְכַפֵּר עֲלֵיכֶם לְטַהֵר אֶתְכֶם מִכֹּל חַטֹּאתֵיכֶם לִפְנֵי ה' תִּטְהָרוּ:

For through this day will He atone for you to purify you; from all your sins before G-d, you will be purified.

Each of these prayers appear to pinpoint and focus on the

various aspects of Shabbos and the Yom Tovim. On Rosh HaShanah, we also recite a *tefillah* which, on the one hand, clearly captures the moment of the day, but at the same time, a phrase is added which begs a question:

תִּקְעוּ בַחֹדֶשׁ שׁוֹפָר בַּכֶּסֶה לְיוֹם חַגֵּנוּ: כִּי חֹק לְיִשְׂרָאֵל הוּא מִשְׁפָּט לֵאלֹקֵי יַעֲקֹב:

Blow the Shofar at the moon's renewal, at the time of the hiding of the moon on our holiday. For it is a decree for Israel, the judgment day for the G-d of Jacob.

Most of this prayer is extremely germane and pertinent to Rosh HaShanah. It talks of the blowing of the Shofar and the fact that Rosh HaShanah is a day of judgment, a day of *din*. However, what is quite puzzling is the term בכסה ליום חגנו – "At the time of the hiding of the moon." I ask you, my friends, what is its meaning? What is its significance? Does it have any relevance for us?

HaRav Soloveitchik zt"l, in the *Machzor Mesoras HaRav* on Rosh HaShanah offers a few explanations. The first answer is that כסה is related to the word כסא, the chair, the Throne of Hashem. On Rosh HaShanah, the main theme is the re-coronation of *HaKadosh Baruch Hu*, the מלך העולם. Thus, the word כסה is not referring to the moon being hidden. Rather, it talks about the sovereignty of G-d and the כסא הכבוד, the Royal Throne upon which He sits.

The second and perhaps the most basic explanation is found in the Gemara Rosh HaShanah. It says that on the other Yom Tovim the moon is quite visible. This is so because the Yom Tovim begin between the sixth (Shavuos) and the 15th day of the month (Pesach and Sukkos). However, Rosh HaShanah begins on the first day of the month of Tishrei, on Rosh Chodesh. At that time, the moon is almost completely hidden; it is practically invisible. We are enveloped in the blackness and the darkness of the night.

The question, my friends, is why does the Torah have to make mention of this fact? What special meaning is there for us? The fact of the matter is that it is both very important and quite significant. It imparts a very unique message for us.

As we look out at the world around us, we see so much darkness. We see almost a total and complete blackout—as if an eclipse of the sun has occurred. Whether it be the leaders of the rogue nation, North Korea, who are flexing their muscles and are threatening to attack the United States with weapons of mass destruction, or the mullahs in Iran who continue to build their nuclear arsenal. They pose a very serious, dangerous and existential threat to our brothers and sisters in Eretz Yisrael.

Countries throughout the world are ramping up the pressure on Medinat Yisrael to reach a peaceful solution with the Palestinian Authority. That would, of course, result in the creation of a Palestinian state. In essence, Israel would be forced to give up hard fought for land which presently serves as a buffer between them and their Arab foes. The world does not see this territory as being part of and belonging to the Jewish historical homeland. Rather, they see it as "occupied territory." The world insists that in any agreement, Israel would have to relinquish at least a part of Jerusalem.

It is quite interesting that in Tanach, in our *Tefillos,* and throughout *Shas,* the word "Yerushalayim" is mentioned thousands of times. In fact, just this coming week, on the third day of *Aseres Yemei Teshuvah* we read a *Selichah* which is entitled "Yerushalayim." In that prayer, the word "Yerushalayim" is mentioned 45 times. Yerushalayim, as the capital of Israel, was established almost 3,000 years ago by Dovid HaMelech. Yerushalayim has always been and always will be our מקום קדש and our עיר הקדש, our most holy city.

I doubt very much that within the many Moslem prayers which are recited daily there is even one mention of Jerusalem. It certainly does not appear even once in their holy book, the Koran. How bizarre, how hypocritical, how counterintuitive it is that we may be forced to compromise and give up a city that is so holy and meaningful to us to a people who do not even consider it important enough to include it in its most holy texts.

Throughout Europe, our fellow Jews are quite afraid and fearful for their very lives. Not since the end of World War II has European Jewry felt so vulnerable and in danger for their safety and for their very future.

In addition, in the past two months, the world has experienced major cataclysmic and devastating natural catastrophes. We have seen three catastrophic hurricanes, two devastating earthquakes, and ravaging forest fires that have gone unabated. All this has caused much carnage and death in a number of communities in this country and beyond. They have practically decimated some islands in the Caribbean and left severe destruction in Mexico.

Here in the United States, we are witness to an enormous and terrible divide. There is so much discontent, division and alienation between different segments of our population. There has not been such hatred and divisiveness in this country in almost 50 years. It seems that each day the situation gets worse and worse. The disunity may G-d forbid, cause us eventual internal catastrophe.

The question, my friends, is why is there so much darkness in the world? Why are we experiencing so many problems and disasters at this very time? We can posit, perhaps, that all the negative and catastrophic events that we are experiencing now is because it appears that Hashem is judging us harshly with his attribute of *Midas HaDin*. Rav Soloveitchik, in *Reflections of the Rav*, explains that "*Midas HaDin* involves a measure for measure punishment commensurate with our sins. This does not signify G-d's withdrawal from the world. On the contrary, it reflects His involvement and concern for mankind. This is intended primarily for one reason to stimulate us to Teshuvah, repentance. This serves as a model for us to do better and to lead a more productive, more fulfilling, and more spiritual life."

In addition, our rabbis say that just prior to the Yom HaDin, Rosh Hashanah, Hashem removes some of His light from the world. Although His presence still remains, it is hidden and barely visible. If this be the case, what can we do to bring it back? Are we capable of turning around this *Midas HaDin*? Are we able to influence *HaKadosh Baruch Hu* to return to us and once again judge us with the attributes of love and forgiveness, *Midas HaRachamim*? Rav Soloveitchik says that it is only through a change in our lives, through *Teshuvah Gemurah*, that G-d's closeness can be restored.

On Rosh HaShanah, Jews the world over acknowledge and honor Hashem as *Melech HaOlam*, the sovereign ruler of the entire universe. Only through our *Tefillos* and our blowing of the Shofar to awaken us from our slumber will Hashem reconnect and reestablish His relationship with the world. Our current state of darkness will be dispelled and we will see His illumination. At that time, we will be witness to a new, different, and most powerful light. Only at that time will the world be able to develop, to grow, and to thrive.

The first move, however, must come from us. We have to take the initiative. We must take the first step. It behooves us to reaffirm our commitment, our faith, and our loyalty to the *Ribono shel Olam*. We can accomplish this with Tzedakah, acts of lovingkindness, with Teshuvah, a complete and total repentance, and of course, we need to give our *Tefillos*, our sincere prayers and supplications.

Perhaps this is the reason that we recite the 27th chapter of Tehillim twice a day from Rosh Chodesh Elul through Shemini Atzeres. In this *kapitel*, we acknowledge that Hashem is our light and our salvation. If we only put our complete trust and *bitachon* in Hashem, we will never fear anyone or anything.

There is, however, one phrase in this chapter that is puzzling. We say:

אַחַת שָׁאַלְתִּי מֵאֵת ה' אוֹתָהּ אֲבַקֵּשׁ שִׁבְתִּי בְּבֵית ה' כָּל יְמֵי חַיַּי ...
One thing I ask of Hashem, that is my request, that You allow me to

dwell in the House of the L-rd all the days of my life.

The Malbim questions this sentence. How can one say that he is only asking for one thing? In essence, we request from G-d a number of things. We continue to ask for many more *bakashos* from Hashem. The Jew requests health, peace, and defeat of our foes. The Malbim answers: while it is true that the Jew is making many requests from Hashem, nevertheless, if he will be granted this one בקשה to live and be in the house of Hashem, then all his בקשות will be answered. If we will be able to cleave to the *Kisei HaKavod,* then all our requests will be heard and responded to in the affirmative. At that time, no force on earth, no evildoers, no foes, not even a great and foreboding army will be able to harm us or destroy us.

We can now understand *Chazal's* interpretation of the *posuk* that Rosh HaShanah occurs at the time when the moon is almost completely hidden, when there is a lack of spiritual light. This teaches us that only through our actions and deeds, our *Ma'asim Tovim*, can we bring Hashem's illumination back into our lives and to all of society. Only by our behavior can we change our judgement from *Midas HaDin* to *Midas HaRachamim.*

Let us therefore resolve on this Rosh HaShanah to do our part to put our complete and total trust, our *bitachon*, in *HaKadosh Baruch Hu.* If we do this, then all our requests will be fulfilled, especially our main *bakasha:*

שָׁבְתִּי בְּבֵית ה' כָּל יְמֵי.

I wish each of you a כתיבה וחתימה טובה; a gut and a gebenched year.

2. One Man's Attempt Does Make a Difference
Rosh HaShanah, Day One, 5738 (1977)

The Torah reading for today centers around the birth of the second Jew: Yitzchak, the son of Avraham and Sarah. This was, perhaps, the most important event in Jewish history, for the entire promise of G-d to Avraham concerning his descendants rested on this one child. He would carry on the teachings of his father and pass them on to his children. The Haftorah for today also discusses the birth of one child, the future prophet and Jewish leader Samuel.

It seems rather strange that the emphasis in the selected scriptural writings for this day of Rosh HaShanah is about one individual, for this holiday stresses the collective unity of the Jewish nation, not the individualistic aspect of our people. As we allude to in today's *Tefillos*, today is the anniversary of the creation of the first man, the father of us all, Adam HaRishon. *HaYom Haras Olam.*

The Gemara in Kidushin, which is elaborated upon in the Rambam, provides us with an answer to our dilemma. Each person, every member of mankind, should regard himself as half guilty and half meritorious. If he performs just one good deed, one mitzvah, he will be saved. If on the other hand he should perform even a single transgression, he will be punished. In the same vein, each of us should consider the entire world as half guilty and half righteous. Whatever action we do will determine the fate of the world. Thus, we see that one man's actions and deeds can indeed help create or destroy an entire world. Thus, our Torah and Haftorah reading.

Rabbi Yitzchak Luria, the Ari HaKadosh, explains why the *viduy*, the confessional, is in the plural rather than in the singular. He says כל ישראל ערבים זה לזה. Each Jew, all of Israel, is one body and each of us is considered as one limb of that body. Thus, even if we may not be personally guilty of the various individual sins for which

Rosh HaShanah

we confess on the *Yomim Noraim*, we nevertheless recite them. We do this because of the cohesiveness and unity of all of Israel. The victories and defeats, the joys and the sorrows of one element of Israel are shared by each of us.

The Midrash Tanchuma on Beraishis sheds light on this idea when it comments on the verse concerning Yitzchak's birth. The Torah says (Genesis 21:1):

וה' פקד את שרה...

And G-d remembered Sarah...

The Midrash says that at the time that Avraham davened for Avimelech to be fertile, the angels said to Hashem: "Almighty G-d, Avraham heals others, and yet it is he who is in need of assistance. Why do You not heal Avraham?"

Then G-d responded, "He indeed is worthy of being healed and granted children." And then the Torah says – וה' פקד את שרה.

On Rosh HaShanah and on Yom Kippur, we pray for a year of health and prosperity. However, we also pray and pledge to work for the benefit of others. Our peace and well-being must be intimately bound up with what we can do for our fellow human beings. Thus, not only can our deeds make a difference in the continuity of mankind, but our personal efforts on behalf of others will in the long run benefit ourselves as well.

This idea is applicable in all areas of life, whether it be our Tzedakah to the poor, aid to religious institutions, helping our oppressed brethren throughout the world, international struggles for Jewish rights and especially in regard to our brethren in the State of Israel. It is absolutely imperative that we not only work diligently on their behalf but we do so with one mind and as one person. We cannot afford to be divided into countless and different camps on the important life and death issues facing the Jewish State.

Israel has been recently under a great deal of pressure to return "conquered territory" and make peace and create a Two-State entity for Eretz Yisrael.

Now that Menachem Begin has been elected prime minister, this will not happen, thank G-d, any time in the near future.

I personally have a great deal of respect for Mr. Begin. He is a man of high principles. He is hard-nosed and has great pride in the historical essence of עם ישראל and ארץ ישראל. It is truly rewarding that we finally have a man at the helm of the Jewish State who is a traditional and proud Jew. He demonstrates his Jewishness unashamedly before the eyes of the world.

The problem is that too many of our coreligionists are still bothered by the fact that a "terrorist" and an "extremist" is the leader of Israel. Many join in the chorus of those who chastise his every move and act merely because he was the commander of the Irgun, the underground Jewish army in pre-statehood days.

Contrary to widespread beliefs, the Irgun was not a murderous and bloodthirsty terrorist group. Their only aim was to rid Palestine of the British who were hindering and destroying the prospects for a free and independent Jewish State.

Our task therefore is quite great. Each of us in our own personal way, in our own communities, must help guarantee the survival of Israel. We must do so by helping the present government remain strong and firm. It must know that it has wide and diversified support from amongst American and world Jewry.

We must in earnest begin a widespread campaign of public relations. We have to inform the entire world about the justness and correctness of Israel's desire to live in peace within secure boundaries. If in the past our brethren in Eretz Yisrael have relied on us for economic assistance, moral support, and public pressure, there is no doubt that they need us now more than ever.

However, many of us will rightfully ask how we, average, middle-class Americans, can influence U.S. policy. How can we alone guarantee that our homeland will be secure and remain strong? The answer is that while we cannot be assured of ultimate success, we are nevertheless not relieved of the duty of working diligently on their behalf.

The Chasam Sofer, the great 19th century scholar and rabbinic leader, sheds light on this problem with an analysis of a sentence in the Parshah of a few weeks ago. In the portion of Ki Seitzei, the first sentence begins:

כי תצא למלחמה על אויביך...

"When the Jewish people go out to battle with their enemy…" Why are the words כי תצא למלחמה, "When *you go out to battle*," used instead of the more proper כי תלחם, "When *you do battle*"? The Chasam Sofer says that man's *Yetzer Hora*, his Evil Inclination, is his greatest enemy. We are, at all times, called upon to battle and attempt to fight him. However, how can we constantly do battle with someone who is so elusive and always on the move? Thus, says the sage of Pressburg, the Torah does not tell us כי תלחם – "When you *complete* the battle," but כי תצא למלחמה – "When you even *go out* to war," when you just attempt and take the first step toward battling your enemy or helping save your brethren. Even then you will be assured of victory and salvation.

Therefore, today on Rosh HaShanah, let us remember that even one person can make a difference. One individual can indeed help change the course of history. Our actions and deeds on behalf of others – if done while we stand united and act as one, with a common purpose – will not only help them but will also help ourselves and our entire people. But most important, we ought to remember that even if we cannot fulfill all of our ideals and goals, as long as we make the effort, we and our people will survive and flourish. Amen.

3. Enthusiastic Determination
Rosh HaShanah Day 2, 5737 (1976)
עקידת יצחק-רחל מבכה על בניה

It is the rare individual who is not stirred or moved to action by an emotional, passionate, and heart-rending appeal. It is only he who is disinterested and self-centered who will sit on the sidelines at a time when he is called upon to perform an act or deed of historic proportions and monumental significance. Oftentimes, the performance of this act is directly opposite and totally contradictory to human intellect and rational thinking. However, one fulfills the request because of his absolute confidence in the person who makes the appeal. Unfortunately, at times, this approach has been used by demagogues to whip crowds and adherents into a frenzy and hypnotize them into doing something which is both incorrect and wrong.

However, this has also been utilized to bring man to the highest degree of spiritual achievement. We read about this in our Torah portion this morning on the second day of Rosh HaShanah – the *Akeidah*.

Avraham, the first Jew, the rationalist par excellence, is asked by Hashem to take his son Yitzchok and offer him as a sacrifice. In yesterday's Torah section, we read how Hashem promised Avraham that Yitzchok will carry on his tradition of monotheism: כי ביצחק יקרא לך זרע – "It is Yitzchak who will be regarded as your son." Nevertheless, Avraham does not stop and think of the contradictory nature of this request. No, Avraham, the true believer, the knight of faith, set aside his own feelings and desires, his hopes and aspirations, in order to unhesitatingly fulfill the will of Hashem.

In fact, the very next morning he arose early and personally prepared for this awesome journey. By this monumental act of faith,

Avraham proved his greatness and his contribution to Judaism and to humanity.

However, the Kotzker Rebbe, the great Chassidic master, explains that Avraham's greatness lies in an altogether different area. While it certainly was difficult for Avraham to accept G-d's decree and to suppress his own very personal feelings, this, he says, was not Avraham's most distinct quality. It is not too difficult to exhibit an initial flash of enthusiasm and zeal at the suggestion of a great undertaking. However, what happens when a day or two passes? Will the same fervor and devotion remain, or will it wane and eventually dissipate? It is this idea, says the Kotzker Rebbe, that made Avraham the great patriarch whose example his descendants were to follow and emulate.

The Akeidah, the proposed sacrifice of Yitzchak, did not occur immediately after G-d's request and Avraham's instant acceptance.

בַּיּוֹם הַשְּׁלִישִׁי וַיִּשָּׂא אַבְרָהָם אֶת עֵינָיו וַיַּרְא אֶת הַמָּקוֹם מֵרָחֹק:
On the third day Abraham looked up and saw the place from a distance.

Avraham, says the Kotzker Rebbe, had the same burning desire, the same willingness to fulfill G-d's command to sacrifice his son on the third day as he did on the first. This is why the *Malach* said to him:

... כִּי עַתָּה יָדַעְתִּי כִּי יְרֵא אֱלֹקִים אַתָּה ...
For now I know that you are a fearer of Hashem…

My friends, so often during these Yomim Noroim we make personal pledges and promises that we will become better human beings. We will be true to our faith and to our tradition. We will become more pious, more devoted to Hashem and to Yiddishkeit. We will observe Shabbos and Yom Tovim to the fullest. We will adhere to the strictest forms of Kashrus. We will attend shul as much as possible. We will always be available to help make minyanim.

The faith of our ancestors will once again become our own and it will be left as an inheritance to our children and our grandchildren. We sit together during these days of awe and make resolutions. We are stirred and awakened by the sound of the Shofar. We are motivated by the moving words and chants of the countless and beautiful *tefillos*.

Today we are filled with enthusiasm, zeal and sincerity. The question is: can this be sustained? Will it last until "the third day," or will it disappear as soon as we begin to rationalize, as we begin to allow our intellect to question the decisions made by our heart? Rosh HaShanah is the first day. Our rabbis tell us that the two days of Rosh HaShanah are considered as a *Yoma Arichta,* one long, continuous day – instead of a two-day festival. Yom Kippur is of course a one-day holiday, and it marks the second day. The challenge that we face is on the third day. Will we still be fired up with the desire and devotion on the day after Yom Kippur as we are today? Will we follow in the path of Avraham and leave our mark on the world, or, will we sink into oblivion and leave no trace of our existence?

All too often, there have been world events and occurrences which could have conceivably helped change the course of human affairs. Unfortunately, however, they were looked upon both by Jews as well as by non-Jews as momentary, fleeting incidents which were relatively insignificant. The 1967 Six Day War and the 1973 Yom Kippur conflict are prime examples. Had those wars been seen not merely as periodic flareups between antagonists but in their proper perspective as further acts in the Divine plan, we would have been much better off today.

In each of these contests, the *Yad Hashem*, the Hand of G-d, was so real and evident. We were, however, blinded by the scent of victory and the exhilaration of conquest. For the first few weeks after these wars, Jews by the thousands purchased and began to daily put on Tefillin. Israelis began to become more concerned with their religion and faith. They made commitments to send their children to yeshivas so that they might be better equipped and prepared to deal with the real problems facing our people. However, after a few months, and certainly after a number of years, the enthusiasm waned. The idealism disappeared and the dreams vanished. We have allowed this golden opportunity to escape us.

However, on July 4, 1976, Hashem, in His infinite wisdom, with kindness and compassion, gave us another chance and another occasion to change ourselves and the entire world. On that day, in which the United States commemorated its bicentennial, Israeli paratroopers flew thousands of miles to Entebbe Airport in Uganda. These brave heroes rescued more than 100 of their coreligionists and the flight crew who were being held hostage by Palestinian terrorists and the Ugandan armed forces who enabled and aided these murderers.

That event, unprecedented in military history, helped raise the morale and served as a shot in the arm to the Jewish community throughout the world. We had been depressed, despondent and pessimistic about our future. For the 2 ½ years since the conclusion of the Yom Kippur War, Israel, both the nation and the people, was subjected to invectives, threats, and economic boycotts. Suddenly it all seemed to turn around. When the same knife that was to slay our father Yitzchak was approaching our own, out of the clear came the Voice and the Hand of the Ribono Shel Olam:

עַתָּה יָדַעְתִּי כִּי יְרֵא אֱלֹקִים אַתָּה

"Now I know that you are a fearer of the L-rd."

But my friends, did we respond as did our father Avraham? Did we become more concerned and dedicated to our people and to Hashem? Yes, for a while, it seemed and appeared that we were about to witness the ביאת המשיח, the coming of the Messiah. Jews befriend Jews. We hugged, kissed and greeted each other with happiness and with hope in the future. The stories from the survivors of Entebbe were filled with nothing but the miraculous details of how they survived. The *Yad Hashem*, the Hand of G-d that was so apparent in the victory by our brethren, now, at last, appeared to be recognized by our people in the aftermath as well. The glow from that fire of enthusiasm indeed remained, but only for a few days. Unfortunately, like the other experiences before it, the great sense of appreciation for this miraculous rescue as part of a Divine plan was discarded on "the third day." It became and remains just one more chapter in the glorious history of our people.

This trend of becoming enthusiastic and eager about either an event or a cause and then allowing our passion to vanish has become quite characteristic of our people. Whether it be our concern with the alarmingly growing rate of intermarriage and assimilation, whether it be the education of our children, be it the future of our brethren in the state of Israel and the physical and spiritual future of our brothers and sisters in Europe and throughout the world, we always begin with a bang. However, after a brief period, it goes out with a whimper. We are satisfied with saving a few lives. We pat ourselves on the back and expect to be congratulated for a job well done. What we forget is the fact that the job has not ended; our responsibility has not been completed.

This, perhaps, could be the explanation for the most unusual and quite difficult Haftorah read this morning from the book of Yirmiyahu. This great and historic Navi who foretold and warned against the eventual destruction of Jerusalem by the Babylonians now presents a most glorious message. He informs his brethren throughout the world that the predicted exile will end and the children of Israel will return to their land. It is a proclamation of a triumphant fulfillment of the prophecy of return and the rebuilding of the Beis HaMikdash and the rebirth of Jewish sovereignty in Eretz Yisrael. In the second part of the Haftorah, he discusses how mother Rachel weeps for her children and refuses to be comforted.

Our rabbis question the entire structure and message of this Haftorah. If the Jewish nation will return to its land and fulfill the prophecy of *Shivas Zion,* why does mother Rachel weep and refuse to be comforted? The explanation is that while mother Rachel, like every other Jew, is thrilled and awed by the dream of the return of the exiled Jewish community, she is not content. The words of the Haftorah read:

רָחֵל מְבַכָּה עַל בָּנֶיהָ מֵאֲנָה לְהִנָּחֵם עַל בָּנֶיהָ כִּי אֵינֶנּוּ:

Rachel is weeping for her children. She refuses to be comforted for they are away.

Rachel is symbolic of all that is good and beautiful with our faith. She is the perfect mother who, although has had all of her children depart and most return, she is still not content. For as long as one of her children is away and has not yet returned home, she continues to shed tears and does not cease to mourn.

Even though the State of Israel has been reestablished and serves as a major focal point for Jewish emigration from tyranny and oppression, as long as some Jews remain away, mother Rachel is disconsolate. Even though we have made major progress toward educating our children and demonstrating to them that assimilation and intermarriage do not work and will not prevent the anti-Semites from attacking them, mother Rachel tells us not to be content. For as long as one Jewish child does not receive a genuine and authentic Jewish education, as long as one Jew marries out of the faith, as long as one Jew does not observe the Mitzvos and uphold our traditions, mother Rachel weeps and will not be consoled. As long as even one Jew is not allowed to worship his faith nor allowed to move to the land of his fathers, mother Rachel is in tears.

And so, my friends, the Navi Yirmiyahu not only transmitted a monumental literary work, he also provided us with a most significant and essential message. This is to be read on the very day when we read of the *Akeidah*. Avraham Avinu, even after a three-day interval with time to think and rationalize Hashem's request, still complies and carries forth the will of G-d. Rachel, who has seen most of her children return from exile, still refuses to be comforted until all of her children have come home. These are our heroes. These are our role models.

On these Yomim Noraim, we must truly ask: what kind of future do we want for ourselves? Will we be content with a superficial recitation of words and another set of broken promises, or will we at last carry forth on our pledges? Will our enthusiasm that we have demonstrated toward Judaism during these holy days continue long after Yom Kippur, on the third day and henceforth, or will it wane and disappear like it does every other year?

Will we be content with the saving of just a few Jewish lives either physically or religiously, and then be happy and rejoice over our work for Judaism, or will we remain vigilant and unswerving in our fight to help all our brethren in every area throughout the world? Will we not rest until every Jew is free to do what he wishes and to live where he desires? My friends, whether we live or die is only in the hands of Hashem. However, the kind of life that we lead is up to us. In order to truly exemplify our Jewishness and pass on our tradition to our children and grandchildren, it would do us well to emulate the lifestyles of an Avraham and a Rachel.

In the city of Beis Lechem in Israel stands the imposing tomb of Rachel. On a wall inside the memorial there is a mosaic which consists of the words from our Haftorah:

וְיֵשׁ תִּקְוָה לְאַחֲרִיתֵךְ נְאֻם ה' וְשָׁבוּ בָנִים לִגְבוּלָם:

"There is hope for your future, says Hashem, and the children will return to their borders."

The mosaic is signed: "This was made by one of her children who returned".

The message before us on this Rosh HaShanah is one of Teshuvah which means both repentance and return. We hope that every Jew will one day be able to come back and return to the borders of Israel. We also pray, we daven that every Jew, no matter where he lives, no matter how far away he is from our tradition, will return and observe the laws, the Mitzvos of *Yahadus*. Through our persistence and determination and our continued zeal and enthusiasm, we will certainly help make this dream into a living reality. It will last and endure for eternity, and it will finally cause mother Rachel to stop weeping and father Avraham to be satisfied and content. Let us do what we can to make this possible. Amen.

4. If I Am Not for Myself, Who Will Be for Me
Second Day of Rosh HaShanah
ספרי חיים וספרי מתים פתוחין לפניו

As the old year fades out and the New Year, Rosh HaShanah, is ushered in, we gather in our shuls to pour out our hearts to the King of the Universe, *HaKadosh Baruch Hu*. Each of us has his or her own individual requests and petitions which we present to G-d. However, the one common denominator which unites all of our prayers is our entreaty for life.

Judaism is very concerned with all aspects of life—from birth to death, from the cradle to the grave. The saving of a life is so sacred that *Chazal* derived that even Shabbos and all its sacred laws and regulations may be violated in order to help save the life of one who is seriously ill or whose life may be in danger. And at all of our happy and joyous occasions – whether it be the Bris of a son, a *Pidyon HaBen*, a Bar Mitzvah, a marriage, or even on all holidays and Shabbos, we make a toast—*l'chaim*—to life.

Our Rabbis inform us that on Rosh HaShanah, *HaKadosh Baruch Hu,* בכבודו ובעצמו, sits in judgment upon each and every one of us here on earth. There are, so to speak, three books in which the proceedings of this Heavenly Tribunal are kept. Inscribed in the first book are all the names of those who, by their meritorious service and good deeds during the past year, are automatically assured another year of life. In the second book, the names of those sinners who have committed unpardonable sins and whose only forgiveness is through death are inscribed. The third book, which is by far the largest of the three, contains the names of all people whose actions during the past year have left something wanting, something to be desired. To these persons, Hashem has given a ten-day reprieve from Rosh HaShanah to Yom Kippur before determining their fate.

It is as if we are given a new lease on life. We have from now until the end of Yom Kippur, until the final chanting of the *Ne'ilah* service, to repent for whatever wrongs we have committed, for whatever transgressions we have performed. If we are found worthy after this period, we will be inscribed into the *Sefer HaChaim,* the Book of the Living. If, G-d forbid, we are found unworthy, we will be inscribed for death into the *Sefer HaMeisim,* the Book of the Dead.

One of the scholars of the Talmud said (Erchin 10b): "The ministering angels appeared before G-d and asked Him, "Why does Israel not sing the song of praise, the Hallel, on Rosh HaShanah and Yom Kippur as they do on every other Yom Tov, on every other holiday?"

The Almighty, blessed be His Name, answered: "Is it possible that the King sits upon the Throne of Judgment with the Books of the Living and the Books of the Dead open before Him, and Israel should sing the Hallel—a song of praise?" The Jewish people utter the Hallel only when their hearts are filled with joy, whereas during the Days of Judgment, during these Yomim Noraim, there is much more fear and trembling in Jewish hearts than there is rejoicing.

The statement that causes us a problem is the mention of the Book of the Dead. Translated accurately, ספרי חיים means the Books of the Living and ספרי מתים means the Books of the Dead. We can understand that a person written in the Book of the Living is alive; but how can a person be written into the Book of the Dead if he has not yet died? Wouldn't the term ספרי מיתה – the Books of *Death* be more appropriate? After all, a wicked man written in the Book of the Dead might live out most of his year. Thus, the term "Book of Death" would be understandable, as this person has received his death sentence. Yet, the "Book of the Dead" would seem to imply that those written into it are already dead. How can this be explained?

After thinking this problem through and analyzing it most carefully, we can understand that life and death in Rabbinic literature and Jewish philosophy has a much greater meaning than the cessation or the continuation of the physical faculties of man. It is said that the righteous after death are regarded as alive while the wicked in life are regarded as dead. Life thus refers to that part of man which can never perish – his acts of kindness and compassion toward his fellow man, the מצות בין אדם לחבירו and his loyalty and commitment toward *HaKadosh Baruch Hu,* the מצות בין אדם למקום. Death, on the other hand, refers to that segment of man which can perish, namely, his physical being, his lusts, his desires, and his hatreds—namely, his manifold Aveiros.

We can now understand this most important statement of Chazal. One whose life is centered on מעשים טובים, good and positive deeds towards his fellow man, one whose entire being and weltanschauung is to help ameliorate the problems and difficulties of his coreligionists will truly live on. This individual who has always performed the מצות בין אדם למקום, who is a genuinely concerned and committed Jew, his name will be inscribed in the Book of the Eternal Living, the *Sefer HaChaim.*

However, he who only thinks of himself and his own selfish needs, he who does not daven, he who does not adhere to the laws of Kashrus, he who abandons the other important Mitzvos of the Torah, he will be considered dead even while he is still alive. He will certainly be inscribed into the *Sefer HaMeisim.*

Our Rabbis discuss a person who sins all his life but, on his deathbed, makes a complete and honest confession for his past transgressions and wrongdoings. If he is truly repentant for his misdeeds and wasted life, *HaKadosh Baruch Hu,* in His infinite compassion and mercy, will truly forgive him. This perpetual sinner who has violated every cardinal rule of Judaism can now attain *Olam HaBa,* the World to Come, through a last-minute change of heart and direction.

In fact, our *Chachamim* implore us to "Repent the day before your death." However, how can we know when one's time to meet his Maker will occur? How do we know when each of us will be called upon to make a *din v'cheshbon*, a complete accounting of our entire lives before the Heavenly Court? If that is indeed impossible, what do our *Chachamim* mean? How can they challenge us with an almost impossible task? The answer to this query is that our Rabbis had great insight into human nature. They knew full well that we cannot predict or pinpoint our own demise. Even if we do know that our end is approaching, we may not have the time or the ability to make our final repentance since man cannot know exactly when he will die. Thus, they are suggesting that we constantly repent. A Jew must always take stock of his actions and performances. In short, man should always remain in a state of *Teshuvah*.

By truly understanding that we may always be just a day or an hour from our physical demise, by fully realizing the real value of Torah, we will then be able to manage and direct our lives carefully and appropriately. We will not idle away our time on foolish, childish, and sophomoric activities. Rather, we will devote ourselves completely to the performance of the will of *HaKadosh Baruch Hu.*

In our capacity as G-d's representatives on earth, we have a great obligation. We ought to channel our energies and our efforts towards the betterment of society in general and to our people in particular. By having been written into the *Sefer HaChaim,* the Book of Life, we must do something positive with that new lease on life.

Our people have been in the forefront of many of the great causes in the general community for the past century. We have not neglected the poor, the oppressed and the downtrodden. We have always been active in every movement whose goal was to improve the world order. All this is exceptionally helpful for *Tikun Olam,* the making of the world into a better place.

However, while this aiding and assisting the general world community is wonderful and commendable, it is not enough. We, as Jews, have an obligation, an אחריות, to put our efforts, all of our כחות, into causes that help support and ameliorate the lives of Jews throughout the world. If we do not take care of ourselves who will? As Hillel HaZakain said in *Pirkei Avos,* "אם אין אני לי מי לי" – *"If I am not for myself, who will be for me?"* We must come to this realization immediately before it is too late to turn the tide as far as Jewish survival and the future of Judaism is concerned.

If we would only focus on the positive way of life, if we do not ever forsake any of our customs, our Mitzvos, and the important and significant Jewish causes, we will certainly succeed. In this way, we will have helped maintain our individuality as a nation and as a people while at the same time continuing to make our mark on the world. The general community will admire us so much more than if, G-d forbid, we assimilate or intermarry. Most importantly, we will earn the respect, the admiration and certainly the love of *HaKadosh Baruch Hu.* We will then certainly be worthy and meritorious of being inscribed into the *Sefer HaChaim,* the Book of the Living. Then, even long after we have left this planet, after our physical demise, our names, our deeds, and our accomplishments will be indelibly written. May we all have a *Kesivah v'Chasimah Tova*, and do our share, so that we can certainly be inscribed into the Book of the Living forever. Amen.

5. To Be Humble and Proud
Rosh HaShanah
שופר של ראה השנה – פשוט או כפוף

Today we begin the *Aseres Yemei Teshuvah*, the Ten Days of Penitence. Today is the *Yom HaDin*, the day of judgement. Today we pray that Hashem will remember us for life. He will, we hope, inscribe us in the *Sefer HaChaim*, the Book of Life, for a year of health, happiness and peace. However, as we appear before G-d and make our requests of Him, as we hope to receive G-d's grace and favorable decree, we must prove and demonstrate our worthiness.

We must approach the Heavenly Throne with a humble spirit and a contrite heart. We should admit our transgressions and vow never again to repeat our delinquent deeds. Finally, we must decide to modify our behavior patterns. We ought to devote ourselves in the future, not to our own self-gratification, but rather to fulfill the will and desire of G-d. We do this in the performance of מצוות מַעֲשִׂיוֹת, the Divine decrees and commandments.

Judaism, my friends, is a religion of action based upon study and introspection. It is not content with mere thought and no discharging of duties. It is a religion of deed, not merely one of creed. There are far too many Jews who are proud of their heritage and delighted with having been born Jewish. They would never hide or deny this fact. However, they do nothing to exhibit their religious attitude and feeling. In fact, their very lifestyle and activities demonstrate just the opposite – a totally un-Jewish, hedonistic, and so-called American existence.

These individuals feel Jewish. They claim that they are Jewish at heart. They cry if another Jew is beaten or oppressed. They rejoice when other Jews are successful in politics, in sports, in military engagements, in business or in the professions. It is, however, at this point that their Jewishness ends. "We need to do no more," they claim, "to show the world that we are different and distinct. Religion, religious observance – that is all a thing of the past. It is outdated, antiquated; a relic of ancient times. We are Jewish by what we think and how we feel." These individuals would do well by reading the words of the great American poet Henry Wadsworth Longfellow. He wrote, "We judge ourselves by what we feel capable of doing; others judge us by what we have done." To perform the will of G-d at the expense of the bending of our own drives and desires in deference to the performance of the will of G-d is Judaism at its finest.

My friends, if our attitude toward Hashem should be one of humbleness and modesty, our actions toward our fellow man should be care and concern for their wellbeing. In other words, what should the Jewish self-image be? Ought it be one of fearlessness, self-respect, and pride, or should it be meekness, submissiveness and subservience? The Mishnah in the tractate of Rosh HaShanah (26b) sheds a great deal of light on this issue.

The Mishnah says that the Shofar which is blown on Rosh HaShanah must be a straight, unbent, horn of a ram. The Gemara quotes Rabbi Levi, who says:

מצוה של ראש השנה ושל יום הכיפורים בכפופין.

"On Rosh HaShanah and on Yom Kippur, the Shofar must be a curved horn." The Gemara asks on R' Levi from the Mishnah which states that the Shofar on Rosh HaShanah must be from the straight horn of the mountain goat. The Gemara answers that R' Levi is ruling in accordance with R' Yehudah who says that on Rosh HaShanah we use the curved horn of the ram. The Gemara then explains these differences of opinion:

מר סבר: בראש השנה - כמה דכייף איניש דעתיה טפי מעלי . . . ומר סבר: בראש השנה כמה דפשיט איניש דעתיה טפי מעלי...

One authority is of the opinion that the more a man bends his mind and his heart on Rosh HaShanah, the more effective is his prayer.

Rosh HaShanah

The other authority maintains that on Rosh HaShanah, the more a man elevates his mind and heart the better the effect.

Rabbi Levi believes that the lesson of the Shofar is one of humility, modesty and self-effacement. Jews must learn how to bend and submit to the word and the will of Hashem. The Mishnah, on the other hand, contends that the message of the Shofar is one of fortitude and confidence. The actions of the Jew must not be bent, curved, or twisted; they should be straight, above board, honest, and sincere.

The fact of the matter is that both of these opinions are correct. We indeed use a curved and twisted Shofar on Rosh HaShanah. However, we turn it upwards towards Heaven.

Although the Halacha is in accordance with R' Levi that one should use a bent Shofar, Rav Yosef Engel cites the Maharam M'Rutenberg who states that in essence, both opinions are correct. This is in consonance with the principle of אלו ואלו דברי אלקים חיים. And the reason is that Judaism insists that we use a dual approach. There are times, specifically in our relationship with our Creator, with *HaKadosh Baruch Hu*, that we must be submissive and compliant. We must bend our will and our inclination. We must subjugate our desires and our pleasures and instead substitute that which Hashem commands us to do. On the other hand, in our relationship to the outside world, as representatives of Judaism, as messengers of our people, we must always stand strong, correct, and tall. We cannot ever waiver in our faith. We must at all times be loyal and devoted to the perpetuation and continuity of Judaism.

This, perhaps, is also the meaning behind the famous epigram of the great Chassidic master, Reb Simcha Bunim of P'shischa, which suggests that every person should carry two pieces of paper—one in each pocket. On one the words inscribed should read: ואנכי עפר ואפר" – "I am but dust and ashes." On the other paper the words should read: "בשבילי נברא העולם" – "For my sake was the world created." These messages, we are told, represent the idealistic nature

Rosh HaShanah

of every person at the start of his life's journey on the one hand, and also sum up the realistic and quite pessimistic views at the end of one's life.

I believe that it can also be utilized to help explain the Gemara in Rosh HaShanah. In our relationship with Hashem, we must always recognize that compared to *HaKadosh Baruch Hu,* the Maker and Creator of the universe, we are but a mere speck, a fleeting second on the clock of eternity. We are indeed "עפר ואפר" – dust and ashes. However, man was created בצלם אלקים, in the image of G-d. He has sanctity, holiness and distinction. And it was for man alone that the world was created, for it was only after man was formed that Hashem said: "והנה טוב מאד", "And He beheld all that He created, and it was very good." Only after the formation of man did G-d rest.

The creation of man was not the end, but rather the first step in the Divine blueprint for the world. Man was to eventually accept, learn and observe the laws and commandments of the Torah. It was only for he who takes this obligation upon himself that Hashem performed the מעשה בראשית, the act of creation. Thus, we Jews who observe and practice even the most miniscule details of the Torah and all of its commentaries can proudly stand up straight and erect. We need not walk with our heads bowed and our backs hunched over.

We should be proud of our heritage, fond of our faith and ever grateful that we have the opportunity to carry out the word of G-d. In our relationship with the non-Jewish world, we should have resolve and remain firm and steadfast in that which we believe. To the rest of the world, which at Mount Sinai and for the past 4,000 years have rejected the Divine Torah and all that it contains, we must proudly say: "בשבילי נברא העולם", "For we and for those of us who accepted the word and the will of the Torah was the world created."

Jews, the world over, continue to observe this twofold approach of humbleness and bending on the one hand, and fearlessness, pride and straightforwardness on the other. The problem is that most Jews get these values confused. In their relationship with the non-Jewish world, they are shy, modest and unpresumptuous. They don't wish to offend the sensitivities of the gentile society. Therefore, they bend, they become obsequious and attempt to curry favor with the non-Jew. Not only do they refuse to flaunt their religious observance, some are even afraid to let it be known that they observe anything other than the more populous religion. They feel compelled to ingratiate themselves with their neighbors and colleagues.

However, when it comes to his relationship with Hashem, then the Jew assumes a completely different posture. Rarely do we find Jews who prepare themselves a full month before the onset of Rosh HaShanah in anticipation of their annual meeting with G-d. Would a Jew a generation or two ago be so presumptuous as to enter the *Yomim Noraim*, the Days of Awe, without making a *Cheshbon HaNefesh*, without undertaking a full inventory of his past actions and deeds? Today that is all passé; it is all considered old-fashioned. There is no longer the fear, the trembling, the tears of Jews when the Shofar is sounded or when the *Tefillos* of *Unesaneh Tokef* and *Avinu Malkainu* are recited. Rather, this has all been replaced by a callous, unemotional, indifferent attitude toward their future as Jews, and especially in their relationship with G-d.

A number of years ago there was a documentary on television entitled "Destination: America." Its theme was the immigration of the east European Jews to America during the last 150 years. The narrator detailed how so many thousands of Jews in just two generations went from squalor and poverty to luxury and wealth. Jews have entered all the businesses and professions, and many have excelled and left their mark on American society. This is a fact which we can all be proud of. However, what I found so depressing and distasteful was the narrator's statement that most American Jews, especially those who have become affluent and successful, hardly maintain any Jewish traditions. However, they continue, nevertheless, to cling tenaciously to their Jewishness. Many support the State of Israel and other philanthropic Jewish causes. Many belong to synagogues, but few ever go there even on the High Holy Days and never during the year. Shabbos is forsaken, Kashrus is cast aside. The Yom Tovim are merely days of history with no celebration or observance. It was this idea of making it big in America, bending your Jewishness before the non-Jew but straightening your back and assuming a brazen and obdurate attitude towards G-d that I found most disheartening. If this is the path that Judaism is taking at the present time, we can all fear for the future of our faith.

These individuals believe quite erroneously that to be a good, proud, and flag-waving American, you must renounce, or at the very least, abandon the traditions of your Jewishness. But the late Justice and first Jew ever appointed to the Supreme Court, Louis Brandeis, once said it quite well when he stated: "By being better Jews, we can become better Americans." The two must go together. As Americans, we must rise to the responsibilities before us in every area of life. However, it must never be at the expense of our faith. It should never occur when it means that the solution is the estrangement from any facet of Halacha and Yiddishkeit.

The teachings and traditions of Judaism must never be forsaken. During our present Golden Age of American Jewry, when most Jews are prosperous, many affluent, and some quite influential, we must never forget our humble beginnings and our point of origin. At all times we must remain a Jew in thought, body and mind. Even in times and eras when we face danger and potential catastrophe, we must always remember the humanistic qualities taught by our faith. At times when the response of the non-Jew would be violence, the Jew reacts in the only way that he is taught – belief and faith in the *Ribono Shel Olam* and his Torah.

Elie Wiesel, the late, great author and conscience of the Holocaust, described the scene at the liberation of Buchenwald in April 1945. 20,000 camp inmates were freed. A number of Russian prisoners of war grabbed some jeeps and machine guns and fired at will at the inhabitants of the neighboring town. The Jews were also freed at that time. And while logic and emotion would have dictated that they should emulate their non-Jewish fellow prisoners and also take revenge, they did not. Instead, they did the only thing Jews could have done. They joined together to daven and to praise Hashem and thank Him for allowing them to remain alive. "We are Jews," they said, "and while the world thinks we should act animalistic, we choose to remain human." This idea of refusing to bend before those who demand that you break and instead fulfill the will of G-d—that is Judaism at its best. Even if we do not understand why we were punished, we still fulfill the Mitzvos. That is greatness; that is *gevurah*.

The Bialistoker Maggid told a tale about an individual who comes to a home and hears crying. He enters the house and sees a *Tallis* weeping. He asks the *Tallis* why he is shedding tears. The *Tallis* responds that his master and his family went on a vacation and took everything tangible with them that will bring them pleasure and happiness. He, the *Tallis,* however, was left behind.

"Weep no more," said the man. "Your master will one day go away on a very long journey, and he will take nothing with him but you."

My friends, must we wait for that long journey to occur before we decide to take our *Tallis*, which is representative of all the other Mitzvos, with us? Will we spend our lives pursuing our own happiness and neglecting the fulfillment of the word of Hashem? What kind of Judaism will we then leave to our children and grandchildren? Will we continue bowing to the pressures of our society at the expense of Hashem and our religion? No, my friends,

Rosh HaShanah

we should, especially during these *Yomim Noraim* when we pray for life and happiness, decide to bend before Hashem but stand tall, straight and erect before the rest of the world. Remember, only he who can truly feel that he is dust and ashes before his maker can declare: "בשבילי נברא העולם" – "For my sake was the world created."

May we all be inscribed in the *Sefer HaChaim*, the Book of Life. May we all have a year of health and happiness from our children and peace in Israel and throughout the world, Amen.

6. To Be Stirred Toward Optimism
Rosh HaShanah
תקיעה-שברים-תרועה

During these *Aseres Yemei Teshuvah,* all of mankind appears before the Throne of Hashem. Like sheep who pass before their master, we come to G-d to be judged. We pray that we, our families, and all of *Klal Yisrael* be granted a favorable and auspicious judgement. We hope to be blessed with a year of health and prosperity. We implore the L-rd to bestow a year of peace, serenity, and growth upon our brethren in Eretz Yisrael. We entreat the Almighty to help all our brothers and sisters who are having difficulty in their lives. We beg Hashem to help our coreligionists worldwide who are being subjected to brutal anti-Semitic invectives and attacks.

When we look out today toward the coming year, we do not see encouragement and optimism. The coming year does not, at least on the surface, appear to be bright, cheerful, and rosy.

We fear for our brothers and sisters in Eretz Yisrael and throughout the world. Some of our people, especially in Europe, are facing virulent, anti-Semitic threats. They fear for their very lives more today than at any other time since the end of World War II.

Jewish survival in the free and democratic countries in Europe and elsewhere cannot be taken for granted. Even here in the United States, the rate of assimilation and intermarriage is growing at a record pace. The general overall complacency and indifference with Jewish life and Jewish values is fast approaching epidemic proportions.

This is the case in the general Jewish population. However, among our college-aged Jews throughout the United States, the figures are even more alarming. So many of the Jewish students on college campuses are alienated and apathetic to Judaism. They do not identify with or think very highly of our faith, our traditions, and our religion

In addition, the virulent anti-Israel sentiment found on so many college campuses even by professors has made life so difficult for any Jewish student who publicly desires to stand up for his faith.

However, my friends, to be depressed and disheartened is very uncharacteristic for the Jewish people. Our philosophy has never been to be מייאש, to give up. That is foreign to our people. We have never abandoned hope in the future. What has continually kept us alive and breathing is hope, faith, confidence, and belief in the future. It was the great medieval Jewish philosopher, Rabbi Yehudah HaLevi, who said that being a Jew means being a prisoner of hope. Buoyancy and optimism have always been our hallmark. Our national anthem does not talk about Jewish supremacy nor Jewish domination. It consists of one mantra: התקוה – hope.

Indeed, hope is one of the underlying themes of today's liturgy. We pray in each *Shemoneh Esrei* on Rosh HaShanah for תקוה טובה לדורשיך – "Good hope for those who seek You." In Yirmiyahu HaNavi's heartrending account of our mother Rachel's cry for her children, we read G-d's response in today's Haftorah:

וְיֵשׁ תִּקְוָה לְאַחֲרִיתֵךְ נְאֻם ה' וְשָׁבוּ בָנִים לִגְבוּלָם:

"There is hope for your future, says Hashem, and the children will return to their borders."

Three times a day we pray to G-d: על כן נקוה – *"Therefore we hope in, O L-rd."* [This phrase is also mentioned during the Rosh HaShanah Musaf.]

We are a people who can stare death in the face on both a personal and national level and can come to grips with it. We can say the Kaddish. We look forward to the time when the Kingdom of G-d, the Sovereignty of Hashem will begin. Then we will be accepted and admired by all mankind.

Our national goal and determination has been, down through the ages, to cheat the Angel of Death. Like our forefather Yitzchak whose participation in the *Akeidah* which we read in the Torah this morning, we too exist against all odds and against all rules of nature. Like Yitzchak, we continue to survive, grow, and flourish. When the world thought we should be dead and buried, our theme has always been לא אמות כי אחיה, "I shall not die because I will live." If called upon, we will fight physically and spiritually both here in the United States and in Israel. We must do so in order to live and guarantee that our people and our ideals will continue to grow and develop.

We have always felt that to despair of *geulah,* redemption, was a major transgression of our faith. Instead, we constantly work to develop Judaism. We look optimistically to the future.

However, what can we do to change our mood from pessimism and depression to one of encouragement and reassurance in the future? We must, I believe, truly study the message imparted to us this morning by the sounds of the Shofar. The Shofar is to serve as an alarm. It awakens us from our slumber. It stirs us from our complacency. It prods us into action.

What is most interesting, however, are the meanings of the different and various sounds of the Shofar. It conveys to us two distinct messages—both equally important and significant for the survival of our people.

There are three sounds of the Shofar: the *Tekiah,* the *Shevarim,* and the *Teruah.* The *Tekiah* is one long and unbroken note. It breaks the silence, the stillness of the atmosphere. It destroys any feeling of complacency and unawareness. It is a sharp and shrill alarm. It cautions us not to feel that our position in the world community is safe and secure. The *Tekiah* comes to wake us up to the danger faced by our people throughout the world – the threat of Iran, ISIS, Hamas, and Hezbollah. We are also quite concerned about the vituperative rhetoric of most of the Arab world against Israel. It also comes to warn us of the unfortunate indifference of the Western democracies toward any tragedy which occurs to Jews in the State of Israel.

The *Shevarim,* meaning "broken fragments," is a thrice-repeated wail. The sounds of the *Shevarim* serve to alert us to the dangers of fragmentation and divisiveness of Jewish life. The *Shevarim* summons us to combat the destructive elements of assimilation and intermarriage as well as the continued infighting and backstabbing of different segments of our community—in essence, the internal threat to Judaism

The *Shevarim* also calls upon us to silence the self-hating Jewish radicals, the non-Jewish leftists, the ignorant—but potentially very dangerous—groups whose primary goal is to influence and subsequently convert Jews to Christianity.

Finally, the *Teruah* is sounded, a 9-part staccato wail. These blasts speak to the cries of depression and hopelessness that threaten to engulf us because of last year's failures. As we observe yet another Rosh HaShanah, we might feel that despite the enthusiasm that we begin each year with, it always ends in a perpetual cycle of self-defeat. The *Teruah* exhorts us to transform those feelings of despair and יאוש into feelings of lasting and effective change. It converts the sighs of hopelessness into tears of authentic *Teshuvah shleimah*.

However, my friends, there is another not too well-known sound which we must also pay strict attention to. This sound is not listed among those that comprise the 30 sounds of obligation nor the 100 sounds that are customarily blown on Rosh HaShanah. Yet, it is indeed most important. In the famous prayer, ונתנה תוקף, written by Rabbi Amnon of Mainz, we read:

ובשופר גדול יתקע וקול דממה דקה ישמע.
A great trumpet is sounded and a still small voice is heard."

What sound was Rav Amnon referring to? And if a great Shofar was sounded, why was only a small voice heard?

I humbly suggest that what Rav Amnon was telling us was that we must not only be moved, stimulated, and impelled to action by the loud, shrill, alarming sounds in life. We should not limit our deeds and activities on behalf of Judaism and our fellow Jews only when the siren is sounded. We must hear much more than great trumpets. We must hear the still, small voice, the קול דממה דקה. This is Hashem talking to each and every one of us on a personal and on an individual level. We are exhorted on a daily and continual basis to be and act as Jews. We must be cognizant and adhere to the eternal messages of the Torah. We then must put into action all that we have learned. By adhering to this formula, we can make ourselves better and more dedicated Jews.

Perhaps this is the meaning of a most interesting halacha regarding the Mitzvah of Shofar. The Shulchan Aruch says that if one Shofar is placed inside another Shofar and is sounded, one fulfills his obligation only if the voice of the inner Shofar is heard. If the outer Shofar alone is heard, the Mitzvah is not fulfilled. This may also be the reason why the blessing on the Shofar is not לתקוע קול שופר – "to sound the Shofar," but לשמוע קול שופר – "to hear the sound of the Shofar." We must not simply sound off. We must listen, pay attention, and comprehend the sounds of the Shofar. We then must act on it. This is so both on an internal level as well as on the global and international stage.

Yes, my friends, there is no doubt at all that when the siren is sounded, when the Shofar is blown, we must rise to the occasion. We must do our part to help ensure that our coreligionists survive and that the light of our tradition will never be extinguished. But we ourselves must also hear another sound. We must hear the קול דממה דקה, the still small voice. We must be moved to act on behalf of our fellow Jews not on a temporary and one-time basis; it must be continuous. The sound that we hear must penetrate our inner conscience and be permanently imbedded in us. It must urge us on to a life of קדושה and טהרה.

Our generation of American Jews is not presently asked to perform any heroic deeds. We are not called upon to sacrifice our sons and daughters like Avraham of old or like the thousands of Avrahams today in Israel. We are not asked to relinquish our life-savings or even risk our future financial and physical security as our coreligionists in the past have done. We are just asked to be loyal and dedicated to the principles of our faith.

Loyalty to Judaism today does not demand acts of martyrdom, deeds of courage, or massive sacrifices. We are asked to hear the sound of the Shofar, internalize its message, act upon it, and allow it to reach the inner recesses of our mind. There it will become part of us. It will gradually and completely transform us into better Jews. We will become more committed and will help guarantee the survival of our people.

My friends, I beseech you. Do not be deaf to the loud and booming alarm nor the still quiet voice of the Shofar. Let us work together to fulfill our dreams. If we can internalize these messages, then, and only then, when we have done all that we can, will we be able to face the New Year with enthusiasm and encouragement. At that time, we will be able to transform our pessimism into optimism. We will then have a good and productive year—one with peace, health, and prosperity.

7. Striving Today for a Better Tomorrow
Rosh HaShanah
היום הרת עולם

Today we begin the most solemn period of the Jewish year. For the next 10 days, from Rosh HaShanah until the final sounding of the Shofar on Yom Kippur, our thoughts and our actions will be pointed upward toward Heaven. We will fervently daven. We will beat our hearts in repentance from any and all personal transgressions. We will implore Hashem to forgive us and to have mercy on the rest of humanity.

The one underlying theme of all the High Holiday Liturgy is that of זכרינו לחיים. We ask *HaKadosh Baruch Hu* to remember us and to inscribe us for a good, healthy, and prosperous year. We beg the L-rd not to forget us. In the Selichos we say during this time period, we cry out, "עננו ה' עננו". Remember our sacred tradition– בזכות אבות:

In honor of the superhuman efforts made by our forefathers, Avraham, Yitzchak, and Yaakov;

In remembrance of the lives lived by Moshe, Dovid HaMelech, and Eliyahu HaNavi;

In recognition of the many martyrs, the קדושים וטהורים, who willingly gave their lives to sanctify and glorify the Holy Name of Hashem. In their merit, we pray that Hashem remember us.

In memory of our ancestors who died defending Yerushalayim against the onslaught of the Roman Legions in 70 C.E.;

In memory of our brethren who were murdered by Christian mobs during the crusades;

In memory of our Six Million brothers and sisters who were barbarically and systematically slaughtered by the Nazi beasts.

Rosh HaShanah

On their behalf and because of the lives lived by our own parents, we beg the L-rd to inscribe us into the *Sefer HaChaim,* the Book of Life.

We are not only concerned with the past. We also think of the future. We say, "*Ribono shel Olam,* please give us another year of life and we will become better Jews. From today, I will donate more Tzedakah. From now on, I will regularly come to shul. Starting today, I will study more Torah. I will immediately be more concerned for the welfare of my fellow Jews.

The fact of the matter is that when Hashem does inscribe us for life, He certainly demands something in return. He wants us to live as Jews. He wants us to be proud and conscientious of our responsibilities to Him. The question is: When does G-d want us to fulfill our end of the bargain? It is not yesterday. It is not tomorrow. Rather, it is now, at this very moment, today.

This, perhaps, can be the interpretation of the famous *Tefillah* recited following the sounding of the Shofar:

היום הרת עולם, היום יעמיד במשפט כל יצורי עולמים.

Today is the birthday of the world; today all creatures of the world stand in judgment.

The usual interpretation is in accordance with the view of R' Eliezer which is stated in the Gemara in Rosh HaShanah (11a). He says that the first day of Tishrei was the day when Adam HaRishon was created. This event completed the creation of the world. He says that today on Rosh HaShanah, two of the three Patriarchs, Avraham and Yaakov, were born. They started a new world – a new and better world after the past sinful generations.

Today also marks the anniversary of the release from jail of Yosef HaTzadik. He had languished in prison for 12 years for a crime he did not commit. Finally, it was on Rosh HaShanah that the forced servitude of *Am Yisrael* in Mitzrayim ceased.

However, historical facts aside, we can humbly offer an interpretation which is applicable to each and every one of us. When we say "היום הרת עולם" – "Today is the birthday of the creation," or, as it should be understood, "the completion of creation of the world," we mean that today, not the yesterday of our ancestors, nor the future of our children, each of us dedicates and commits himself to lead a complete and total Jewish life. If we are willing to sacrifice and guarantee the survival and perpetuation of Judaism, then indeed this היום, this "today," can and will certainly mark the completion of a new and better world. It will be a society in which all will live in peace, harmony and brotherhood. It will be a world where every human being, regardless of race or color, irrespective of political or nationalistic inclination, will bend their knees in prayer to He Who is the Master of us all, to the מלך מלכי המלכים.

This *Tefillah*, "היום הרת עולם", is recited three times during the *Musaf* service. It follows the sounding of the Shofar at the conclusion of each of the three central components and orders of this day's *Musaf Tefillah*. These are the blessings of *Malchiyos, Zichronos,* and *Shofaros.*

Malchiyos means kingship and majesty. Today we acknowledge the authority and reign of the Almighty. We testify that His sovereignty exists over the entire world. We accept His dominion over all of mankind.

Zichronos means remembrances. We proclaim our faith that we are subject to Divine remembrance as well as the fact that G-d manifests His Divine care and concern for all His creations. While He bestows reward and punishment in accord with man's actions, Hashem is a merciful and forgiving G-d and Master.

Shofaros refers to the blasts of the ram's horn. This was sounded at Har Sinai. It also can be interpreted to mean to beautify and improve. When we begin this section of *Musaf,* we willingly, as

Rosh HaShanah

did our ancestors, accept the yoke of the Torah. We do so just as if we too were receiving the Torah now for the first time. We pledge ourselves to learn and study it and to fulfill all its precepts and ordinances. We must constantly strive to improve ourselves spiritually, and by doing so, we improve the world around us.

The arrangement of these prayers in the *Machzor* presents a difficulty. What is the relationship between היום הרת עולם and the three orders of the *Musaf* service? The commentaries explain that this *Tefillah* is recited after each of the three sections because Rosh HaShanah resembles the three fresh starts that the world has experienced:

1) The *Sheishes Yemei Bereishis* – the Six Days of Creation
2) The rebirth of the world following the Great Flood
3) The day of the giving of the Torah.

During the *Sheishes Y'mei Bereishis,* the Six Days of Creation, the world was created in a state of *Malchiyos,* reflecting the sovereignty and majesty of G-d. Indeed, as we begin the section of *Malchiyos* in our prayers, we recite the glorious words of Yehoshua, recalling G-d's majesty in connection with the Creation:

עלינו לשבח לאדון הכל – לתת גדולה ליוצר **בראשית.**

When Hashem created Man on Rosh HaShanah, he was created in the image of G-d. Man was destined to be immortal, and as such, his role as a reflection of G-d's image was quite apparent. As G-d's direct handiwork, it was the most natural thing for man to coronate G-d as King over the whole world. However, the first man and woman were unable to conform with G-d's sovereignty, violating their single command to avoid eating from the Tree of Knowledge. Adam and Chava were banished forever from the idyllic and majestic Garden of Eden. Man was now mortal, and his G-dlike stature—and hence, his relationship with G-d—became diminished. Instead of his original task of cultivating and protecting the royal gardens of the King of the world, man was now required to work by the sweat of his brow just to live and survive.

Nevertheless, for the first 10 generations of this world, mankind continued to live a G-dly existence. The lifespan was close to 1,000 years. While man was banished from Gan Eden, the world's year-round spring climate was certainly Eden-like. G-d's grandeur should have been clearly evident to all. However, mankind failed at this task. Without the threat of imminent death, man felt free to act according to his own capriciousness and never take a reckoning of his deeds. And so, instead of beautifying and bettering the world, Adam's descendants filled it with lust, ugliness, and wickedness. After 10 generations of this base and negative attitude, G-d decreed the obliteration of the world with the Great Flood, the *Mabul*.

Hashem then began anew; once again, *HaYom Haras Olam*. After the *Mabul*, man's lifespan gradually diminished, introducing a state of *Zichronos*. Man was forced to reckon with his impending death and come to terms with the consequences of his actions. Noach was the harbinger of this era, as he was the sole person to live with a reckoning in the antediluvian era. It may be for this reason that Noach holds such a prominent place in the verses recited in the *Zichronos* section.

However, mankind as a whole failed in this task of *Zichronos*. The wickedness of Nimrod, the treason of the Tower of Bavel, the depravity of Egypt, Sedom, and Amorrah – all of these demonstrated that mankind had once again fallen into the abyss. The world sought to fight against G-d instead of recalling His judgment.

Finally, our Patriarchs, Avraham, Yitzchak, and Yaakov came onto the scene. They understood the responsibility of caring for the world. The Avos were determined to save mankind from backsliding and relapsing into the state of תהו ובהו – void and emptiness.

Thus, the era of *Zichronos* which began with Noach and his family was saved and transformed by the Patriarchs. They lived a life where they recalled and reckoned with the Master of the World, and in their merit, we implore G-d in *Zichronos* to recall us for life. Remember us, G-d, because of the kind of lives which our Patriarchs lived.

The *Zichronos* section concludes with the recollection of Avraham's ultimate sacrifice when he was willing to bring up Yitzchak as an offering to G-d. This act served as the harbinger of the third Genesis, *Shofaros*. When the angel called out for Avraham to spare the life of his son, G-d provided Avraham with a ram as a substitute. The Shofar from this very ram proclaimed the third *HaYom Haras Olam* at Matan Torah, when the nation of Avraham, Yitzchak, and Yaakov accepted the Torah. It was as if on that day the world was reborn and reestablished – this time, on a permanent basis. Finally, the world had a complete nation who would live in the image of G-d. They would coronate G-d with *Malchiyos*, live a life of reckoning with *Zichronos*, and accept G-d's Torah with *Shofaros*.

The element of *Shofaros* is the ability of man to hear the sound of the Shofar, of his inner conscience which awakens him from his self-imposed slumber. It implants in him a desired willingness to correct and change his ways. As we learn in Pirkei Avos, this call of the Shofar at Mount Sinai does not cease. We can always hear it within ourselves, reminding us to lead lives suitable for a people created in the image of G-d.

Thus, my friends, the recital of the *Tefillah* of *HaYom Haras Olam* at these three junctures is most appropriate on Rosh HaShanah.

As we approach Hashem and ask that He inscribe us for a year of life, health, and happiness, we must acknowledge our responsibility. We must, first and foremost, understand how small and puny, how insignificant we are in comparison to the majesty of *HaKadosh Baruch Hu*. We must first be aware that G-d is a קל עורך דין, a G-d of Judgement, pure and unadulterated. If one does the right thing, he will be rewarded. If, on the other hand, he does evil, he will suffer the consequences.

We must also always remember that Hashem is a most loving and compassionate Father. He is merciful and forgiving no matter how far we have strayed from the correct and straight path. No matter how severe our transgressions are, if we do תשובה גמורה and change our ways, we will be forgiven and pardoned.

Finally, in order to be able to carry on the Divine will and demonstrate to Hashem that our verbal utterances are sincere, we must accept and practice the yoke of Torah. We must hear the Shofar which prods our inner conscience. It calls upon us to improve ourselves and the world around us. We must do so by subscribing and adhering to our blueprint for survival, our Torah.

We must also always keep in mind that what we personally do today will have a very profound impact on the world of tomorrow.

Perhaps this is what the Rambam (הלכות תשובה פרק ג') had in mind when he said:

לפיכך צריך כל אדם שיראה עצמו כל השנה כולה כאילו חציו זכאי וחציו חייב, וכן כל העולם חציו זכאי וחציו חייב, חטא חטא אחד הרי הכריע את עצמו ואת כל העולם כולו לכף חובה וגרם לו השחתה, עשה מצוה אחת הרי הכריע את עצמו ואת כל העולם כולו לכף זכות וגרם לו ולהם תשועה והצלה.

> A man should always regard himself as though he was half meritorious and half guilty. Likewise, he should regard the world as half innocent and half guilty. If he commits even one sin, he tips the scale of guilt for himself and for the entire world. He will then cause its destruction as well. If he performs even one Mitzvah, he tips the scale of merit for himself and for the entire community. He causes its salvation and deliverance.

Today on Rosh HaShanah, we have the opportunity to rescue the world from abyss and destruction. On the other hand, we can be responsible for destroying it. The choice, my friends, is ours.

In our personal religious lives, as well as in our collective lives, let each of us guarantee the survival of mankind. If we internalize this message and act on it, we will help guarantee the future of the world. Then, we will all say in unison, *HaYom Haras Olam* – today on this Rosh HaShanah we are responsible for the rebirth and the new creation of a stronger, a better, and a more religious and secure world. It truly rests with us. Only we can create the dawn of a new tomorrow.

8. The Sounds of the Shofar: Laughter and Tears
Rosh HaShanah 5735 (1974)
לידת יצחק - עקידת יצחק

The holiday of Rosh HaShanah is one of a number of biblically ordained festivals that the Jewish people are commanded to observe. As with the other festive occasions, there are many rituals, *Halachos*, *Minhagim*, and traditions that we uphold. However, Rosh HaShanah is, in at least one notable respect, very different, and uniquely separated from every other biblical holiday. On Pesach, Shavuos and Sukkos, there is a distinction and differentiation between the observance in Israel versus חוץ לארץ, the Diaspora. It has become a custom in communities outside of Israel to observe all holidays for two days. In Israel, however the same Yom Tovim are celebrated for only one day.

This same Halacha does not apply to Rosh HaShanah. Even in our ancient homeland, Rosh HaShanah is observed for two days. The reason is not because of the uncertainty as to when this festival will occur. Rather, the Sages during the Second Temple era ordained that even those who are aware which day the new moon appeared must observe two days of Rosh HaShanah. This has become tradition and law. In fact, both days of Rosh HaShanah contain the same degree of sanctity. Both are considered as a *Yoma Arichta*, one long, continuous day.

I ask you, my friends, how is this to be understood? Are the customs and traditions – and especially the Torah readings for the two days – so similar so as to convince us that they are considered as one? Upon closer analysis, while the Torah portions for these days are divergent, they really are quite analogous. While they may, on the surface, express two separate and dissimilar ideas, a closer scrutiny and a more thorough reading will demonstrate that they are very much alike. Indeed, all that we read about and all that we recite on Rosh HaShanah indicates the likeness, the resemblance and the parallelism of the two days being considered as one.

The Torah portion for today, the first day of Rosh HaShanah, describes the birth of a son to our first patriarch and matriarch, Avraham and Sarah. They anxiously awaited this event for many decades and were overjoyed by this gift of Hashem that they were presented with in old age. Their progeny will carry on their ideals, goals, traditions, and faith. The religion which they conceived of, the belief which they developed, and the creed that they nurtured would not die with them. Their faith in Hashem as the Creator and Master of the universe will live on in the son, whom they named Yitzchak.

Indeed, Yitzchak is a most interesting and yet peculiar name. It is the future tense of the root צחק, to laugh. Thus, the son of the first patriarch and matriarch of Judaism, persons who stood on one side against all of mankind in their belief in Hashem is now named, "He will laugh." How strange, how odd. This name is even more difficult to understand when we realize that tomorrow's Torah reading describes the *Akeidah*, Avraham's attempted offering of Yitzchak as a *korban* to G-d. Yitzchak represents גבורה and עבודה, strength and sacrifice—certainly not attributes that imply laughter and joy. It is thus ironic that he is given such a name. Who shall he laugh at? And why?

Chazal tell us that the laugh of Yitzchak really expresses not only his laugh but also the laugh of his descendants. The vision and hope of his parents was that he would laugh and find joy in the ideals and G-dly life that he would inherit from his parents. His laughter would be that of carrying the banner, the flag of a new faith proclaimed by his father Avraham and his mother Sarah.

Some of our other Rabbanim explain this name differently. They say that the fact that the word Yitzchak is written in the future tense indicates the dominant role that laughter will have played in the history of our people. In fact, our chronicle is made up of both past and future, history as well as prophecy. Normally, Yitzchak and his descendants should have at one point or another given up. Human logic would dictate that at any given time in our traumatic and troublesome history, we should have put an end to our agony and suffering. It appears that perhaps we really should have renounced our faith. We should have abandoned the apparently sinking ship and parachuted to safety away from the burning wreckage of the plane called Judaism.

Fortunately, with the help of Hashem, this has never occurred. A violent, selfish, and treacherous world has repeatedly called out to us saying, "Your G-d has forsaken you; He cares nothing for you. Join with us. Desert your foolhardy, senseless and ludicrous religion. You will then know no more suffering or discrimination." How did we respond? We laughed. We looked to the outside world and refused to be taken in by their hypocrisy, double-dealing, and duplicity. No matter what the sacrifice, what the difficulties, what the price, our faith in Hashem never weakened or wavered. And like our father Yitzchak – we laughed. This was not because we were mocking them or deriding them. We laughed because we rejoiced with the heritage and faith that is uniquely ours, no matter how many sacrifices go with it. Thus, today's Torah reading is, in the final analysis, a message of hope and optimism, confidence and buoyancy.

This theme of laughter amid sacrifice is underscored in the following account by Moshe Prager in his book *Sparks of Glory:*

> The Jews were forced back against the barbed wire. The barbs pierced their flesh, pricking their bones, and the blood began to trickle and run. The Jews huddled and crowded together, stumbling and falling as more kept coming, colliding against the fallen ones and falling with them. In the midst of this confusion the shrieking voice of the murderous chief was heard again: "Sing, arrogant Jews, sing! Sing or you will die! Gunners, aim your machine guns! Now listen, you dirty Jews.

Sing or you will die!" And at that horrifying moment, one man pried himself loose from the frightened mob and broke the conspiracy of total silence. He stood there all alone and began to sing. His song was a Chassidic folk song in which the Chassid poured out his soul before the Almighty:

"Lomir zich iberbeiten, iberbeiten, Avinu shebashamayim, Lomir zich iberbeiten, iberbeiten, iberbeiten—" "Let us be reconciled, our Heavenly Father. Let us be reconciled, let us make up—"

A spark of song was kindled, but that spark fell short of its mark. The Jews had been beaten and recoiled. The voice of the singer did not reach them. His song was silenced. There was no singing.

But something did happen at that moment. A change took place.

As soon as the solitary voice was hushed, humbly, another voice picked up the same tune, the same captivating Chassidic tune. Only the words were not the same. New words were being sung. One solitary person in the entire humiliated and downtrodden crowd had become the spokesman of all the Jews. This man had composed the new song on the spot, a song derived from the eternal wellspring of the nation. The melody was the same ancient Chassidic melody, but the words were conceived and distilled through the crucible of affliction:

"Mir velen zey iberleben, iberleben, Avinu shebashamayim, Mir velen zey iberleben, iberleben, iberleben—" "We shall outlive them, our Heavenly Father. We shall outlive them, outlive them, outlive them—"

This time the song swept the entire crowd. The new refrain struck like lightning and jolted the multitude. Feet rose rhythmically, as if by themselves. The song heaved and swelled like a tidal wave, arms were joined, and soon all the frightened and despondent Jews were dancing.

As for the commander, at first, he clapped his hands in great satisfaction, laughing derisively. "Ha, ha, ha, the Jews are singing and dancing! Ha, ha, the Jews have been subdued!" But soon he grew puzzled and confused. What is going on? Is this how subdued people behave? Are they really oppressed and humiliated? They all seem to be fired up by this Chassidic dance, as if they have forgotten all pain, suffering, humiliation, and despair. They have even forgotten about the presence of the Nazi commander . . .

"Stop, Jews! Stop at once! Stop the singing and dancing! Stop! Stop immediately!" the oppressor yelled out in a terrible voice, and for the first time his well-disciplined subordinates saw him at a loss, not knowing what to do next. "Stop! Stop! Stop at once!" the commander pleaded with his soldiers in a croaking voice. The Jews, singing and dancing ecstatically, were swept by the flood of their emotions and danced on and on. They paid a high price for it. They were brutally beaten for their strange behavior. But their singing and dancing did not stop.

This most promising and reassuring thought stands out in stark and marked contrast to the Haftorah which we will read tomorrow morning. The section is taken from the book of Yirmiyahu, the great prophet who lived at the end of *Bayis Rishon*. That ancient Jewish leader foretold and then witnessed the cataclysmic and catastrophic ruin and ravage of Yerushalayim and the end of Jewish sovereignty by the Babylonians in the year 586 B.C.E. The major sentence of the reading relates how mother Rachel, Yaakov Avinu's beloved wife, continuously cries for her children:

רָחֵל מְבַכָּה עַל בָּנֶיהָ מֵאֲנָה לְהִנָּחֵם עַל בָּנֶיהָ כִּי אֵינֶנּוּ:

Rachel is weeping for her children. She refuses to be comforted for they are away.

What a total contradiction to today's Torah reading. Laughter and tears, happiness and sorrow, joy and despair, optimism and pessimism. How do they go together? What common bond do they share? The truth of the matter is that these two ideas are not really diametrically opposite each other. In fact, they go together and

Rosh HaShanah

perhaps even complement each other. Modern psychologists tell us that there is a very narrow line that separates love from hate, affection from animosity. I humbly believe that the same can be applied to grief and sadness on the one hand and happiness and joy on the other.

We can understand this more fully with a brief explanation of the central and most important symbol of Rosh HaShanah, the Shofar, the ram's horn. Both the Rambam and Rav Saadia Gaon and many other scholars have offered countless reasons why the Shofar is sounded on this day. However, what we need to understand is the meaning of the different sounds of the Shofar and its significance. It has a three-fold message: the Tekiah, the Shevarim, and the Teruah. The Tekiah, is a straight, calm, even blast. It was the sound that was used to gather our people together in the Midbar. It was sounded in the Beis HaMikdash on Yom Tovim and in times of peace and happiness.

The Teruah, a staccato, wailing, broken sound was sounded as an alarm. It is a siren announcing trouble, impending attack, and imminent war. The Shevarim, according to many authorities, is but a variant of the Teruah and contains the same meaning. Thus, while in essence, we sound three blasts, there are really two, the Tekiah and the Teruah.

It has been suggested that the sounds of the Shofar represent the history of the Jewish people. It recalls its high moments and its periods of despair, its light and darkness, epochs of optimism and pessimism. Following the sorrow, tragedy, and suffering of the Egyptian bondage, the Tekiah was first sounded at Har Sinai at the great moment in Jewish history – the revelation of the Torah, the great theophany. We were at that time formed as a nation and molded as a people dedicated and devoted to G-d. This continued, with certain exceptions, throughout the periods of the two Batei Mikdash, first during the reigns of Dovid HaMelech and Shlomo as well as during the period of the leadership of the Maccabees.

All too soon, however, the sound of the Tekiah came to an end and was replaced by the Teruah, the sighing of men, the wailing of women, and the constant crying of children. The Beis HaMikdash was destroyed, our young noble sons were killed, and the nation was exiled from its land. We were forced to wander the face of the earth. We were continuously harassed, persecuted and slaughtered.

Each time when we thought that we had finally reached the nadir, the lowest point of despair and sorrow, we discovered that we were wrong. Cruel fate demonstrated that the sound of the Shevarim could be fragmented even further into the sound of the Teruah. The Teruah became the sound of our brethren crying out and weeping during the pogroms of czarist Russia and during the Siberian exile of the Stalin era. Most notably, it was represented by our Six-Million brothers and sisters who stoically went to their deaths without begging for mercy in total defiance of the Nazi monsters.

My friends, the Teruah is not the final sound of the Shofar. The Teruah is not the epilogue of Jewish history and Jewish survival. No. Thank G-d, there is a final Tekiah, a Tekiah Gedolah, a long glorious sound which will herald in the messianic era. It will be a sound which will indicate the end of our wandering, the termination of Jewish suffering. It will be the conclusion of the Jewish people being a pariah, the outcast of society who was spat upon, pitied at the least, detested and killed at most. The note which indicates gladness, hope and beracha follows on the heels of the sound of the Teruah. All that for which we have wept, all that for which we have sacrificed and for which we have striven and bled will not have been in vain. G-d, my friends, certainly has not forsaken us.

This also is the message of the tears of mother Rachel. Her constant, ongoing, unending desolation, her weeping and lamenting will not have been in vain. Her refusal to be comforted until her children will return, her constant sorrow has kept the determination

Rosh HaShanah

and dream alive. The Navi records *HaKadosh Baruch Hu's* response to her:

כֹּה אָמַר ה' מִנְעִי קוֹלֵךְ מִבֶּכִי וְעֵינַיִךְ מִדִּמְעָה כִּי יֵשׁ שָׂכָר לִפְעֻלָּתֵךְ נְאֻם ה' וְשָׁבוּ מֵאֶרֶץ אוֹיֵב: וְיֵשׁ תִּקְוָה לְאַחֲרִיתֵךְ נְאֻם ה' וְשָׁבוּ בָנִים לִגְבוּלָם:

So says the L-rd: Restrain your voice from weeping and your eyes from tears, for your work shall have its rewards, says Hashem, and they shall return from the hand of the enemy. There is hope for your future says Hashem, and the children shall return to their own land.

During my last visit to Eretz Yisrael, I had the *zechus* of visiting many sites of religious and historical significance. The emotional pull was quite great at each and every one of these memorials. However, at two major Israeli landmarks, I literally poured out my heart and wept. These two sanctuaries represented to me all that is holy, precious, and dear about Israel. At one spot, my tears were of joy and happiness. At the other, my weeping was one of sadness and mourning. One site of course is the Kotel, the Western wall, the holiest of Jewish possessions. There, my tears were of gratitude and appreciation. I offered my thanks to Hashem who gave me yet another opportunity to daven at this Makom Kodesh, at this holy wall for which our ancestors died defending and our contemporaneous heroes died recapturing it in the 1967 Six-Day War. There, my tears of joy and happiness were transformed into the laughter of Yitzchak Avinu.

I also visited a monument which is not unfortunately so well-known. It is the Holocaust cave and memorial on Mount Zion in Jerusalem. Included there along with all the tragic physical reminders of the Nazi madness is a simple but emotionally moving well. The well has water which continuously flows out from it sides. There is also an inscription on the bottom which reads: רחל מבכה על בניה – "Rachel cries out for her children." She cries out for her children who were killed for no reason other than that they were Jews.

From there I immediately returned to the Kotel and was comforted. For after the sound of the Teruah, we must once again experience the sound of the Tekiah. Out of the ashes of Bergen-Belsen and Buchenwald, Auschwitz and Treblinka, came the nation of Israel – strong and erect, joyful and happy. From the tears and sadness emerged laughter and music. "There is hope, says Hashem, and your children shall return to their own land." That dream, that hope, that aspiration has begun to be fulfilled in our own lifetime.

Mother Rachel, with our help and assistance, will one day in the near future cease to cry and mourn. She will instead rejoice and be happy. For her children, all her children from the four corners of the globe, will all be free at last and will all be able to come home. Finally, the sound of the Tekiah Gedolah, will be heard worldwide. Nations will live in peace with nations. They shall not lift the sword against one another and shall never know any more war. We hope and pray that this will be the year that the great Tekiah Gedolah will be sounded and will be heard. Let us all do what we can to truly make this happen. At that time, we will know that we have certainly been granted a *Kesivah v'Chasimah Tova*, Amen.

YOM KIPPUR

9. Judaism in Action
Yom Kippur – Kol Nidrei 5838 (1977)
יונה

We have just completed the first of five services of Yom Kippur. Tomorrow evening, when we conclude the *Ne'ilah* service, the *Sha'arei Teshuvah,* the gates of repentance, will be closed. And while it is always possible for one to repent and change his ways even until the day of his death (Rambam, *Hilchos Teshuvah*), it is most effective and efficacious on this day of atonement. Today Hashem listens and hears our pleas more acutely than at any other time of the year. If we wish to have our fate sealed for a שנה טובה ומתוקה, a happy, healthy, and sweet year, the time to make any last-minute, genuine resolutions is during this 25-hour period while the *Sha'arei Teshuvah* are wide open. We can sincerely and earnestly pledge to lead better lives as both Jews, loyal and dedicated to our faith, and as decent members of the human race. If we act upon our oaths, only then can we be certain of G-d's favorable judgment.

It is most interesting that the last scriptural reading before *Ne'ilah* is the Mincha *Haftarah* taken from the Book of Yonah. The question that is asked is why do we detail the life of this relatively obscure and little-known prophet? There are so many other great Jewish personalities whom our Rabbis could have chosen for this very distinct and significant honor. Why Yonah?

Yonah was chosen for a very specific purpose. The 14th century Rabbi David ben Joseph Avudraham explained that the Book of Yonah is read to teach us that no man, no matter how righteous or wicked, how rich or poor, can flee and escape from G-d and from one's responsibilities to Him.

Yom Kippur

Yonah was told by the Almighty to travel to the iniquitous city of Ninveh and tell its inhabitants to repent from their transgressions and do *Teshuvah* or else they will be completely destroyed. Yonah refused to fulfill G-d's command and instead boarded a ship headed for the legendary city of Tarshish. He eventually realized his mistake and was saved from certain disaster by carrying out the word and dictate of the L-rd. However, even while fleeing, while attempting to avoid G-d and His duties at a time when anonymity would have saved him, when he was asked who he was, Yonah replied "עברי אנכי" "I am a Jew." Even when defying the will of G-d he loudly proclaimed his Jewishness and his attachment and link to עם ישראל. And while Yonah did perform a fine act, a positive feat, it was simply not good enough for G-d. For to be Jewish means a great deal more than announcing and publicizing our faith. It means that we must live and act as Jews in every form and fashion, at every opportunity that we have.

There are those who maintain that simply by affiliating with Jews, by identifying with Jewish causes emotionally and intellectually, they will do their share toward preserving Judaism. If they see Jews who are victorious, they are happy and proud. If they observe some who are in difficult straits, they are sad and depressed. If they read and personally witness how certain individual Nazis who methodically and barbarically were responsible for the deaths of tens of thousands of Jews are not only not punished for their crimes but are allowed to assume positions of wealth and leadership in this country, they are appalled and shocked. While feeling for our people and faith is certainly one aspect of Judaism, it is only a start and cannot end there.

The cardiac Jew, he who is a Jew only at heart and does not allow his mouth to eat Kosher food, his hands to lay *Tefillin*, his legs to rest on Shabbos, his eyes to behold the lights of the Yom Tov candles, will soon suffer spiritual cardiac arrest from all the pressure being placed upon his heart. To be Jewish in mind only, in creed and not in deed and action, is in the final analysis worthless and absolutely meaningless. This approach was tried often in the past by different generations of Jews and all have failed. It is exemplified mostly by the Marranos.

These victims of the Spanish Inquisition were coerced to embrace Christianity but inwardly remained loyal to Judaism. Yom Kippur, especially Kol Nidrei, is associated with them. The melody of tonight's prayer is credited to their secret worship on Yom Kippur night. Then, once a year, they renounced the imposed vows of a religion to which they were forced to accept. They could not practice their true faith, but their loyalty was with Judaism.

The problem with the Marranos and those that followed them is that Jewish feeling and empathy with Jewish causes is just not enough. Thinking and feeling Jewish or subscribing to a specific creed will not guarantee the continuity or the furtherance of our faith and religion. The Marranos, who were only Jews at heart, who only showed an inward feeling for Judaism and demonstrated no outward manifestation, they who were not completely and totally Jewish, did not survive. They left no descendants who today are Jewish. There are only some vestiges of the Marranos today. There are perhaps some Jewish family names. Some people light candles on Friday nights without knowing the reason behind it and then hide them in a jar.

Judaism is a religion of deed, not just of creed. We believe in מצות מעשיות. We first have to perform good works and accomplishments in our relationship to G-d and to our fellow man and only then will we have better Jewish hearts. We first say: קדשנו במצותיך ותן חלקינו בתורתיך: "O L-rd, bless us with Thy commandments" and only then "וטהר לבנו" – "will our hearts be pure and holy." We can neither reverse the order nor totally eliminate the

Mitzvah system. For to do so is not only a distortion of our faith, it is not real, genuine, and authentic Judaism.

In fact, while we place much emphasis upon the study of Torah and the learning of Jewish tradition and law that in itself is insufficient in the overall Jewish balance sheet. The Torah in Parshas Re'eh (11:32) says:

וּשְׁמַרְתֶּם לַעֲשׂוֹת אֵת כָּל הַחֻקִּים וְאֶת הַמִּשְׁפָּטִים אֲשֶׁר אָנֹכִי נֹתֵן לִפְנֵיכֶם הַיּוֹם.

"And you shall observe and perform all the statutes and judgments which I set before you this day."

The *Sifree* comments on this verse and says:

ושמרתם זו משנה, ועשיתם זו מעשה.

"משנה" refers to our learning, studying, and internalizing Jewish tradition. "מעשה" is the application of this knowledge to good and proper use. While Judaism has always stressed the importance and significance of proper knowledge of Torah and Jewish values, it has always been quite sensitive to the inherent dangers of משנה without מעשה. One's knowledge and study of Torah by itself is insufficient. If it is not used to the benefit of one's fellow man, he too is castigated as neglectful in his duties. The *Yerushalmi* in *Shabbos* (א:ב) says:

הלומד שלא על מנת לעשות נוח לו שלא נברא.

If one studies Torah without the intention to fulfill its Mitzvos, it is more desirable that he had never been created.

No one, no matter what his station in life is exempt from the commandment of ללמוד וללמד לשמור ולעשות – to learn, to teach, to observe, and then to perform. To act on behalf of our religion, to put into effect the teachings of our faith and to help our fellow Jews are of paramount importance in Judaism. This, in essence, is the real message of the *Yomim Noraim*.

In order to be worthy of the blessings and grace of Hashem, we must assume our responsibilities and fulfill our obligations. This

Yom Kippur

applies to all areas of life. We have to observe the מצות בין אדם למקום, the commandments that pertain to man in his relationship with his Creator: the observance of Shabbos, Kashrus, prayer, and family purity, etc. We also have an obligation to fulfill the מצות בין אדם לחבירו, the duties between man and his fellow man: charity to the poor and the needy and assistance to our brethren throughout the world.

Our brethren in Eretz Yisrael, our ancient and holy land, stand alone, apart and isolated from the rest of the world community. The only people that Israel can depend upon completely and totally are its own brothers and sisters – the Jews of the Diaspora and, more specifically, we of the United States. Whether through helping to gain American public opinion, diplomatic maneuvering, or even the election of political leaders who will be strong supporters and defenders of Israel, we have always done our share to help our embattled brethren.

While Israel has been pressured into making concessions and taking actions which she feels are not in her best interests, we here in this country have a great responsibility. We have the duty to truly understand the relevant issues. We must interpret them properly to the American people and to the highest circles in Washington.

We must convince the U.S. Government that continued support for a strong, vibrant, and dynamic Israel is ultimately in the best interest of America and all freedom-loving people throughout the world. Our leaders and the American people as a whole have to be inundated with facts and information as to the peace-loving desires of Medinat Yisrael. They must know in no uncertain terms that we American Jews have been loyal and dedicated to our country since its very inception. We have fought in all her wars and helped mold all her eras of peace. At the same time, we are as steadfast and fanatic in our wish to see a continually strong and secure State of Israel. That will only occur when she is allowed to defend her own borders, thwart any terrorist activity, and crush any external attacks.

Our government must know that we speak with one voice, we act with one voice, and we will vote with one voice. Israel must continue to receive the latest military equipment which she is requesting, for she must have the deterrent power to discourage the rejectionist Arabs from starting yet another war. And it is our responsibility to help her and put into action the teachings of our heritage.

The *Chasam Sofer* explained this idea with his commentary on the opening sentence of Parshas Netzavim. The Torah says:
אַתֶּם נִצָּבִים הַיּוֹם כֻּלְּכֶם לִפְנֵי ה' אֱלֹקֵיכֶם.
"You shall all stand this day completely before the Eternal, your G-d."

Most commentaries explain this to mean that all the people of Israel must stand *together as one* before the L-rd. However, the *Chasam Sofer* explains that each Jew should stand up *completely and totally* for the service of G-d. Especially on these *Yomim Noraim*, these days of Awe, we should be completely aware of our transgressions. Our *Teshuvah*, our return back to G-d should not be half-hearted or haphazard. Rather, it should be כלכם, total and complete. Our entire person must be involved in our loyalty to G-d and our service to our people.

Thus, this evening, as we begin the holiest day in our calendar, let us resolve to dedicate ourselves, body and soul, to our faith. Let us not have to go through the ordeal of a Yonah and only later respond adequately. Let us – when we are called upon to act – do so unquestionably and unhesitatingly on behalf of all our people. And then, when we have fulfilled all that is required of us, we can be assured of having our fate sealed in the Book of Life for a year of health and happiness. Amen.

Yom Kippur

10. From Confusion to Understanding
Yom Kippur—Kol Nidrei 5734 (1973)
על חטא שחטאנו לפניך בתמהון לבב

Throughout this solemn and sacred 24-hour period of Yom Kippur, we consistently recite the various and numerous *"Al Chet's,"* the emotional and soul-searching confessional. Among the many confessions for which we beat our breasts, there are some that many will question as to whether we have actually been guilty of them. In response, we are told that even though individually we may not have committed each sin, as a people, as a nation, we have collectively committed the sins. This is due to the principle taught in the Talmud of: כל ישראל ערבים זה לזה, "Each Jew, all of Israel, is mutually responsible for the deeds and actions of every other Jew." For this reason, the *Al Chet,* the long and all-encompassing list of confessions is recited in the plural:

על חטא שחטא**נו** לפניך בכפת שחד.

*"For the transgression which **we** have committed before Thee through bribery."*

על חטא שחטא**נו** לפניך בלשון הרע.

*"For the sin that **we** have sinned before Thee by evil speech."*

Over and over again, we employ the plural: "***We*** have sinned," "***We*** have transgressed," "***We*** have performed iniquities."

In addition to the חטאים for which we must confess, there is another puzzling aspect of the על חטא. We find one for which we ask forgiveness, the very last על חטא, in fact, and our Rabbis wonder why it is even considered a sin:

על חטא שחטאנו לפניך בתמהון לבב.

"And for the sin that we have sinned before Thee with bewilderment of the heart."

How is it possible that one sins because his heart is bewildered? No one wishes to be bewildered. There certainly is no benefit in being confused, mixed up, and distraught. Why do we then regard this sad state of affairs as an Aveirah, a transgression for which we must plead – *"O אלוק סליחות, סלח לנו, מחל לנו, כפר לנו – G-d of forgiveness, forgive us, pardon us, and grant us atonement"*?

    We can better understand the nature of this confessional and plea by turning back the pages of history to the dramatic scene of *Kol Nidrei* night many centuries ago in the Iberian Peninsula. During the Spanish Inquisition of the 15th and 16th centuries, the Marranos openly professed Christianity so that their lives may be spared. On the sacred night of Yom Kippur, they gathered in underground tunnels and basements to renounce their vows against G-d and Israel and to renew their allegiance to the faith of their ancestors. In fear of their own lives they assembled this night to declare their resistance as much as possible against being cut out of the Jewish fold, against being apart from their faith.

    These people were torn between external pretenses and inner self-convictions. They knew, however, in what and in Whom they really believed. They considered themselves to be and desperately wanted to be Jews—members of *Knesses Yisrael,* the Assembly of Israel. They sought to cling to the dedication of their heart in spite of the oppression, the torture of the Inquisition, and their outward appearance as Christians.

    Contrast this poignant and heartrending *Kol Nidrei* picture with the present-day American Jewish scene. We live today in the greatest democracy that the world has ever known. We are totally and completely free. We can be Jews and worship and live as Jews. We face no Inquisition. We face no persecution, no threat to our lives. Yet, what are the headlines we read? What are the problems facing our generation? "The Vanishing Jew," "The intermarrying Jew," and "The Assimilating Jew." The Jew is and has been accepted for decades as an individual and an equal in American society. However, by so doing, he is losing his commitment and dedication to his faith. That, taken together with the high rate of intermarriage and low Jewish birthrate, undermines our people and puts our future in jeopardy.

But why this alarming threat? Perhaps because we are bewildered as Jews. For after 3,500 years of our history, we are suddenly confronted in the State of Israel with the question of "מי הוא היהודי" – "Who is a Jew?" After living as Jews for three and a half thousand years, we still do not know who we are and why we are. We have more segments, more branches of Judaism in which to attract our people, and yet, an ever increasingly percentage of our people continues to leave our ranks. It thus appears that freedom, equality, and independence has become a road which leads to the abandonment of Jewish values and their leaving the fold more easily than was the persecution, oppression, and torture in the days of the Marranos. Our brethren in Spain knew where they stood, and their convictions were strong. The current Jew, unfortunately, does not even know what his convictions are. Our generation, it appears, stands in almost total and complete confusion.

The question is: Why do our people, especially our young people, leave the fold? The answer is quite obvious – because Judaism has little meaning to them. They believe it offers them nothing. It is a source of utter confusion. They have not learned the truths, the beauties, and the eternal values of our religion, all of which make for a happy and complete Jewish life.

In a classic study entitled, "Intermarriage," Dr. Albert Gordon wrote that there is a close relationship in inverse proportion between the practice of Judaism within a family structure and its members marrying out of the fold. There must be a strengthening of the ties which bind the Jewish child to the Jewish religion. What is most essential is a good and thorough Jewish education and most importantly – parental example through the performance of the Mitzvos, the commandments of the Torah.

Yom Kippur

When we fail in our devotion and dedication to our faith, when our Jewish quality of life is a hodge-podge of bits and pieces, then it is only a token practice of Judaism. We then invite confusion and תמהון לבב – bewilderment of the heart.

There is, however, a great contrast in the response of our people today to that of other lands during the days of the Spanish Jewish exiles who indeed left their homeland rather than convert to Christianity. In those days, Jews raised funds for the redemption of their fellow Jews and prayed to G-d for His compassion. They also opened their communities and homes in North Africa, Holland, Greece, France, and Turkey to receive their brethren. They redoubled their efforts to build Jewish life and learning to replace the loss of the great Spanish center. Their pious response, their prayers and their tears brought courage and aid to their suffering brethren. It reassured them that Judaism would live in spite of oppression. Jews knew where they stood and strengthened one another in the face of martyrdom.

Today, our response has quite a different sound. Our sporadic meetings and political actions are not followed with continuity because we are not sure what good it will do. We might ask ourselves whether a mother seeing her child in a flaming house stops to consider what good her shouting, her screaming, her prayers, and her leaping into the fire will do? She knows what she wants and doesn't become confused by such considerations.

Genocide, my friends, is an involuntary oppressive denial of right. Jewish suicide, however, violating the Torah and Mitzvos, is as great a crime against Jewish society as is genocide. Even if it is voluntary, do we want our shuls and other areas of Jewish life to continue? Are we proponents of Aliya or not? Are these ideals good enough for others but not for ourselves? If the significant aspects of Yiddishkeit such as Shabbos, Kashrus, and Taharas HaMishpacha are essential to Jewish life, then disregarding these values destroys

Yom Kippur

Judaism and Jewish life itself. To live in a society which protests genocide and is guilty of suicide is to be guilty of תמהון לבב. It renders us helpless to advance the cause of our endangered brethren.

Let us resolve in this land of the free and home of the brave to be very free. Many of our Marrano-coreligionists would have given their right arm for even a moment of the privilege of freedom which we have. Let us learn and live up to the meaning of Judaism and Torah as the *Am Kadosh LaHashem*, the holy and sacred people of the Almighty. Let us work for our shuls and the development of its religious life. Let us spread Torah learning by helping Yeshivos to flourish. Let us join adult education classes at our shul and elsewhere. Then will the vanishing Jew and the intermarrying and assimilating Jew stop in his tracks and return to Judaism. Then will there be a new ring to the cry we give for our brethren throughout the world who are experiencing difficult times. We will lend them courage by building what their oppressors seek to destroy. We will be leading lives in which G-d plays a most important role. His very positive response will be forthcoming.

Let us, on this night of Kol Nidrei, the start of Yom Kippur, erase the sin of confusion and bewilderment. Let us replace it with understanding and dedication. We will then be able to build and develop a good and glorious new life for the coming year and for many more years to come.

גמר חתימה טובה to all. אמן.

11. From Darkness to Salvation
Yom Kippur – Yizkor 5735 (1974)
עשרה הרוגי מלכות

A few weeks ago, I watched a most fascinating interview with one of the great Jewish personalities of today, Elie Wiesel. As a child, Mr. Wiesel was an inmate of the Buchenwald concentration camp. Upon his release, he vowed to devote his life's work to reminding the world of the Holocaust, the greatest catastrophe and most cataclysmic event to befall the Jewish people in our present exile. His numerous books, articles, and lectures have truly inspired his title, "The Conscience of Our Times."

In this interview with ABC's Gary Essex, Mr. Wiesel described the complex problems faced by the Jewish survivors of Hitler's madness. After their release from bondage, their freedom from human Hell, the newly liberated Jews were undecided as to how to relate their nightmare. Should they commit their experiences to writing and leave an everlasting and enduring memorial? Should they tell their story orally? Should they be silent? The fear of expressing their tale in print was that, once published, they and the world might feel that there is no more to say, nothing else to tell.

This, says Wiesel, should not, nor can it ever occur. The story must be told over and over again. It must be related continuously until mankind understands it, until humanity will never again repeat it. The point that Elie Wiesel emphasized time and again was that no matter what the final decision was – to write or to relate orally or through publication, the tragedy must be told. The world in general and the Jew in particular must never forget. We must always remember how our brethren were mercilessly butchered. We must constantly recall how our brothers and sisters were slaughtered a mere 30 years ago.

Yom Kippur

This idea of remembering an event which occurred to our people has become a tradition and a way of life with us. On every holiday, at every festive occasion, we remember what the L-rd has done for Israel. We fondly recall the goodness that He has performed for our ancestors and what He continually does for us. In fact, the concept of remembering in general is almost synonymous with that of Judaism.

Today, Yom Kippur, is a Day of Remembrance. We join with Jews the world over and pray, fast, and afflict our souls. We beseech the Almighty that He remember us. We pray that He inscribe us into the *Sefer HaChaim,* the Book of Life. We beg Him to seal our fate today for a year of peace, health, and prosperity.

We pause briefly, however, from our personal requests and desires. We forget for just a moment about our fate, our future, and our destiny. In this brief interlude, we remember those of our people who have departed and are no longer with us. We remember the great heroes of Judaism, the Avos, Moshe Rabbeinu, and Dovid HaMelech. We recall their contribution to our nation, our faith, and in turn, to all of mankind. We are so grateful that they existed. Because of them, our lives are more meaningful today.

In a little while, during our *Musaf* prayers, we will read one of the most moving and heartrending sections of the entire Yom Kippur service. We will recite the prayer *"Eileh Ezkarah,"* "These I remember." This elegy describes in a most mournful manner the circumstances under which ten Jewish martyrs were put to death by the Romans. This occurred during the Second Century C.E. during the Hadrianic persecutions. It followed the tragic and ignominious end of the Bar Kochba revolt against the mighty Roman Empire.

The *"Eileh Ezkarah"* prayer is the story of the truly dedicated individuals who offered themselves knowingly and with much courage for a faith which they desperately wished to preserve. They allowed themselves to be killed so that authentic and genuine

Yom Kippur

Judaism could survive and grow. What was their crime? Why did they deserve to be so cruelly murdered? They dared to defy the decree of the Roman Emperor and taught Torah. They dedicated their lives to their people, to the Torah, and to all the laws and principles contained therein. They knew that without the Torah, without the core and essence, the very lifeline of Judaism, the Jew would be no different than other persons. There would then be no reason for the Jew to exist as a separate and distinct entity.

The story is related (Berachos 61b) that one of these martyrs, the great and incomparable Rabbi Akiva, continued teaching the Torah long after the Roman decree was promulgated. One of his students/colleagues, Papus ben Yehudah, approached him and asked: "My dear teacher, are you not afraid of the Roman law? Why do you go on teaching the Torah? Don't you fear for your life?"

Rabbi Akiva smiled and answered, "My son, a Jew with Torah is likened unto a fish with water. Remove the fish from its natural habitat, take it out of the water, and the fish will surely die. The same is true with the Jew. His natural habitat, his life-sustaining source is the Torah, the Word of G-d. Remove the Jew from Torah or take the Torah from the Jew, and he will perish. Force the Jew to forego his laws and traditions, prevent him from learning its precepts, and the Jew will surely die. The Jews will expire physically as a nation and more importantly, they will perish spiritually."

Rabbi Akiva and the nine other Martyrs lived by the dictum of כי הם חיינו וארך ימינו. The study of the Torah was so much more important than that of even life itself. Each of these martyrs died a horrible death. None, however, cried out for help. No one begged for mercy. They, like their Six Million descendants 2,000 years later, went to their deaths stoically and proud. They realized that they were sanctifying the Holy Name of G-d in dying *al Kiddush Hashem.*

We are commanded today to consecrate and hallow the memory of these men. We must sanctify they who gave their lives in order to perpetuate Jewish learning and scholarship. We do this with the full knowledge of the importance and the most significant role that the Torah plays in our lives as a people and as a nation. These Ten Men, the *Asarah Harugai Malchus,* have come to symbolize all Jews throughout our history who willingly gave their lives in order to immortalize our people as a value-bearing and G-d witnessing entity.

We also recall today the memory of two men who could potentially have become outstanding Jewish leaders. Unfortunately, however, they never actualized that potential, as they were stricken down in the prime of life. Our Torah portion this morning recalls the tragic deaths of Nadav and Avihu, the eldest sons of the High Priest, Aharon. On the eighth day of their consecration as Kohanim of the Mishkan, tragedy struck. Like a bolt of lightning, the calamity of their deaths occurred.

Why were they killed? What transgression did they perform? What commandment did they desecrate which caused them to be condemned to death? Our Rabbis offer several reasons. First, we are told that they entered the holy sanctuary while intoxicated and inebriated. Other Scholars state that they introduced an *Aish Zarah,* a strange and alien fire into the Priestly service which was prohibited by Divine Law.

However, there is yet a third reason presented. The Akeidas Yitzchak in his commentary notes that Nadav and Avihu were filled with unbridled *ga'avah*, haughtiness. They were fired with unwarranted, and uncontrollable ambition and desire. When they saw Moshe and Aharon walking through the Camp of Israel, they remarked: "How long will it be before these two old men will die and we will replace them as leaders?" They were opposed to the policies and ideas of their elders. They looked upon their father and uncle as two archaic individuals who had far outlived their usefulness. It was

Yom Kippur

time for a change, they said. They wanted to be free from the imposition and limitations of an antiquated philosophy of life.

These two immature, inexperienced youths were certain that they knew more and were more qualified to lead Israel than Moshe and Aharon. They were better prepared to lead the Chosen People than the tried and tested men who had helped redeem them from the yoke of slavery and presented them with the Divine message. It was for that iniquity that Nadav and Avihu met an untimely and most tragic death.

I ask you my friends, does this passage have any message for us today? Is there any significance? Is there any reason for its being read on the day of judgment, Yom Kippur? While numerous opinions have been presented by our commentators, I would like to humbly suggest one which I believe is most appropriate for today, Yom Kippur, 1974.

In a few moments, as we do on three other occasions during the year, we will recite the Yizkor memorial prayer. We remember our relatives and loved ones who have departed from this world. We recall the memory of a dear departed mother or father who sacrificed of herself or himself to give us life, values, and Jewish education. We fondly remember a brother or sister who stood by our side in times of joy and happiness and during periods of sorrow and disappointment. We lovingly reminisce about a grandfather or grandmother who nursed our hurts and who transmitted their tradition which they received from their elders. We implore the Almighty to remember those of our loved ones who have died and passed on to the Hereafter. We plead before the Heavenly Throne that He cherish the memory of these who lived and died so that we might remain Jews.

This Yom Kippur, my friends, Yizkor is like no other Yizkor in our lifetime. Today, in addition to our remembering our precious dearly beloved, in addition to our recalling the souls of our ancestors

Yom Kippur

and martyrs of the past, we unfortunately have a new, long list of Jewish martyrs of the present. Today is indeed the Day of Remembrance. Today is the day that we and all Jews world-wide stand together and say, "We remember and we recall." We shall never forget the tragic, treacherous, callous, and unprovoked Arab-Pearl Harbor-like attack on Israel last Yom Kippur, "a day which will live in infamy."

Just one year ago today, I stood before you from this pulpit. I described the events as they had been related to me. Who then could have imagined that at that very moment, 60,000 Egyptian soldiers with 600 tanks were crossing the Suez Canal. They were attacking the Bar-Lev line which was defended by fewer than 500 Israeli soldiers and less than 10 working tanks. Who thought it possible that 1,200 Syrian tanks were then overrunning sparsely defended Israeli positions on the Golan Heights. I remember stating with uncalled for optimism and confidence that this sneak-attack will be repulsed in a matter of days at most and our losses will be minimal. How *haughty*, what great *pride*, what *superiority* we truly felt last year. How very *sober* we all are today.

Yom Kippur 1973 saw thousands of young and middle-aged Israeli men mobilized into action. They were summoned from their synagogues still wearing their Talaisim, Kittels, and sneakers. They went off to fight for and preserve the independence of their country and the future of every one of us, their people. The wave goodbye, the loving kiss, the sincere prayer which they received from their families inspired them and provided many of them with a morale booster during the horrors of war. To 2,800 young precious and holy brothers, this, unfortunately, was their last farewell.

When the smoke cleared, when the bullets stopped flying, when G-d's children ceased dying, Israel experienced a great military victory. The victory of the מלחמת יום הכיפורים was not as decisive as in the past. This time it took Israel three times longer to defeat the

Arab states than it did in 1967. However, defeat them soundly they certainly did. Instead of Egypt and Syria recapturing Israeli held territory, the end of the war saw Israel 35 kilometers from Damascus and 60 miles from Cairo. It is one thing to win a preemptive offensive war. It is quite another thing and far more difficult to be on the defensive and then push the enemy back as Israel did.

The Yom Kippur War was, I believe, a turning point in Israeli history and, perhaps, in the destiny of the world. Israel and world Jewry will never again be the same after the events of last Yom Kippur and its aftermath. There is a distinct possibility that peace can now occur in the Middle East. One could perhaps say that the Yom Kippur War made possible political achievements for Israel which even the Six Day War failed to produce. Before last Yom Kippur, no Arab nation ever wanted to sit down with Israel or even sign an interim agreement. But now both of these have taken place.

The Yom Kippur War also produced cataclysmic events in and around Israel. The Golda Meir government was held responsible for the initial state of military unpreparedness and was forced to resign. Great leaders and heroes of the past, so-called sacred cows of modern Israel history – Moshe Dayan, Abba Eban, and even Golda Meir, were ousted from office and power. Israel saw herself isolated, set apart from the world community. Only world Jewry and the U.S. were solidly on her side. Israel's citizens became disillusioned. They seemed to have lost their confidence. They appeared depressed and bitter. Israel today, my friends, is a different country. Its citizens are different people from what they were 13 months ago. But, despite all her difficulties and woes, Israel is presently much stronger physically, morally, and psychologically than she was last Yom Kippur. If the Yom Kippur War taught Israel one thing, it is that she will never again be caught napping. Never again, with G-d's help, will Israel be the victim of a surprise attack.

Yom Kippur

The problem of Israel just one year ago, and perhaps with all of us, was that we walked in the footsteps of Nadav and Avihu of old. We were complacent. We were overconfident. We had an unquestioning belief in Israel's invincibility and her military superiority. We were intoxicated with the pride of our army and our impregnable borders and defenses. We fully believed in the military inferiority and ineptitude of the Arab armies. "They would never dare attack," we reasoned. "Why should they risk senseless suicide?" We were filled with that pride, that *ga'avah,* that hubris. And for this sin, for this transgression, for this very severe iniquity, Yom Kippur had to come and humble our hearts into contrition.

Because we failed to see that the *Yad Hashem* alone was responsible for our past victories and glories, we were forced to endure the trauma of Yom Kippur 1973. Shall we continue to be blind to the miracles that occur in our own day? Have we become so sophisticated, so cynical, that we cannot sense the Hand of the Almighty controlling our destinies? Are we so ignorant, are we so void of feeling that we cannot sense when the spirit of G-d brushes up against us even for a brief moment? Will we not learn any lesson from the past? Will we not correct our mistakes?

This is not a new message that G-d is conveying to us. After the Jewish people defeated the mighty giants Sichon and Og, they were filled with a sense of pride and invincibility, just as we felt on Erev Yom Kippur 1973. At the end of Parshas Ki Savo, they stood on the borders of Eretz Yisrael with a smug assurance that nothing could stand in their way. Moshe therefore exhorted the Jews, as explained by Rashi: "Now you see yourselves in a state of exaltedness and glory. Do not dare forsake G-d *and do not become haughty of heart.* Rather, you must guard the words of this covenant."

After having witnessed the miracle of G-d, after having felt the presence of the L-rd, can we ever again be the same? In other words, did the Yom Kippur War have some value? Was there some positive purpose to it? If we have learned and internalized this lesson, then this could be, G-d willing, the last war, "המלחמה האחרונה".

This is what we must remember this morning. We must recall not only those who have died long ago but also those who have perished so very recently. Those 2,800 holy and pure martyrs are the latest names to be included in our long and all too numerous Scroll of Martyrology. We must say and we must always remember that their lives and deaths were not in vain, that it had a distinct and real purpose.

We must also maintain that the sacrifices of our loved ones, the labors and efforts of our parents, were not failures and unimportant. If today we feel drawn closer to the memory of our relatives and their Jewish ideals, if through them the Shabbos becomes a meaningful day of spiritual and physical rest, if because of our grandparents we have a greater devotion to our faith and our people, we can then say that their sacrifices were not made in vain. If because of our dear departed we have learned to share our riches and our wealth with the poor and with the synagogue, we will then have truly internalized their teachings and taken them to heart.

Therefore, on behalf of the memory of all our relatives, on behalf of the memory of the bravery of the holy martyrs of Judaism, on behalf of our Six Million brothers and sisters, and lastly, on behalf of our 2,800 latest Jewish martyrs, I appeal for your help. I ask you to help maintain and sustain not only the past of Judaism but its present and future as well. I urge you to aid our synagogue, our shul, the very core of our faith. I ask you to contribute funds in the memory of all who were so precious and dear to us in a most direct and immediate way. I implore you to donate in memory of those members of our family of Jews who gave their lives in the past so that we may live today. By doing so, we will help guarantee the future of our nation, the future of our synagogue, and the future of

Yom Kippur

our community. Then the memories of our dear and beloved departed will remain everlasting. Then will our devotion to Judaism and to the Jewish people endure and live eternally.

I pray that you should all be blessed with a *G'mar Chasimah Tova*. May you all be inscribed and sealed into the Book of Life for the coming year, a year which we hope will bring health, happiness, and prosperity. Mostly, may it bring שלום על ישראל to our people and to the entire world. Amen.

12. Remembering the Past, Living the Present, Striving for the Future
Yom Kippur – Yizkor 5737 (1976)
וידוי

Jews the world over are greatly concerned with the concepts of exoneration, forgiveness, and pardon. Today is the last day of the Ten Days of Penitence, the conclusion of the period known as the עשרת ימי תשובה, the Days of Awe, and thus we pray and ask for G-d's mercy and compassion.

Before reciting the *Viduy,* the confessional, we say:
ובכן יהי רצון מלפניך ה' אלקינו ואלקי אבותינו שתכפר לנו על כל חטאתינו ותסלח לנו על כל עונותינו ותמחל לנו על כל פשעינו.
And so let it be Your will, L-rd, our G-d and G-d of our fathers, that You forgive us for all our unintended sins, and You pardon us for all our intended sins, and You cleanse us of all our rebellious sins.

The idea of Yom Kippur being a day of forgiveness began 3,300 years ago. The *Seder Olam Rabbah* (6) relates that Moshe descended Mt. Sinai on the 10th day of Tishrei with the second set of *Luchos* bearing the Ten Commandments. He brought Israel the news that the L-rd had finally accepted their plea for forgiveness after their abomination and transgression with the Golden Calf at the foot of Mt. Sinai. Moshe ascended the mountain twice after that awesome day and pleaded Israel's case until the L-rd said סלחתי, "I have forgiven." This day has therefore remained as a statute and remembrance for over three millennia. It continues to be a most propitious day for eliciting the magnanimity, compassion, and exoneration of the Almighty.

However, my friends, in order to receive G-d's absolution and amnesty, we need do more than just request it. That is, of course, a first step, a mere knock on the Divine door of forgiveness. It is an indication that we are admitting our transgressions and we require

Yom Kippur

G-d's exculpation. But it is not enough. In fact, one of the confessionals that we recite today is:

על חטא שחטאנו לפניך בוידוי פה.

We admit our sins without really feeling regret for having committed them, or without resolving to genuinely attempt to correct them. It is incumbent upon us to demonstrate our ability to do *Teshuvah*. We must indicate to G-d in clear and unmistaken words and actions that we are truly sincere. Our ancestors in the Sinai desert were not given a complete and total pardon until they authentically and honestly repented for their gross transgressions.

The Midrash in Vayikra Rabbah (3:3) quotes Rav Bibi bar Abaye who said, "How should a person confess on the eve of Yom Kippur? He should say: I confess all the evil I have done before Thee; I stood on an evil path; and as for all the evil I have done, I shall not do this again. May it be Thy will, O L-rd, my G-d, that Thou should forgive my transgressions, pardon my iniquities and forgive me for all my transgressions, and grant me atonement for all my sins. Therefore, it is written:

יַעֲזֹב רָשָׁע דַּרְכּוֹ וְאִישׁ אָוֶן מַחְשְׁבֹתָיו.

"Let the wicked forsake his way and the man of iniquity his thoughts" (Yeshayahu 55:7).

While many people are indeed guilty of עוונות ופשעים, performing sins and transgressions against G-d, there are very few Jews who take a perpetual oath and vow never to repent and return to the right and proper path. The problem is that too many of us keep on procrastinating and postponing this act until it is far too late. It is for this reason that Rav Eliezer in the second chapter of Pirkei Avos, *Ethics of the Fathers,* says:

ושוב יום אחד לפני מיתתך.

And repent one day before thy death.

The Gemara in Tractate Shabbos (153a) elaborates on this statement and adds:

Yom Kippur

שאלו תלמידיו את רבי אליעזר, וכי אדם יודע איזהו יום ימות? Rav Eliezer's disciples asked him, "Does a man know which day he will die?"

He said to them, "Let him therefore repent today, for he may die tomorrow without having repented." This concept of doing penance, humbling yourself, admitting your guilt and changing your course of action immediately and not putting it off until it is too late can be better understood with a story related by Rav Chaim of Sanz, the great 19th century teacher.

Rav Chaim tells about a poor countrywoman who had many children but precious little with which to feed them. One day she found an egg. She was excited and exhilarated with her discovery. She hurriedly ran home and told her children about it. However, being a prudent woman, she said, "We will not eat the egg. Rather we will ask our neighbor to sit it under her hen until a chick is hatched. And this chick of ours will produce its own eggs and will hatch them into other chicks. We will still not eat any of this. Instead, we will sell the chicks and buy a calf, raise it to a cow. We will then wait until the cow has its own calves and we will sell our cattle for a field and then . . ." Suddenly in her excitement, the woman, while holding the egg, lost her grip. The egg fell to the ground and broke. It was of no use to the woman and her family, and they continued being penniless and hungry.

The moral of the story, says Rav Chaim is that when the High Holy Days arrive, each Jew resolves to do Teshuvah immediately. However, the days pass by and the weeks turn into months, and thought and contemplation are not translated into action and deed. The individual who made the resolution, instead of elevating himself, falls deeper and deeper into an abyss. Therefore, each of us ought to exercise great caution in not postponing to tomorrow that which we can and should do today. In that way, we will guarantee that not only will our present be secure, but our future will likewise be guaranteed.

Today, we are concerned about the future. We ask G-d's forgiveness and mercy and we pray that the L-rd will remember our families and ourselves and inscribe and seal us in the *Sefer HaChaim* – the Book of Life. On this day, when all our thoughts are geared ahead toward the future, we are also told to stop for a moment and reflect backwards. Think of your past and those who were an integral part of it.

It states in Deuteronomy (21:8):

כַּפֵּר לְעַמְּךָ יִשְׂרָאֵל אֲשֶׁר פָּדִיתָ....

Atone for your children Israel whom You have redeemed.

The *Sifrei* comments on this verse: כפר לעמך ישראל refers to those Jews who are alive. אשר פדית refers to those who are dead.

This atonement is found in the *Tefillos* and the Tzedakah of the living on behalf of the dead. Thus, while we have a הזכרת נשמות – a memorial service on every Yom Tov, it takes on even greater significance and importance on Yom Kippur. This is so because the very essence of Yom Kippur is a quest for forgiveness and atonement which is, says the Sifrei, necessary for the dead as it is for the living. Therefore, Yom Kippur is not only considered as a יום של רחמנות, a day of G-d's compassion and mercy; it is also a day of remembrance, a period to reminisce.

Today we bear in mind the memory of our parents and loved ones who have passed on to their eternal reward. We are reminded of the great heroes and martyrs of Judaism who have lived and died so that we and our children could remain as practicing and observant Jews. Today, we fondly recall the names of Moshe, Eliyahu, Channah and her seven sons, Rabbi Akiva, Rav Amnon, and hundreds of thousands like them. They were truly מוסר נפש, people who gave their lives in order to be מקדש שם שמים, so that the Holy Name of G-d would be sanctified and made sacrosanct.

The question for us is what will we do with our remembrance on this day? Will we remember and always do justice to the memory of all our *Kedoshim*, those that gave their lives defending Judaism down through the ages, as well as our holy and sacred Israeli martyrs who died protecting Eretz Yisrael from those who wished to destroy her? Will we remember the kind of lives that our parents and loved ones lived? Will we recall the Jewish values that they sacrificed and left us? Will we internalize them and incorporate them into our own personal existence?

My friends, even if our parents were uneducated or untrained, we always lovingly refer to them as אבי מורי and אמי מורתי, "My father, my teacher," "My mother, my teacher." The reason for this is that whether our parents were great scholars or very simple people – the values, traditions, and the ideals that they imparted to us, the kind of lives that they lived serve as eternal lessons for ourselves and our descendants. Will we emulate their lifestyles, or will we just remember them on this day of memorial for a few brief moments and then return to our normal daily activities and routine?

The Dubno Maggid explains this problem with a parable. A father once walked along a road with his young son. Whenever they reached a difficult or narrow crossing, a river, a mountain, or a valley, he would lift his son upon his shoulders and thus enable the child to cross over. Once they came to a fortified city at the approach of dusk. The gate was locked and the only openings in the wall were small windows. The father said to the son: "Know my son that until now I treated you with love and compassion. I bore you upon my shoulders and carried you in my arms. But now you see that we cannot enter the city unless you help and assist me. Only if you climb through the window and open the gates for me can we both get inside the city."

My friends, our parents and loved ones were kind, gracious and loving toward us. They gave of themselves body and soul. They sacrificed for us so that we would have a better and easier life than

Yom Kippur

they experienced. However, they always clung tenaciously to their religion and faith. Now that they are no longer physically here to lead us onto the right path and to carry us on their shoulders, we must lead the way. We must assume our responsibilities. We must become the torch lighters and help guarantee that Judaism will remain strong, secure, and vibrant. In that way the Yom HaZikaron, this day of memorial and remembrance will have genuine meaning. We will then truly merit the complete and total forgiveness, amnesty, and pardon of the L-rd. Let us do what we can. Amen.

13. Living Through Our Actions
Yom Kippur – Yizkor

Today marks the completion of the *Aseres Yemei Teshuvah,* the Ten Days of Awe which began with Rosh HaShanah. We have all fervently prayed. We have repented from any and all personal transgressions, and we have implored the Almighty to forgive us and have mercy upon the entire universe. In just a few hours, the final verdict will be brought in and the Chief Justice of the Court of Humanity will pronounce judgment on us all. We have either brought enough evidence and character witnesses to have Him inscribe us in the Book of Life, or else, G-d forbid, we have failed and our sentence of death will soon be given. But, as optimists, as people with faith in the future, we eagerly await the return of the jury. We hope that we will be granted a favorable decree and will be given yet another opportunity to serve Hashem faithfully and truthfully.

Thousands of years ago on this day, another group of Jews eagerly awaited the judgment of the L-rd. They did not face possible death sometime in the next year. Rather, nothing less than their imminent destruction was at stake. I refer, of course, to our ancestors who were recently liberated from their servitude in Egypt. In the dessert, at the foot of Mt. Sinai, they desecrated the Holy Name of G-d and worshipped the Golden Calf, a sin punishable only by death.

Moshe, their teacher and mentor, the individual who had nurtured them and transformed them from slaves to free men, was completely pained by the prospect of Israel's death. He pleaded before the throne of the Almighty to spare his people. He beseeched Him, he implored Him, he begged Him. Ultimately, Moshe cast his lot with them. "If they die, Moshe declared, then "מחני נא מספרך" – "Blot out my name from Your book." "Their fate is my fate; their doom is my doom." And so, after 40 days of fasting and supplication,

Yom Kippur

on Yom Kippur, on the tenth day of Tishrei, Hashem said "סלחתי" – "I have forgiven."

We have, my friends, reason for being optimistic. These historical facts indicate that today, Yom Kippur, is indeed a day of pardon and forgiveness. We can believe that just as G-d forgave our forebears who were unequivocally guilty, so too will He completely and totally absolve us, declare us innocent and give us life and health.

We must ask ourselves if this is really so. Can we merely rely on the nature of Yom Kippur as a day of forgiveness and be sure that we too will be acquitted of any wrongdoing, or is something else required? Perhaps we, by our actions and deeds, have to demonstrate that we have done Teshuvah, that we are basically different than that person who previously committed the transgression. This is the subject of a fundamental debate in the Talmud (Shavuos 13a) between Rebbe (R' Yehudah HaNasi) the codifier of the Mishna, and his teacher, R' Yehudah bar Ilai on the very nature of the day of Yom Kippur:

דתניא, רבי אומר: על כל עבירות שבתורה, בין עשה תשובה בין לא עשה תשובה - יום הכפורים מכפר, חוץ מפורק עול ומגלה פנים בתורה ומפר ברית בבשר, שאם עשה תשובה - יום הכפורים מכפר, ואם לאו - אין יום הכפורים מכפר.

Rebbe says, on all sins in the Torah, whether one repented or did not repent, the day of Yom Kippur, by its very nature of holiness and efficacy, will forgive the transgressor. This is so for all sins except for the transgressions of:
   a. one who disregards Hashem by denying His existence,
   b. one who speaks with insolence about the Torah, and
   c. one who refuses to undergo circumcision, or one who attempts to conceal his circumcision so as to resemble the non-Jew.
In these cases, the day of Yom Kippur does not atone until the sinner actually repents.

Yom Kippur

Rav Yehudah disagrees with Rebbe. He said, שבים אין לא שבים לא – If a person truly repents from each and every transgression, regardless of whether it is considered "major" or "minor," then that repentance, coupled with the holy nature of Yom Kippur, will bring forgiveness to the individual. However, if one does not do penitence for his Aveiros, Yom Kippur alone will not help him; he will not be pardoned.

R' Yehudah understood that unless the individual Jew is made to personalize the religious and spiritual implications of this day through absolute and genuine Teshuvah, its significance would be lost on him. In truth, the Shulchan Aruch in Hilchos Yom HaKippurim (607:6) certifies R' Yehudah's position that Yom Kippur without real, bona fide Teshuvah will not pardon the sinner.

No, my friends. Yom Kippur day does not automatically guarantee Hashem's forgiveness and compassion. He will have mercy on us only if we use this day to our benefit. Only if we willingly internalize the message and promise of a meaningful life – and we do something positive with it – will we guarantee our complete and total pardon.

In a few moments, we will begin one of the most solemn and poignant supplications in all of these Yomim Noraim. We will recite the Yizkor prayer. This meditation is of course offered four times during the Jewish year. Yet, at no time is it more touching, more moving, and more obviously relevant than during these High Holy Days.

As we recite Yizkor on Yom Kippur, we bid G-d to remember those of our loved ones who have died and passed on to the hereafter. We pause, reflect, and ask the *Ribono shel Olam* to recall those who were closest to us. We remember those who formed and fashioned our lives and those to whom we owe a great deal more than just a debt of gratitude.

Yom Kippur

As we recite our personal Yizkor, we must also keep in mind those thousands, nay millions upon millions of our coreligionists down through the ages who lived and died so that we today might be Jews. The memory of each Jew is holy and dear to us. It is not only because of the life that he lived, but because of what that life represented. So many Jews throughout all of the generations that preceded us made that conscious choice of remaining a Jew and guaranteeing a Jewish future for his children and grandchildren. We are indebted to each of our ancestors as far back as those who stood at Mt. Sinai with Moshe and accepted the challenge of G-d.

When we utter the Yizkor prayer, we ought to keep in mind that it is an expression of our awareness that we owe a debt to those who preceded us. It was by virtue of their lives, and often, unfortunately, by their deaths that Jewish survival was insured.

We remember the heroes and martyrs of our people – the incomparable Rabbi Akiva and the rest of the *Asarah Harugei Malchus*. We remember Rav Amnon and how he was literally butchered to death for adhering to Yiddishkeit and refusing to convert to Christianity. Just prior to his death, he composed one of the most well-known *Tefillos* of the *Yomim Noraim* liturgy – *Unesaneh Tokef*. We will never forget the Crusades or the Spanish Inquisition. We will never remove from our memory the atrocities and the inhuman slaughter of our brethren in Auschwitz, Treblinka, and the many other concentration and death camps.

Who can ever forget the cowardly and dastardly Arab attack on Israel in the Yom Kippur War? How can we erase from our memory those beautiful innocent Israeli teenagers and young men not praying in shul where they had been, not fasting, not supplicating to G-d as you and I were doing? Rather, their bodies lay unburied in the hot sands of the Sinai and still unmourned in the wild fields of the Golan. This we can never forget. This we must always remember.

Yom Kippur

Today, can we do anything but remember our Six Million brethren who were mercilessly butchered and categorically destroyed just 70 years ago? How dare we forget to say and recite the Kaddish for the hundreds of thousands who have no one left alive to memorialize them personally?

It is forbidden for us to allow the world to forget the real meaning of the terms "Holocaust" and "Genocide." We must strongly object to the many instances of the application of these terms. In fact, we must vehemently oppose the use of these expressions when they are applied to Israel. The world community perversely accuses the State of Israel of mistreating their "poor Palestinian residents." Not only is this charge ludicrous and absurd, it is totally false and a complete distortion of the truth. In years to come, I am afraid that the non-Jewish world will forget that the Holocaust was primarily and distinctively the destruction of European Jewry. It is not a catch-all word for all murder and mayhem that occurs throughout the world. The fact that our own people, our fellow Jews, are desperately trying to forget is almost as tragic. There are many young people born after the conclusion of World War II who do not want to know or take the time to learn about it.

What is also so very painful is that many of our fellow Jews who do come to shul to remember and say Yizkor do not know or understand what they are actually saying. They are totally unaware and ignorant of the importance and the significance of Yizkor.

Yizkor, my friends, is much more than just an utterance of the lips or going through the motions. Our loved ones who are no longer with us will not be remembered any more or less by G-d because we come to shul and say a few words. Rather, their lives and even their deaths will have some meaning and will not have been in vain only if we do more than lip service. Their lives are intertwined with ours. While they are no longer alive physically, only we can keep them alive spiritually. We do so by leading meaningful and purposeful Jewish lives.

What about the majority of you who will remain with us until the conclusion of the Yom Kippur service? You have attended shul now at least three times during the past Ten Days – some even more. You have prayed, fasted, and repented. You have pledged to become better Jews who are more committed and dedicated to your faith. However, will your lives be any different starting tomorrow morning? Will you attend shul more often than in the past? Will you become more religious? Will your homes and your personal lives become kosher? Will you observe the Shabbos as it should be observed? Will you respond to an appeal for funds and not sit back sheepishly and say, "I gave at the office"? Will you respond to the call and cry of our beleaguered brethren the world over? Will you make their cause, your cause, their troubles, your troubles, or will you continue on the same path as before? Will you be saying to yourselves, "It makes no difference what I do or perform; it is my heart that counts, and I have a good Jewish heart"?

My friends, that is one of the primary differences between the Jew and the non-Jew. While we believe very much in *creed*, it is the *deed* that counts in the final analysis. When we become satisfied with our feelings and meditations, when we substitute them for deeds, we are guilty of the sin of הרהור הלב, "of meditations of the heart," for which we confess on Yom Kippur. What we do is much more significant and meaningful than what we say or think.

The actions of the Jew determine what he feels as a Jew. The pulse in the hand of the Jew tells us a great deal about the heart of the Jew. The Jew who puts all his religion in his heart may feel for his people, may cry over their suffering, and may give a sigh of relief when they succeed. However, he does absolutely nothing to shape and mold the Jewish future.

The issue of being only a Jew at heart and nothing more was the dilemma which faced the Marranos – the hidden Jews of the Spanish Inquisition. They were Jews who outwardly were forced to accept Christianity, but inwardly remained committed to their ancestral faith. Yom Kippur has been identified with them. The melody of last night's Kol Nidrei prayer is associated with their underground worship on this day, renouncing imposed vows of an oppressive religion.

They were given a distinct status and they needed dispensation. This was because, while they felt like Jews, while they counted themselves as Jews, this was not enough. Today, other than a few symbols of Judaism that some non-Jews have, such as candle lighting on Shabbos and wearing a Magen Dovid around their necks, there are very few Jews who can trace their ancestry directly to the Marranos. The essence of Judaism is not only to believe as a Jew; one must act as a Jew.

Judaism, my friends, does not begin with the heart. The core and the essence of our faith is in deed and performance of מצות מעשיות. קדשנו במצותיך precedes וטהר לבנו. First comes the act; through that our hearts will be purified and sanctified. Preaching without practice does not lead to a noble or pure heart. The Mitzvah must precede the heart.

The Sanzer Rebbe once asked: Why was the Beis HaMikdash built on Mt. Moriah and not on Mt. Sinai? He answered: On Sinai G-d gave us the Torah. He came down and told us what to do. On Mt. Sinai we learned how to act as Jews.

On Mt. Moriah, however, we demonstrated to G-d what we could do. Avraham was willing to bring Yitzchak as a sacrifice to G-d. Yitzchak allowed himself to die if necessary in order to demonstrate his faith in fulfilling G-d's will. We are thus reminded that the Beis HaMikdash was not to be linked with instruction primarily but with deeds of grandeur and self-surrender. For as

Yom Kippur

important as instruction is, it is far more important to perform deeds: לא המדרש העיקר אלא המעשה.

We are not presently required to be among those who were forced to sacrifice their lives for Torah, Mitzvos and Jewish learning. It is also not required of us to put our lives or the lives of our children on the frontlines to defend the physical future of our people worldwide. It is, however, incumbent upon us to do what is asked of us. It is imperative that we fulfill and uphold the Mitzvos of the Torah. By doing so, we will help guarantee that our people will not die. Rather, they will continue to live, succeed, and thrive.

The test of our strength as Jews will be neither Yizkor nor the fervor of the prayers we will recite during the remainder of Yom Kippur. It will be the way we will act and perform during the coming year.

Will we honor the memory of those who died by our commitment to greater Torah learning?

Will we honor the memory of those who perished על קידוש ה' by observing more Mitzvos and thereby living על קידוש ה'?

Will we glorify the remembrance of those who gave their lives defending the future of Israel by strengthening our own commitments? If we do so, then this will lead to action which will guarantee that the Jewish people in Israel and the Diaspora will survive.

Will our recollection of the past prompt us to consider the future?

Will we, by our actions, determine that we will have a share in securing and enriching that future?

Then, and only then, will we have truly said and understood the significance of Yizkor. The memory of our loved ones and all the righteous in Israel will thereby be a blessing and will live on through us and in our actions.

Yom Kippur

Let us resolve on this holy and sacred day to do what we can to carry on the deeds and actions of our loved ones and all the *Kedoshim* and *Tzadikim* throughout our history. Amen.

14. Linking the Past to the Future
Yom Kippur - Yizkor
יום שנתנו בו לוחות שניות

All of the Jewish festivals commemorate some historic incident. They all relate to at least one element of the past. Pesach recalls the Exodus from Egypt. Shavuos is the anniversary of the theophany, G-d's revelation and His presenting the Torah to the Jewish people. Succos reminds us of the wandering of our forebears in the Sinai dessert. Rosh HaShanah commemorates Hashem's creating the world. The Rabbinic holidays, Chanukah and Purim, also call to mind victories of our ancestors over those who wished to destroy them. The only Yom Tov which, on the surface, appears to have no connection with the past is Yom Kippur, the Day of Atonement. Superficially, it seems that this, the holiest day of the year, is concerned with the tomorrows of our faith and totally ignores any historical national event. However, if we would analyze this more carefully, we would see that Yom Kippur does commemorate an historic event. It also serves as a vital and significant link between the past and the future.

While on Yom Kippur we ask G-d for forgiveness and pardon, we also observe and commemorate an event of monumental proportions which occurred more than 3,000 years ago. The Seder HaOlam explains that Yom Kippur was the day when Moshe returned from atop Mt. Sinai with the second set of Tablets for the Jewish people. It was also the day that Hashem forgave Israel for their grievous and heinous sin of the golden calf. After countless prayers by Moshe Rabbeinu, G-d said, "*Salachti*," "I have forgiven them." Thus, Yom Kippur became the day on which Jews annually ask the L-rd for His continuous and non-ending forgiveness.

Yom Kippur

We observe this day due to the courageous act of Moshe when he returned with the first set of Tablets. When he saw the abomination of the Golden Calf, he smashed the Luchos in front of Klal Yisrael and, by so doing, brought about Israel's salvation. The question that is asked is why did Moshe obliterate G-d's gift to Israel? What is even more puzzling is the Gemara in Menachos (99b) which is also quoted in the last Rashi in V'Zos HaBeracha. The Talmud states: אמר לו הקב"ה למשה יישר כחך ששברת. It commends and praises Moshe for shattering the Tablets. Why the accolades for an act which surely desecrated G-d by destroying His very gift? The Rav, Rabbi Joseph Soloveitchik זצ"ל explains this dilemma by saying that Moshe was afraid that Israel would continue sinning and transgressing with the calf and would hold up the banner of the Luchos to show that it was all very kosher and proper; it had even G-d's sanction. This was because they were delivered in the midst of Israel's serving the *Eigel HaZahav*. Thus, Moshe shattered the Tablets to indicate to Israel in the strongest possible terms that Judaism does not allow perversion, hypocrisy or phoniness. The only Judaism that can be demonstrated and held up for the whole world to see is real, genuine, and authentic.

The message of Yom Kippur then is the ever-present link between the past and the present. It serves as the tie between the heritage of our parents' lives which were dedicated to Jewish values and our own modern, contemporary times in which we attempt to emulate them. This link, this connection, must be pure and unadulterated. It cannot be false and disingenuous. We cannot worry about the future of our shuls if we rarely or never attend them. We cannot be concerned about Jewish education if we never give our children an authentic Jewish training. It is absolute hypocrisy for us to clamor about the rights of Jews throughout the world to observe the Shabbos and Festivals while we never commemorate them. No, my friends, our Judaism must not be tainted and false. We cannot dance with the calf of iniquity and hold up the Luchos to show that

Yom Kippur

all is kosher. This brings to mind the humorous but, unfortunately, true story of a Rabbi who passed a non-kosher restaurant and saw one of his most devoted congregants enjoying a hearty *treifa* meal. When he emerged from the restaurant the Rabbi greeted him and said that he saw him eating the forbidden food. The congregant thereupon responded: "If that be the case, then my food was under constant Rabbinic supervision."

Yom Kippur, and especially Yizkor of Yom Kippur, concerns itself with the past as well as the future. It is not a day just to recall the names of our departed loved ones. Indeed, one individual I know observes Yizkor by bringing forth a hidden picture of his bearded and very religious father immersed in prayer. Yizkor is a great deal more than a momentary recollection. Yizkor means keeping alive the memories of those loved ones who have passed on to their external rest. We perpetuate their memory by pledging to lead Jewish lives, internalizing their traditions, and by so doing, passing them on to our children.

An advertisement from the Bureau of Jewish Education of New York recently appeared in the Anglo-Jewish press which described the true message of Yizkor. The ad says: "Give your children a gift for the future; give them the past." In order to guarantee that Judaism will survive, in order to make certain that our children will remain Jewish, we must act as Jews. In order to be certain that our departed loved ones will not be forgotten and will not also die spiritually, we must leave a heritage to our children and grandchildren as our parents and grandparents left for us.

The Gemara in Ta'anis (23a) relates the story of Choni HaMa'agel, the famous Tana and Jewish Rip Van Winkel, who slept for 70 years. The Talmud tells how Choni once passed a man who was planting a carob tree. He asked him how long it would take for this tree to bear fruit. "70 years," responded the gentleman.

113

"Then, if that be the case, why do you plant it? You certainly will not live 70 more years?"

"I am not planting it for myself. Rather, I am doing this so that my descendants will have fruit. My grandfather planted a tree so that I may benefit from the fruit. I too am planting a tree for the well-being of my grandson."

My friends, what this aggadic incident teaches us is that we must begin today to plant the seeds for tomorrow. Even though we ourselves may not personally reap the rewards, our children and grandchildren will profit from our endeavors.

If we wish to bring back to life and spiritually immortalize those whom we fondly recall today, we can do it in no better way than by dedicating ourselves to their way of life. Judaism is not a relic of the past; it cannot be consigned to obsolescence. It is modern, contemporary, and vibrant. We cannot rely on our father's religion, our mother's piety, our grandmother's saintliness, and our grandfather's knowledge of Judaism for us to be relieved of our duties. No, my friends, the obligation is upon us. We have the duty to be Jewish for ourselves and to demonstrate it in no uncertain terms.

The Gemara in Sanhedrin (21b) comments on the sentence in Parshas Vayeilech (31:19):

וְעַתָּה כִּתְבוּ לָכֶם אֶת הַשִּׁירָה הַזֹּאת ...

Now you shall write this song...
This is the command for each Jew to personally write a Torah. The Talmud comments:

אמר רבה: אף על פי שהניחו לו אבותיו לאדם ספר תורה - מצוה לכתוב משלו.

Even if one was left a Torah by one's parents, it is incumbent upon him to write his own.

If we want our children and grandchildren to grow up being Jewish, then we must observe the Torah and teach them its values. If we wish to prevent the ever-spreading rise of intermarriage, if we wish to further Jewish survival both in this country and abroad, we must enhance our Yiddishkeit and set an example for our children and grandchildren. We have to change our lives and our lifestyles. We ought to make the Jewish community and especially the synagogue a most integral part. The shul should not be a place which we visit infrequently. Rather, we should make our synagogues our second home. We should come not only on sad occasions such as deaths, Yahrzeits, and Yizkor. Rather, we should join with our brethren at joyous times as well. It is incumbent upon us to pray in shul not only on Rosh HaShanah and Yom Kippur but on Succos, Pesach, Shavuos, and Shabbos as well. In other words, if we genuinely wish to promote Jewish survival, we, and not just the memory of our loved ones, must be the link between the past and the future. We must act without any kind of phoniness and hypocrisy, without perversion and distortion. We cannot hold up the Luchos while dancing with the *Eigel HaZahav.* We must be pure, wholesome, and unadulterated in our belief and faith, or else our children will totally and completely reject all of our overtures.

We must begin transforming and changing ourselves and our lives. We should then carry over our newfound lifestyles to our houses of worship, our shuls. The Synagogue, the miniature Temple, the מקדש מעט, represents the very essence of Jewish holiness. It has served from time immemorial as the embassy of our people. Wherever we were, no matter what country we found ourselves in, no matter how far we were from home, we always knew that we were amongst family. We were always able to go to the synagogue, meet our fellow Jews, and speak and pray in the language which unites us all—לשון הקדש.

Today, while this may not necessarily be the case in the United States and Western Europe, it was certainly so in Eastern Europe, behind the Iron Curtain. Why did the Russian Jews, who were mostly ignorant of their heritage come to congregate on Yom Kippur,

Simchas Torah, or on any other occasions? They all came to the synagogue to pray and also to meet other Jews. The synagogue was their primary Jewish address. Our brethren may not have understood all the prayers and Torah readings, but they knew that if they wished to protest and decry the Soviet persecution and harassment of Jews, there was no better place to do so than at the synagogue. The Beis Knesses, the house of worship which represents and symbolizes the past heritage of our people, was their very link to the future. It was their embassy to their fellow Jews throughout the world and their hope for a better tomorrow.

It is our obligation, here in the free and democratic Western countries, to do the same. We should, like them, be drawn to our synagogues. We should understand and realize the important part that our shuls have had in shaping our people's past. What a glorious role they can indeed play if we only let them do so in our future.

There is a story told about a Maggid, an itinerant preacher, who traveled from town to town exhorting the people to perform various good deeds. One day he came to an impoverished hamlet, and all the people gathered in their synagogue to hear him. Upon entering the shul, he was astonished to find that the townspeople were so poor that they did not even put down a floor in the shul. All that their synagogue consisted of was four bare walls and a naked earth. He began to admonish the inhabitants about at least placing a floor in their house of worship.

"When the Moshiach comes," he said, "all the Jews in the Diaspora will gather in their shuls and fly together with the synagogue to Israel. If there is no floor in your shul, your house of worship will fly to the holy land and you will remain left behind."

The question which we must ask ourselves, my friends, is – will we allow our shuls to fly away and be redeemed without us, or will we be there to hold on to the floors and be saved as well? Only if we begin to make our shuls our second home which we visit frequently and which we support wholeheartedly will we be assured of success in the future. Only if we dedicate ourselves to the values and traditions of our elders will we guarantee that spiritual continuity. Only if we are genuine and authentic and not pretentious and sanctimonious, only if we do not hold up the Golden Calf and the Luchos together will our prayers be answered. And, like Moshe before us, the *Ribono shel Olam* will say to us, "סלחתי": "I have pardoned you of your transgressions and I have inscribed and sealed you in the Book of Life for a year of health and prosperity." אמן.

15. Not Dying in Vain
Yom Kippur – Yizkor
עשרה הרוגי מלכות

Today is the Day of Remembrances. Today, as we gather in our synagogues and in our houses of worship, we join with Jews throughout this country and around the globe. We all pray, we all fast, and we all afflict our souls. We beseech the Almighty to forgive us for all our sins which we committed during the past year, and we ask and beg Him to inscribe us into the *Sefer HaChaim*, the Book of Life, and seal our fate today for a year of peace, for a year of health, and for a year of prosperity. But for a short period this morning, for a brief interlude, we pause and forget about ourselves, about our future, about our fate and destiny. We instead remember, ever so briefly, our loved ones—our fathers and mothers, our husbands and wives, our dear relatives who have departed this world. We will concentrate solely on those who are no longer within our midst, those whose souls have returned to their source and Creator—*HaKadosh Baruch Hu*—Almighty G-d.

The Hebrew word for remembrance—זָכוֹר—or זֵכֶר—is very much part of the Jew. It is uppermost on his lips throughout the entire year. On Purim, the Festival of Lots, we are commanded:

זָכוֹר אֵת אֲשֶׁר עָשָׂה לְךָ עֲמָלֵק בַּדֶּרֶךְ בְּצֵאתְכֶם מִמִּצְרָיִם:

Thou shall remember that which Amaleik did unto you when thou went forth from Egypt.

On Yom HaShoah, one of our newest commemorative days on which we memorialize the six million victims of Hitler's madness, we say over again and again, "Do not forget. We shall not forget. We will always remember you."

Just last week on Rosh HaShanah, one of the major sections of our *Musaf*, the additional service, was entitled *Zichronos,* "Remembrances." The Almighty, we are told, remembers all our

Yom Kippur

deeds and makes an accounting of each and every one of them. And at that segment of the service, the Shofar horn was sounded to remind us that each of us still has time to repent for all of our sins and all of our transgressions. We are still able to change our ways. There is yet an opportunity to turn over a new, a different, and a better leaf in life.

At all times during the year, the Jews is commanded to remember that the Almighty redeemed our ancestors from the yoke of oppression and servitude in Egypt, and that He brought them forth into the Promised Land—Eretz Yisrael—the Land of Israel.

The theme of the *Shalosh Regalim*—Pesach, Shavuos, and Succos center around the remembering, the *Zichronos*, of G-d's acts of kindness and love toward the Jewish people. Pesach, of course, symbolizes the actual physical Exodus. After 210 years of unbearable and inhumane torture and bondage, the Almighty redeemed the Jewish people with a *Yad Chazakah*, with a strong hand, and with a *Zeroa Netuyah,* with an outstretched arm.

On Succos we remember the kind benevolence of the Almighty in providing the *Ananei HaKavod*, the Clouds of Glory, which hovered over Israel throughout their 40-year sojourn and wandering in the Sinai desert.

The Festival of Shavuos recalls that one great historic moment in all of human history when man actually encountered and had communion with the Almighty. Shavuos commemorates the revelation of the Holy Torah, the heart and soul of Judaism, by the Almighty to the Jewish people at Mt. Sinai.

Remembering, however, is insufficient and does not within itself make a major impact upon our lives and the lives of our people. To truly remember, we must be able to link the past with the present and to go forth proudly toward the future.

Twice a year on Yom Kippur and on Tisha b'Av, our most solemn day and our saddest day, we read the very special Tefillah of

אלה אזכרה. We remember the heroic martyrdom of the עשרה הרוגי מלכות, the slaughter of 10 of our finest and greatest *Tana'im* and teachers who lived during the second century, CE.

These 10 leaders and *manhigim* of Klal Yisrael, including the incomparable Rabbi Akiva, died horrific and brutal deaths after *Churban Bayis Sheini* and the Bar Kochba revolt. They were beautiful and bold. They were courageous and defiant. They refused to buckle under to the brutal Hadrianic regime. They were forbidden from teaching Torah. They were prohibited from performing many of the most significant Mitzvos. In spite of the extreme likelihood of being caught and killed, they continued teaching and leading until they were captured and so viciously murdered.

They taught us a most important lesson. No matter where you find yourself, no matter where you are, or who the enemy is, Torah and Mitzvos must always be taught. We must internalize it. This must then be transformed into the constant performance of מעשים טובים. Only in this way will we help, preserve, maintain, and continue the growth of *Am Yisrael*.

The lesson of זכור was taught to us by our leaders, our Tzadikim, our *Kedoshim*, in every era and in each century.

We were hated and discriminated against by the countries in which we lived. There was only one reason for this behavior: we were Jewish, and we were different. We were deported from our homes. We faced forced conversions. We were thrown into ghettos. We had to endure the Inquisition. We managed to survive through pogroms. Most heinously, we experienced the worst living hell in human history, the Holocaust, the Shoah.

When we read the stirring account of the *Asarah Harugei Malchus*, when we recall all the atrocities that our people had to endure, when we read about the hardships we faced in every country and in every century, we must ask ourselves a very basic and fundamental question: was it all really worth it? Consider the

Yom Kippur

haughty and disdainful manner with which our more recent generations have treated our traditions, our teachings, and our Mitzvos for which millions of our people have given their lives. Pause and reflect on the attitude which leads so many to take the Torah for granted, which leads them to eliminate observances, to forget traditions, and to ignore ancient lessons. The purpose of the Ten Martyrs was to teach future generations that there is no greater vocation than that of Torah study and of Torah practice. To them Torah was life itself—no my friends—it was more important than even life. According to their scale of values, according to their *Cheshbon HaNefesh*, it was indeed worth every ounce of the sacrifice.

A modern story I recently read best reflects the elegy of all the *Kedoshim,* all of our Martyrs down through the ages. There was a recently married young couple, deeply in love and blessed with true understanding and feeling. They had great hopes of raising a large and happy family. However, during the first ten years of married life, in spite of all medical attention, in spite of all prayers, they were not blessed with any children. Suddenly, a miracle occurred and the woman became pregnant. They were soon to become parents. There was much joy and gladness in their home and throughout their families.

The long-awaited day finally arrived. But it was not a day of gladness and joy but rather, one of gloom and grief. Complications arose and the mother's life was endangered. A team of specialists were called in, and they decided that the only action which would save the mother's life was that of a therapeutic abortion. The choice was to be either the mother or the child. The two could not both live. The husband grievously insisted that his wife make the decision. And without a moment's hesitation, she declared, "Let me die, but let the child live." And so it was. As the mother's life slowly ebbed

Yom Kippur

away, the baby's life began. The baby was a boy, and his father never told him the tragic story of his birth.

When the son grew up, he went off to college. There, like so many of his colleagues and contemporaries, he met a young lady of another faith. One day, he returned home and informed his father of his great love for this girl and of his desire to marry her. Her religion? "That doesn't matter," he said. "We live in the 20th Century. We live in a new and different world. So she isn't Jewish, but we will use a judge anyway—who uses a Rabbi today to perform weddings? And besides, Dad," the son said, "today each of us lives for himself and for no one else. This is my life. I want to lead it as I see fit."

"Yes," said the distressed and distraught father. "It is your life, and you have every right to lead it as you want. But, before you proceed with your plans, just grant me one request." The son agreed, and his father drove him to an older Jewish cemetery. He led him right to his mother's grave. "20 years ago, when a little baby was about to be born, his mother became gravely ill. The doctors, with the father's consent, gave her the choice. 'It could not be both,' they sadly informed her. It was either her life or that of the unborn child. The woman in this grave would be alive today had she not cried out, 'Let me die, but allow the baby to live.' You, my son, are that baby, and this is your mother's grave. Your mother would be alive today had she not given her life so that you could live. Yes, my son, you have your own life to live. But before you go on living it the way you see fit, answer just one question: Did your mother die in vain? Was it worth the sacrifice?"

My dear friends, on this holy day of Yom Kippur, we recall the memory of a dear departed parent who sacrificed of himself and herself to give us life. We remember a beloved relative who taught us Jewish values and Jewish education. We recall our ancestors who were at our side both in our joys and happiness and during our sorrows and disappointments. The question to which we must

Yom Kippur

address ourselves is: Was their sacrifice worth it? Were their labors in vain? Were we left with an everlasting and enduring heritage? If we feel drawn closer to the memory of our relatives and to their Jewish ideals, then it was worth it. If through them the Shabbos becomes a meaningful day of spiritual and physical rest and we have greater devotion to our faith, then, my friends, we can all say in unison that it most certainly was worth the sacrifice. We thus have a tremendous burden on our shoulders. In order to give meaning to the ultimate sacrifice that our ancestors gave by dying as Jews, we must commit ourselves to living as Jews.

In the memory of our loved ones who are no longer with us, to the millions of our holy and pure Jewish *neshamos* who have given their lives so that Yiddishkeit can remain alive, to these people we loudly say: אלה אזכרה ונפשי עלי אספחה: "To these great heroes I will remember and for them I pour out my soul."

It is also quite instructive that when we discuss memory and our need to recall these tragic events, we find it written so clearly in the Torah in Parshas Ki Seitzei. The Torah says:

זכור את אשר עשה לך עמלק.

Reb Bunim of Peshischa, the great Chassidic Rebbe, wonders why the word זכור is in the singular. If the entire Jewish people has to recall the עמלק experience, should it not say זכרו in the plural?

The Torah, he says, wrote it in the singular to teach us a very important lesson. Amaleik, Israel's arch-enemy, cannot attack us successfully if we are as one. Then עמלק – and all her modern successors – have no power over us. However, if we are separate and divided, if we do not act in unison, nor are we as one mind, if we have *machlokes* and divisiveness, then, and only then, will עמלק be able to pierce our veil and attack our nation. When we are united כאיש אחד בלב אחד, he has no power over us at all. Thus, the singular זכור. He says:

סימן הוא לדורות שכל זמן שישראל באחדות אין עמלק שולט בהם.
If we constantly remember our beloved relatives and they remain in everlasting memorial to us, they then will have succeeded. If they propel us to increase our devotion and dedication to Torah and Mitzvos, then we can truly say in the words found in נצח: ספר שמואל ישראל לא ישקר, "The eternity and destiny of Israel will not fail and will not die." It will continue to live and be strong לעולם ועד. Amen.

***

Postscript: In the tragic story of the mother who sacrificed her life on behalf of her child, it would appear, at first glance, that the actions of this mother conflict with Halacha. The Shulchan Aruch in Choshen Mishpat 425:2 rules that if a mother's life is in danger during childbirth, the fetus may be aborted so long as its head did not protrude out of the womb. The reason for this is that we view the fetus as a *rodeif*, one who is pursuing another with intent to kill. One may kill a *rodeif* to save the life of the one being pursued. However, it is unclear from the language of the Shulchan Aruch (מותר לחתוך העובר במעיה) whether one is *obligated* to abort the baby or if it is merely *permitted* to do so. In *Shailos U'Teshuvos Mishneh Halachos* (14:277) Rav Menashe Klein understands the *obligation* to kill a *rodeif* to apply only where the pursuer has intent to kill. In the case of the fetus, however, since the fetus does not intend to kill its mother, although one is *permitted* to kill the fetus, one is not *obligated* to do so. According to this ruling, the mother in this case was within her Halachic rights to sacrifice her life on behalf of her baby.

This comment should not be construed as a halachic ruling. May we never be faced by such a tragic decision.

16. The We of the Jew, the I of the World
Yom Kippur—Ne'ilah
אשמנו

There is a story told about a group of men who were sailing together on a ship. Suddenly, one of them began boring a hole in the boat. The others confronted him with the terrible danger to which he was subjecting them: "Do you want to drown us all?"

To this the man calmly replied: "Why, I'm not harming you. I am only boring under my own seat."

This, my friends, is one of the saddest commentaries on our times. Our society believes in individuality, in each person thinking and performing for his own benefit. "Will what I do be beneficial or harmful to me and those closest to me?" is the only concern of one contemplating some form of activity. "I do not care at all how my deeds will affect anyone else or any group of others."

The Ari HaKadosh says that this is why the confessional which we continuously recite on Yom Kippur is composed in the plural and not the singular. We say, *"Ashamnu, bagadnu, gazalnu."* *"We* have sinned," rather than *"I* have sinned." *"We* have acted aggressively. *We* have acted slanderously." All Israel is one body, and every Jew is a limb of that body. We are therefore responsible for one another when we sin. Therefore, if our fellow Jew has acted perniciously and fraudulently, it is as though we have sinned ourselves. Despite the fact that we have personally not committed any of these *Aveiros,* we must nevertheless confess to it. This is because "כל ישראל ערבים זה לזה": "Each Jew is responsible for his fellow Jew."

In addition to our mutual responsibility, we have another area which we must rectify. We have a tendency of attempting to try to be that which we are not. We put on a charade. It is one of our favorite pastimes to delude ourselves and make ourselves think that

Yom Kippur

we are something or someone that we are not. Children often do this when they wear a baseball uniform and pretend they play for a major league sports team. Fantasizing is wonderful when you are between the ages of five and twelve. However, if an adult pretends to be someone other than himself, he requires psychological help.

Unfortunately, the Jew has also been guilty of this self-deception. The problem is that the only one whom he fools is himself. The Jew tries to hide his religion; he attempts to conceal his origin. When living in a secular or Christian society, the Jew has begun to feel guilty for his birth as well as his heritage. Therefore, he attempts to hide this fact.

Even when people are truly religious and observant, quite often, they never admit it. I am sure that we all know Jews who observe and practice all the Mitzvos of the Torah, but if they need to take off from work on a Yom Tov, they would never give the real reason. Rather, they concoct some fabricated story which will satisfy their employer. If one has to take a client out to dinner to a restaurant which is not kosher, this Jew very often will not state unashamedly, "I cannot eat because I am an observant Jew, and the restaurant does not meet my religious standards." Rather, he will give all sorts of stories such as, "I am a vegetarian," or, "I am on a diet," instead of admitting loud and clear, "I am a Jew. I cannot eat non-kosher food."

The Jew has attempted to assimilate himself into American society with such impetus and with such speed. This is done so often that it is impossible to detect the fact that he is Jewish. The great Kotzker Rebbe once talked about such behavior. He said that all letters of the Hebrew alphabet can be made larger and still retain their identity. The only one which cannot is the 'י. If it is made larger, it becomes a 'ו; still larger and it turns into a 'ן. So it is, said the Rebbe, with a Jew, the *"Yud"* or *"Yid."* If he attempts to make himself bigger, if he becomes haughty and proud, he then changes himself, and in essence, ceases to be Jewish.

Yom Kippur

The first step in the total elimination of Jewish values and concepts from the individual and eventually the whole form of Jewish life is to try to be that which you are not. When you try to conceal your Jewishness, then you are on the road to extinction. However, no matter how far you try to separate yourself from Judaism and Jews, no matter where you hide, you will be found and be counted among the Jewish people. This is so on a halachic basis: ישראל אף על פי שחטא ישראל הוא. "A Jew, no matter how far he has strayed, is still considered to be a Jew." And this is also the case in the eyes of the non-Jew. Jean Paul Satre, the French existentialist, once said: "A Jew is one whom the world considers a Jew."

We cannot hide the fact that we are Jews. We should not conceal our identity. We ought not try to be what we are not. We must fulfill our duties as Jews both to G-d and to our fellow man. We dare not shirk our responsibilities to our fellow Jew. This, in essence, is the message of Yom Kippur.

The Mishnah in Yoma (8:9) says that Yom Kippur atones for transgressions committed in man's relationship with G-d. However, Yom Kippur does not atone for transgressions committed in man's relationship vis-à-vis his fellow man. This only occurs when the transgressor has appeased his fellow man.

If we have harmed another individual in any way – physically, economically, or psychologically, we must make it up to him and ask him to forgive us. If this be the case with any one individual, על אחת כמה וכמה, how much more is this true with many people. If we have not helped nor come to the aid of our fellow human beings, then we have sinned against our fellow man and we must seek his forgiveness.

Are we acting as did the prophet Yonah and attempting to shirk our responsibilities to Hashem and to our people? Instead of heading to Ninveh and warning them of the impending danger faced by their continuous involvement in the disintegration of the moral fiber of the community, Yonah fled. He boarded a ship headed for Tarshish. As the Malbim explains, Yonah's goal was simply to remain on the ocean so that he could not receive prophecy and get Hashem's instructions on how to influence the people of Ninveh to do Teshuvah. He never reached his destination. He could not escape from his mission and from his moral duty. Eventually, after the extraordinary episode of being swallowed by a whale, Yonah returned and fulfilled his obligation. I ask you my friends: must we experience what Yonah did? Must we rely on others to do our work and fulfill our responsibility?

It has been said that the whole lesson of Jewish responsibility can be summed up in three words of the Passover Haggadah: אני ולא שליח – "It is my job and not that of a messenger." It is the lesson of personal, not vicarious participation, which has sustained and nurtured Judaism. In Halacha there is a concept known as "מצוה שבגופו", a Mitzvah which one must fulfill with one's own body. Although there are many Mitzvos which one can fulfill by listening to others, such as listening to Kiddush, the מצוה שבגופו must be fulfilled by oneself. Yom Kippur teaches us that one must hold up his Judaism as a מצוה שבגופו – a personal obligation. Too many of our coreligionists are content with passive membership in the Jewish community and its organizations. The actual conduct of religious and communal life is left to others. However, no religious life, no religious community can ever flourish by the delegation of authority. We cannot rely on others; we must rise to the occasion and assume our responsibility.

We must decide to become more dedicated and committed Jews in every sense of the word. We must become concerned with the *achdus,* the unity of the Jewish people. The words "I" and "you" must be changed to "we." I recall a very dear friend of mine in the army. He was a captain who taught in the infantry school of Ft. Benning, Georgia. He was a highly intelligent non-Jew. Often,

Yom Kippur

during our numerous discussions, I would tell him, "John, you know you have a Jewish head on your shoulders." But as bright and as perceptive as he was, he could not comprehend why, when I discussed Israel, I would use expressions such as: "We won," or "We lost," or "We suffer." He said, "They are in Israel, and you are in the U.S. Use the 'I' and 'They.'" And, as hard as I tried, I could not make him understand that when a Jew in Russia is beaten, we feel the blow. When a Jew in Israel is shot, we bleed. When a Jew in Iraq is humiliated and tortured, we experience his anguish. We are one with all Jews throughout the world. This is a purely Jewish idea. This is a concept that only an authentic and genuine Jew can truly understand.

We dare not remain on the sidelines as mere passive spectators when great and momentous events are occurring. We cannot be silent and powerless against the great tide of history. We dare not rationalize away our inactivity by saying, "What can we do to help the cause of Jewish survival?"

Our Rabbis tell us that before Moshe and Aharon went to Pharaoh to demand the release of the Jews, they held a mass demonstration. All the Elders, all the important Jewish personalities attended. But the next day when the meeting occurred, no one accompanied Moshe and Aharon to the palace. Why? Where were the others? Our Rabbis tell us that in the final confrontation, the people relied on Moshe and Aharon. They felt that they had done their share. It was not necessary for them to put their personal bodies on the line and possibly risk their lives. For this they were chastised and condemned.

My friends, I call upon you to join together in this great project of aiding and assisting Jews the world over and especially in Israel. Can we join together to help our Israeli brethren to live, grow, and flourish? If you do so, you will truly internalize the Tefillah which we recite at *Ne'ilah* which we will recite in just a few minutes:

Yom Kippur

בספר חיים ברכה ושלום ופרנסה טובה נזכר ונחתם לפניך אנחנו וכל עמך בית ישראל.

May we and all Israel, Your people, be remembered and sealed before You in the Book of Life, Blessing, Peace, and Prosperity.

Only when we do not rely on others to fulfill our responsibilities, only when we think of our brethren as we do ourselves, will we be truly remembered, written, and sealed in the Book of Life. We will then merit to live a life of peace, serenity, and happiness. We pray that all of our בקשות will be מקויים, and may we all have a happy and healthy year. אמן.

17. *Ani Yehudi* – I am a Jew
Yom Kippur—Ne'ilah, 5735 (1974)
מפטיר יונה

"I am a Jew. I want to live in the Jewish State. This is my right. Just as it is the right of a Ukrainian to live in the Ukraine, the right of a Georgian to live in Georgia, I want to live in Israel.

"… As long as I live, as long as I am capable of feeling, I shall devote all my strength to obtain an exit permit for Israel. And even if you should find it possible to sentence me for this, I shall anyway—if I live long enough to be freed—be prepared, even then, to make my way, even on foot, to the homeland of my ancestors."

This was the declaration of a great and courageous Jew, Boris Kochubiyevsky, in 1968. He dispatched this in a letter to the Soviet Party Secretary, Leonid Brezhnev, when his request to emigrate to Israel was denied. This is the cry of thousands of Jewish prisoners of conscience. Their only crime is that they desire to uphold the faith of their ancestors. All that they want is to live as Jews and give their children an opportunity to learn their heritage. They wish to fulfill the Biblical command of *Aliyah*. They desperately want to settle in Israel.

What is so touching about Kochubiyevsky's declaration and the cry of these magnificent Jews is their comradeship and solidarity with World Jewry. After almost 60 years of living under communist rule, after more than a half century of being denied their culture and faith, their religion and heritage, they still remember. They desperately want to come home. Their cry for *Aliyah* is preceded with two of the most beautiful words in the Hebrew language: *"Ani Yehudi,"* "I am a Jew." No matter what you do to prevent me from learning and studying about my tradition and my faith, I shall not waver. I am a Jew. I am proud of my Jewishness and the more you

Yom Kippur

try to suppress it from me, the more steadfast will be my determination to fight for my heritage and my people.

These truly great Jewish heroes—the Kochubiyevskys, the Sylvia Zalmansons, and the thousands of others—have a tradition and history to follow. The Russian Jews are not the first group of our people to make this declaration. They were preceded by millions of Jews down through the ages who offered their lives for the preservation of our faith and for the furtherance and continuity of Judaism. One of the first to make such a statement was the ancient prophet Yonah.

The Haftorah, for our Mincha service today was taken from the Book of Yonah. What was the significance, what was the special quality about this book that it alone, to the exclusion of every other prophetic writing, was chosen to be read on the holiest day of the year?

A comprehensive reading of the book reveals a lucid and clear call to an acceptance of responsibility, a striking message of faith. On account of this one man, Yonah, who abandoned his Divine mission temporarily and fell asleep in a moment of extreme danger, an entire vessel with all its passengers was brought to the brink of disaster. And thanks to the same man who eventually carried out his responsibilities and obligations, an entire city was saved from obliteration.

Yonah was commanded to fulfill a Divine mission. He was told to travel to the evil ancient city of Nineveh, the capital of Assyria. Its citizens were guilty of various transgressions, most notably, thievery and robbery. He was to warn its inhabitants that they faced annihilation at the Hand of Hashem because of their wickedness, thievery, and corruption. However, instead of heeding the call of the Almighty and fulfilling his mission, Yonah tried to escape and flee from G-d. He boarded a ship in Jaffa and headed for Tarshish.

Yom Kippur

A fierce and treacherous storm overtook the ship and put it in immediate danger of sinking. The sailors aboard believed that the storm was out of the ordinary, seeing in it the wrath of an offended G-d. Yonah was awakened from his peaceful sleep and placed aboard the ship's deck. He joined the other passengers in praying for their safety. They believed that someone aboard had caused this to occur. They cast lots and Yonah was chosen. He was to be thrown overboard as an appeasement to G-d. He was then asked a whole series of questions: Where do you come from? What is your occupation? Who are your people? The time was a most serious and soul-searching one. It was not a moment for evasion; it was a time for affirmation. It was an instant when what was required was a proud and loud clarion call, a declaration of faith. And this time, thank G-d, Yonah met the challenge. Unhesitatingly and unequivocally, Yonah declared: *"Ivri Anochi,"* "I am a Jew and I fear the L-rd, G-d of Heavens."

Yonah as a person and prophet was a parable of our people. He was trying to achieve the impossible. He tried to flee from G-d. He tried to shirk his responsibilities. Had he been true to the faith of the Torah, had he adhered to the word of G-d, he would not have been tossed about in the violent storm, the convulsion which always disrupts the placid and calm sea of life. He would instead have dwelt securely in his own land. But Yonah tried to flee from his responsibilities and he was thus faced with the prospect of being cast into the sea.

However, when Yonah realized that he was about to be thrown overboard, when he fully understood that his patriotism and his aid to society in general was all meaningless, he burst forth with his declaration, "I am a Jew." The message of Yonah should become our own declaration. We must state: "I am not an American who is Jewish." "I am not a Frenchman of the Hebraic persuasion." "I am not a Canadian of the Mosaic faith." "I am a Jew. I am a descendent

Yom Kippur

of Abraham, Isaac, and Jacob. I am a follower of the Torah of Moshe and the Talmud of Rabbi Akiva and Rabbi Judah the Prince. If I am to be killed, if I am to be destroyed, then let me go down fighting. Let me go down together with a declaration of undying and never-ending faith." And we shall truly find that in the final analysis, we will not really go down. We shall yet emerge to safety and peace. And we will ultimately fulfill and carry out the will of G-d.

For too long, our people have acted in the manner of a Yonah. We have shirked our responsibilities both to our G-d and to our co-religionists. We thought that if we adhere to the rules of the general gentile society around us all will turn out all right. We honestly believed that if we didn't rock the boat, if we didn't make our specific presence as Jews felt, we would be allowed to live in peace and tranquility. O, how wrong we were. As long as the Sea of Life was calm and serene, as long as the sun continued to shine, no questions were ever asked of us or our allegiance. But when the storms of war, the ravages and violent catastrophes began to shake the foundation of society, the Jew was made the culprit, the Jew was made the *kaparah*, the Jew was made the scapegoat.

We witnessed this during the period of the Middle Ages and early modern times with the *shtadlan*. This Jewish lobbyist represented the interests of the Jewish community with the local authorities. We observed this during the Russian pogroms, and we saw this ever so clearly and tragically in Germany of the 1930s and 1940s. While we have not, thank G-d, experienced this here in the U.S., we cannot be blind to its potential. We must learn a lesson from our history. If we do not want to repeat our past tragic mistakes, we must finally come to grips with reality. We must declare once and for all: "I am a Jew. I believe in G-d. I will fight for the destiny of my people. If I must, I will even give my life." Such a bold and courageous declaration has unfortunately been made by too few of us.

Yom Kippur

There is one group of our people who have, for over a quarter of a century, raised the banner of Judaism to unparalleled heights. They have declared in no uncertain terms their adherence to our faith and tradition. They have announced from the highest rooftops, *"Anachnu Yehudim!"* "We are Jews! We are proud to be members of the Holy Covenant of G-d." They have demonstrated their courage. They have proven their bravery. They have truly sanctified the very concept of Judaism. I speak, of course, of our brethren, our holy and precious brothers and sisters in the State of Israel. While we play the wishy-washy game of avoiding our responsibility and denying our tradition, our Israeli coreligionists die to preserve their Judaism and ours.

For 26 years and through four life-and-death wars, Israel has been the focal point, the very core of Judaism. Our hearts turn Eastward not only when we pray but every waking hour of the day. Israel, her successes and failures, her achievements and frustrations, her hopes and her shattered dreams have become internalized by almost all thinking Jews. We rejoice over her victories and we cry over her defeats.

While not all of us have had the truly uplifting experience of visiting Israel, I am certain that you have been told what you are missing. When a Jew comes to Israel, it is not as if he is touring a foreign country. One doesn't feel strange or alien; you feel like you really belong. It is as if you have come home. At last, you have returned to the Land of your Fathers, the birthplace of our heritage.

American Judaism has a very unique relationship with the State of Israel. The only type of alliance which this can be compared to is that of the relationship between Yissachar and Zevulun and their descendants. These two sons of our Patriarch Yaakov made a pact and signed an agreement. Yissachar and his Tribe symbolized the Torah and all that it stood for. They continually studied the Word of G-d. Zevulun, on the other hand, was a merchant and businessman.

Yom Kippur

These two Tribes worked together. Yissachar would constantly immerse himself in the Torah not only for his own benefit but also for the virtue and spiritual well-being of Zevulun. The Tribe of Zevulun supported their brothers with material wealth and prosperity. This was a most unique and different type of relationship. It has become legendary in the annals of our history.

This beautiful association and partnership has occurred often throughout our history. It was common for such a partnership to be set up among families. One family member would dedicate his life exclusively to the learning of Torah. At the same time, one or more of his siblings would work and support him and his family. The two brothers would together share in the heavenly reward of Torah study.

A poignant example of this was the arrangement made by the Rambam and his brother David. The Rambam dedicated himself to learn and write his great works. He was supported by his businessman brother, David. This arrangement ended only when David was tragically drowned at sea in a shipwreck.

Even today, in our own times, many such Yissachar-Zevulun relationships are active. In fact, in my own family, such a relationship was in effect for a number of years. My paternal great-uncle, R' Moshe Yehuda Genauer *alav hashalom*, owned a very successful business. He had six wonderful sons. All of them went to yeshivah and were quite learned. However, one of his sons had an exceptional talent. R' Heshy Genauer *zt"l* was a *Talmid chacham* of the highest order. In fact, he was one of the original *Talmidim* whom R' Aharon Kotler *zt"l* chose to begin Beth Medrash Govoha in Lakewood, New Jersey. In his *tzava'ah* (will), Uncle Moshe Yehuda wrote that his business was to be divided six ways. However, only five brothers were to work, and R' Heshy would devote his life to Torah. He nevertheless would continue to receive his share of the business. This arrangement lasted for a number of years, until tragedy struck. On *Yom HaAtzmaut*, 1953, R' Heshy and a beloved

Yom Kippur

niece, Debbi Genauer, were tragically murdered in his home in Yerushalayim by an Arab intruder. They became two of the first victims of Arab terrorism since the founding of the State of Israel.

While this formal arrangement was suspended, the loyalty and love of the Genauer brothers remained intact. After giving his *almanah* her share of the business, the five surviving brothers helped support their sister-in-law and her children. They paid for the children's education and helped make all their weddings. It is acts of love and affection and familial responsibility like these that make me so proud to be a member of such a marvelous family.

This arrangement also exists today on a national scale. Our brethren in the State of Israel are the present day Yissachars. They give us confidence. They boost our morale. We can lift our heads a little higher. We can boast of our accomplishments and successes because of the work and sacrifice of the Israelis. We, in turn, are the modern-day reincarnation of Zevulun. We reap the rewards of Israel's strivings and challenges and we help support and maintain them in their very difficult struggle.

Each time that war broke out in the Middle East in the past 26 years, our Israeli brethren have risen to the occasion. They forgot their petty differences. They put aside their internal disputes. They faced the enemy as one. They fought, they defended, and they died to preserve their land – our land – and our heritage.

We too in the Diaspora and especially here in the U.S. have also responded in a most magnanimous manner. During the 1967 Six Day War for example, the amount of money that American Jewry raised exceeded even our wildest expectations. During the Yom Kippur War last year, our solidarity, our comradeship and our partnership with Israel reached its zenith, its highest peak. As the Yissachars of today sacrificed their *"damim,"* their blood, their youth, their very lives, we too did our share. We were asked to give our *"damim,"* not our blood, not our limbs, but our funds. For, indeed, the word *"damim"* encompasses both meanings—blood and money, life and that which helps sustain and continues life.

In a matter of 18 days, Israel overwhelmingly defeated the combined armies of three Arab nations. But the price she paid was very dear and extremely high. Over 2800 potentially great Jewish leaders had their lives snuffed out in this three-week period. The extent of their loss is even magnified when we realize that it was the equivalent proportionally to 200,000 American boys killed in the same time span. The war was also economically disastrous. It cost the Israeli government $8 billion, which could have been used to continue developing industries and expanding the economic growth of our homeland.

As Israel was donating its *damim,* so were we. American Jewry donated $650 million to the Emergency Fund of the UJA. It was 3.5x the amount it raised in the Six Day War in 1967. Over $1 billion of Israel bonds were purchased. There was a tremendous degree of vitality and a spirit of unity. Yom Kippur 1973 demonstrated a spiritual and material generosity that was unprecedented in the annals of human history. We cared and we were concerned. In fact, Israel's gravest hour produced American Jewry's finest moment.

Only we, world Jewry, and especially American Jewry, stood by Israel's side during the Yom Kippur War. Only we, more than any other people or nation, can stand by her side and be of help to her even now. Hopefully, as she is going forward to a potential peace, we pray that she continually become a strong and prosperous country. Only with our help with our *damim,* with our encouragement, and with our *Tefillos* will Israel live, grow, and flourish in the future.

At this late hour of Yom Kippur, when the *Sha'arei Teshuvah*, the Gates of Repentance will soon close for another year, let us together make a resolution. Let us here and now resolve to adhere to the call of a Boris Kochubiyevsky of today and a Yonah the prophet

Yom Kippur

of yesterday. Let us declare with them, *"Ani Yehudi," "Ivri Anochi,"* "I am a Jew," in every sense of the word. In all the nuances and all the specifics, I am willing to make the commitment and sacrifice to preserve my faith and defend my people.

With our giving our charity to Eretz Yisrael, we will have fulfilled our three-pronged approach. Our *Teshuvah, Tefillah,* and *Tzedakah.* We will certainly then be assured that we will be blessed with a year of health, prosperity, and most importantly, peace for Israel, for all of *Klal Yisrael,* and for all of mankind. אמן.

18. Yom Kippurim—A Day like Purim
Yom Kippur 5778 (2017)
על חטא שחטאנו לפניך בפריקת עול

Since the conclusion of the Holocaust 72 years ago, Jews the world over have been confronted with two serious problems:
1. Why were we chosen to survive while six million of our brethren perished?
2. Where do we go from here?

Some have responded that since G-d neglected our people in its most perilous moment, since He appeared to have abandoned His children, it is only right and proper that we forget Him as well as our religion. We ought to attempt to hide our tradition and faith and become universalists. If G-d does not care for the Jewish people, why should we? We should begin to think of ourselves, our own gratification and glorification. The fact that we were chosen to survive was due to some quirk of fate, some inexplicable accident. We owe nothing to anyone. We owe everything to ourselves.

Fortunately, most of our coreligionists have not responded in such depressing and caustic terms. They know that G-d's actions are beyond human comprehension and rationalization. If we cannot understand either an overt act of the Almighty or why the L-rd allowed such an event to occur, it does not decrease or diminish in any way our love, fear, and devotion to the מלך מלכי המלכים הקדוש ברוך הוא.

The late great author and "conscience of the Holocaust," Eli Wiesel, tells of an incident which he observed in Auschwitz. This story truly underscores this dialectic approach—our inability to understand G-d's ways and yet simultaneously adhere to our faith.

Three rabbis convened a Beis Din to put G-d on trial for the murder of His children. After listening to testimony and deliberating

Yom Kippur

on the matter over several days, the court concluded that G-d was indeed guilty. After what seemed like an eternity of silence, one of the rabbis looked up to the sky and announced that it was time to daven Ma'ariv. And the members of the Beis Din proceeded to pray.

We survived and the Six Million Jews went to their deaths because that was the will of G-d. Hashem has a Master Plan to which we are not privy. Even the great and incomparable Moshe Rabbeinu, who stood at the zenith of Har Sinai and spoke פנים אל פנים – face to face with Hashem—could not understand the inner workings of *HaKadosh Baruch Hu*.

In Parshas Ki Sisa, Moshe asks Hashem:

וַיֹּאמַר הַרְאֵנִי נָא אֶת כְּבֹדֶךָ.

"Please allow me to see Your Glory."

Hashem answers:

וַיֹּאמֶר לֹא תוּכַל לִרְאֹת אֶת פָּנָי כִּי לֹא יִרְאַנִי הָאָדָם וָחָי.

"You cannot see My Face. No man is able to see My Face and remain alive.

וְרָאִיתָ אֶת אֲחֹרָי וּפָנַי לֹא יֵרָאוּ.

"You may, however, see My Back. My Face, however, shall not be seen."

The Chasam Sofer explains this very puzzling dialogue. He says that very often, we do not understand the reasons and purpose for events that occur in our lifetime at the time they transpire. It is only after a period of time elapses, whether it is a few years, decades, or even centuries that the meanings of these events and the reason Hashem brought them become clear to us.

"You may not see My Face; My Back, however, I will allow you to see."

Perhaps we can see it with the passage of time. We or our children and grandchildren will learn the reason and the rationale of the workings of Hashem.

Yom Kippur

In order to put this matter of survival into perspective, we must examine the stories of two individuals whom we recall today. Their lives and sacrifices have greatly affected our people and their actions have had a profound impact on our history and on our way of life. Internalizing their messages will provide us with a significant lesson for Yom Kippur.

The first individual at first failed in his mission. Only later, after some time, did he fulfill the will of G-d. The second person passed the test presented to her with flying colors.

The central character of the last segment of Yom Kippur is undoubtedly the prophet Yonah, whose book we read during the Mincha service.

Yonah was commanded by G-d to travel to the wicked city of Nineveh. He was to warn its inhabitants that unless they repent from their immoral behavior, the Almighty will destroy them. Instead of meeting up to the challenge of G-d, Yonah shirked his responsibility and defected. He attempted to flee from his mission and from his G-d by boarding a ship headed for Tarshish, an idyllic, utopian location. However, we are told that as much as man tries to flee from G-d and from his responsibilities, he can never travel far enough. A storm overtook the ship, and Yonah was cast overboard after it was learned that he was responsible for provoking the wrath of the L-rd.

The second historical figure who occupies a leading role in the Yom Kippur drama is none other than Esther of the Purim festival fame. And as unlikely as the mixture of these two festivals appear on the surface, in truth, they have quite a bit in common. Our Rabbis tell us that the holiday of Yom Kippur is considered in some ways as Yom Kippurim, a day like Purim. The theme of both festivals is quite similar. On Yom Kippur, the Children of Israel rise above nature by nullifying the bodily aspects of their existence. They attain atonement for their physical transgressions. On Purim, the Jew achieves the same through eating and merrymaking. His physical

Yom Kippur

pleasures therefore become sanctified, consecrated, and dedicated to G-d.

Yom Kippur contains a Mitzvah of eating and drinking on the 9th day of Tishrei followed by the commandment of fasting and afflicting the soul on the following day. Purim, likewise, contains these two Mitzvos – fasting as well as eating – except that the order is reversed. First, on Ta'anis Esther, on the 13th day of Adar, we refrain from food and drink. Then, the next day, on Purim itself, we are commanded to eat, drink, and rejoice. In fact, many have the custom to eat *kreplach*, a 3-cornered baked food, on both Erev Yom Kippur and on Purim but on no other holiday.

However, besides these similarities, I believe that there is another and more significant connection between these two Yom Tovim. Among the enumeration of the *Viduy,* the confessional which the Jew recites during Yom Kippur, is one phrase which seems to serve as a most important link between these two festivals. Ten times, from Erev Yom Kippur through Ne'ilah we say:

על חטא שחטאנו לפניך בפריקת עול.

We confess for the transgression which we sinned before You by shirking our responsibility and duty.

Each of us during the course of the year has been guilty on certain occasions of thinking only of ourselves and our family at the expense of our religion and our people. When crisis and difficulties arose at which time our participation and involvement was of the utmost importance, did we shirk our duties and relegate our responsibilities? When a friend or neighbor was ill or needed a favor were we always available to be of help and assistance? When our Congregation called and asked if we would help with a minyan or contribute funds so as to help meet the budget, were we always magnanimous, altruistic, and charitable?

If this was true on the local and personal level, when it involved people with whom we have daily and personal contact, על

Yom Kippur

אחת כמה וכמה, how much more so was this the case when it concerned our brethren in general throughout the world. On the national Jewish scene as well as on the international arena we must ask ourselves: Were we at all times caring, considerate, and compassionate? Were the needs of the Jewish people at large placed above our own petty and insignificant desires and gratifications? If the answer is in the negative, then the specific confessional of פריקת עול, shirking our responsibility, should be taken to heart by each of us individually.

The same lesson can be learned from the Purim narrative. A few years after Esther's rise to the royal throne as queen and wife of King Achashveirosh, Haman, the archenemy of the Jews, put forth his diabolical plan of slaughtering the Jewish population. When Mordechai, Esther's relative, learned of this plot, he called upon her to plead her people's case with the king. Esther hesitated. "It would be suicidal," she rationalized, "to enter the King's chambers without a formal invitation."

She was rebuked and chastised by Mordechai. "How can you possibly hesitate and think of your own selfish needs when your people are in serious danger, when their very future hangs in the balance?" And with classical words which have become a source of inspiration and motivation to Jews down through the ages, Mordechai said:

וּמִי יוֹדֵעַ אִם לְעֵת כָּזֹאת הִגַּעַתְּ לַמַּלְכוּת:
"Who knows but for such a time have you attained royalty?"

"Why do you think that G-d chose you above all the other maidens in the land to become Queen? It was not that you should be happy and content as Queen of Persia. Rather, you were placed in a position of royalty and leadership so that you can help bring about the rescue, survival, and perpetuation of His people." And with these words of admonition and encouragement, Esther put her own fears and anxieties aside and thought only of her people. She entered the

King's chambers, carried out her task, and began the process of saving her coreligionists.

My friends, on this, the most solemn and holy day of the Jewish year, we must ask ourselves, "Which personality will we emulate and follow?" Will we be like a Yonah and flee from our responsibilities? Will we run away and forsake our fellow Jews? Will it only be in the face of a great calamity that we will be ready to assume all our obligations, or will we follow in the footsteps of Esther? Even though she fully realized the dangers involved in her mission, she discharged her duties in a most effective manner and, together with Mordechai, was responsible for the salvation of her people. Yes, she wavered at first. Yes, she needed encouragement and persuasion. However, she did not procrastinate until she saw the imminent danger as did Yonah. She acted firmly, sincerely, and without any equivocation.

If, upon reflection, one looks upon the past year and sees that one has acted more like a Yonah than an Esther, one need not despair. This is a great lesson in our reading the Book of Yonah on Yom Kippur, the Day of Atonement. Yes, Yonah attempted to flee from his responsibilities to the point of despair. True, he was thrown off the ship and all seemed lost. However, G-d gave Yonah another chance. After being saved from the sea in a miraculous fashion, Yonah regrets his ways and finally heeds G-d's call. Thus, even if we may have shirked our duties in the past, we must learn from the story of Yonah to seek forgiveness and try again. However, as we begin the new year, we must strive to emulate the example of Esther. We must step forward and fulfill our responsibilities, for we may not rely on a miracle. If one shirks one's duties now, who knows if one will ever be given another chance.

Jews living in the United States and in the other democratic countries are faced with a similar challenge. By virtue of our dwelling in these countries which provide us with an unlimited

Yom Kippur

opportunity to build, develop, and grow internally, we can do one of two things. We can use this chance to our advantage and create a *Beracha*, a true blessing. We can perform acts of affirmation, positive deeds which will enhance our status in our various communities and aid and assist our brethren the world over. Or, on the other hand, we can use our freedom and independence to our detriment. We can, by our indifference and complacency toward Judaism and Jewish causes, make a *"Gehenim,"* a hell, out of our potential for greatness.

The Gemara in Eiruvin (19a) comments on this thought:

ואמר רבי ירמיה בן אלעזר: שלשה פתחים יש לגיהנם, אחד במדבר ואחד בים ואחד בירושלים.

There are three things which are openings to purgatory but also affords one an opportunity to get out – a desert, a sea, and Jerusalem.

A desert is a wilderness, an undisciplined way of life. It is a wide-open area which is barren and a wasteland. However, a desert also has great potential for growth and development. We are not restricted by any past mistakes or actions. We can build from nothing. We can create a יש מאין and mold and develop it into the right and proper path. The *Midbar*, I believe, represents our uneducated and uninitiated Jewish youth – the college students who have abandoned any and all forms of superficial and peripheral Judaism. They are looking and searching for a meaningful answer to their existence. We have the opportunity to build from nothing. We have the means to take the assimilated and intermarried Jews who have discarded authentic Judaism and transform their desert of apostasy into a blooming and blossoming garden of faith.

Some might argue that once a Jew has left the fold, there is not much we can do for him. Why even try? However, sometimes all it takes is a tiny spark to fan the flame of the Jewish soul.

There is a story told about a Jewish survivor of the concentration camps who, after the war, abandoned his faith and

Yom Kippur

belief in G-d. One day, he happened to be traveling by plane and found himself sitting next to an Orthodox Rabbi. They talked together and exchanged their views on religion. Suddenly, they were told that the plane would land in Germany and all passengers had to disembark. The Holocaust survivor became quite agitated, saying that when he left the concentration camps he took an oath that he would never again set foot on German soil. He was told that it was absolutely impossible for him to remain on the aircraft; all passengers had to deplane. Suddenly, he turned to the Rabbi sitting next to him and asked if he could borrow his Talis and Tefillin, objects which he had long ago discarded. Naturally, the Rabbi was delighted to comply with his request. The gentleman donned the Talis and Tefillin and stepped from the plane. He walked over to the first German guard he saw and said in a bold and proud voice, "Ich bin a Yid!" "I am a Jew! I have returned!"

What amazing courage. While this survivor appeared to be a "desert," he proved that he could bloom under the right conditions.

My friends, will we respond to our challenges? Will we be like an Esther, or will we take the easier and less controversial path of a Yonah?

The *Yam,* the raging sea, is symbolic of the dangers of nature – tidal waves, floods, thunderstorms, monsoons, and drownings. But the sea also represents a connecting link between nations and people. The sea serves as an endless source of supply of food and energy. The sea can be dangerous and deleterious, but it can also be quite good and beneficial if it is only harnessed and used properly.

The *Yam,* as I see it, represents the second great danger facing Judaism. It is a symbol for our brothers and sisters throughout the world who are literally drowning religiously and physically in a sea of hatred, animosity, and anti-Semitism. It represents the Jews living in Western Europe who are extremely worried about the new rise of anti-Semitism on their continent. They are petrified about the radical

Yom Kippur

Islamic hoodlums who constantly harass and threaten them with bodily harm.

With the challenge of the raging sea before us, what will we do? Will we respond with folded hands and shrugged shoulders? "Yes, I am very sorry for them. I wish they were in a safer place, and I pray they would be better off. However, what can I do?" Will we respond in such a manner, or will we react in a bold and daring way? Will we write letters, send emails, or make telephone calls to our elected officials, begging them not to forget our very frightened brethren? Will we implore our government to try to influence their counterparts in Europe to take necessary measures to help protect our brethren? Will we ask them to help try to stem the tide of radical Islamic and ISIS immigration? What will we do with the *Yam*, with the raging sea before us? Will we make it into a *Klalah*, a curse, which will lead to purgatory, or will we make it into a *Beracha*, a blessing, which will bring us to *Gan Eden*?

Yerushalayim, the capital of Israel, the Eternal City, the עיר דוד, represents all that is holy and sacred. It is the embodiment of *Kedusha*, purity and elevation. It is synonymous with brotherhood, loyalty, and heroism. However, to the non-Jewish world, it is seen as one of the great problems of our day. It is a barrier to world peace and tranquility. "It will," say our enemies, "be the cause and the battlefield for the third world war." It is representative of *Gehenim*, the very embodiment of perdition.

Whether Jerusalem and all that it stands for to us will indeed be a *Beracha* or a *Klalah*, a blessing or a curse for the future is, in many ways, in our hands. Whether Israel survives as a free and independent nation, a strong and secure force able to make its own decisions, is dependent in a great measure on American Jewry. We are the most numerous, the most powerful, and the most influential group of Jews in the Diaspora.

Yom Kippur

What will we do? How will we act? Will we become complacent and indifferent to the cries of our embattled brothers and sisters? Will we choose as our model the Prophet Yonah and attempt to flee from our commitments and obligations, or will we make the link between Yom HaKippurim and Purim ever stronger? Will we emulate the conduct and behavior of Esther? In the paraphrased words of Mordechai:

מי יודע אם לעת כזאת הִגַעְנוּ למלכות?
Who knows but for such a time that we have attained royalty?" Why were we rescued from the burning inferno of the Holocaust? Why were we fortunate enough not to have been ensnared into the inferno of the Nazis ימח שממ while Six Million other Jews died? Perhaps, my friends, we were saved and placed in a position of leadership in the Jewish community so that when the times come when our people will need us, we will be able to offer help, assistance, moral support, and financial aid.

If these words are taken to heart, if we act on them faithfully and honestly, then we will certainly succeed. Perhaps the next generation of Jews will not have to refer to themselves when they recite the על חטא שחטאנו בפריקת עול for we will have indeed fulfilled our responsibilities. By so doing, we will make a *Beracha* out of the desert. We will sanctify the sea. We will perpetuate the sanctification of Jerusalem. May we all be זוכה to be able to act like Esther HaMalkah and make Yom Kippur a Yom Kipurim, a day like no other. Amen.

Succos

19. The Unity of Israel
Succos 5738 (1977)
זמן שמחתינו – ד' מינים

Each Jewish festival is replete with symbols which are quite representative of its major theme and which provide a most instructive and significant lesson. On Pesach, we partake of matzah, unleavened bread, the poor man's food. This reminds us of our humble beginnings, the earliest period of Jewish history. Our ancestors were enslaved in Egypt and finally, the L-rd redeemed them with a strong hand and an outstretched arm. On Shavuos we study the Torah, decorate the synagogue with flowers, and eat dairy meals. All this reminds us of the theophany, G-d's revelation, His choosing Israel over the other nations of the world to be the *Am Kadosh* and the *Am Nivchar.*

On Rosh HaShanah and Yom Kippur, we sound the Shofar. We fervently pray and supplicate G-d, and we afflict our souls. All this is done to stir and motivate us to do Teshuvah, to reflect upon our past actions. We repent and vow never again to repeat our transgressions and mistakes. It also serves to demonstrate to the L-rd that we are different people. We have changed and we deserve another chance, one more opportunity to better ourselves.

Succos, one of the major pilgrimage festivals, has as its most noticeable symbol – the frail and hastily constructed hut – the Succah. This reminds us of the temporary quarters in which our ancestors wandering in the Sinai desert dwelled. It recalls the *Ananei HaKavod*, the Clouds of Glory which hovered over our forefathers and protected them from all dangers. The Succah also teaches the Jew to be happy and content with a little less in life and place his faith

Succos

and future in the hands of the L-rd. However, the Succos festival represents, I believe, another idea which is of paramount importance to Judaism.

Succos is the only holiday which is subtitled *Zeman Simchaseinu,* the season of our rejoicing and happiness. On the surface, this means that in ancient times the Jew, living primarily in an agrarian society, rejoiced and was exhilarated on this festival which marked the culmination and completion of the harvest season. He celebrated his yearly supply of crops and bounty and the blessings of the soil. However, he recognized the fact that while he certainly worked by the sweat of his brow – all that he produced, all his possessions and resources were presented to him by the Almighty, Who alone is the Master of the earth and all that it contains.

I would humbly suggest another interpretation which is not bound or limited to any form of occupation or trade. It relates one idea which remains constant throughout the Jewish community no matter what continent, regardless of century or era. This can be understood with an analysis of one of the most mystifying but beautiful Jewish traditions, the Mitzvah of the Lulav and the Esrog.

On Succos, the Jew is commanded to take the *Arba'ah Minim,* the four species – the Lulav, the Esrog, the Hadasim, and the Aravos – in his hands, make a blessing over them and wave them in all directions – east, south, west, north, up and down. And while many reasons have been advanced as to why these specific agricultural products are used on our holiday, the Rabbis in the Midrash of Vayikra Rabbah (30:12 and 14) offer two ideas which I believe best explain our tradition.

The first Midrash says:

רב מני פתח "כל עצמתי תאמרנה ה' מי כמוך."

Rabbi Moni opened his discourse with the text (Psalms 35:10): *"All my bones shall say, 'L-rd, who is like unto thee.'"*

Succos

This verse is said as an allusion to the Four Species since the rib of the Lulav (palm branch) resembles the spine of a human being. The Hadasim (the myrtle) represents the eyes. The Aravos (willow) resembles the mouth, and the Esrog symbolizes the heart.

A short while later the Midrash offers another comment. It says that our Rabbis expounded that the four agricultural products represent the four different types of Jews – the Jew who is loyal both to G-d and man; the Jew who is dedicated solely to G-d; the Jew who is devoted to his fellow man; and he who by his callousness and capriciousness cares neither for G-d nor for man. The fact of the matter is that both of these interpretations are equally correct and vitally important for a true understanding and analysis of this practice.

The Lulav, the branch of the palm tree, the כפת תמרים, contains fruit and has taste. However, it possesses no fragrance. This is symbolic of the human spine. It also stands for the Jew who may be derelict in his duties toward his fellow man – מצות בין אדם לחבירו. He, however, does not bend or break in his performance of the will of G-d, in the carrying out of מצות בין אדם למקום.

The Hadasim, the twigs of the myrtle tree, the ענף עץ עבות, contain no fruit but have a very pleasant aroma. This is similar to a human eye which sees and cries for his fellow human beings who suffer and are afflicted and tortured. This same eye is nevertheless blind to the words and commands of the L-rd.

The Aravos, the willows of the brook possess neither taste, fruit, or smell. They are compared to the human mouth which can speak *Lashon Hora.* It can talk evil, spread malicious gossip and tales about one's fellow man. It can also curse G-d, use foul language, and refuse to obey the dictates of the L-rd.

Finally, the Esrog, has both good taste and a most pleasant aroma. It represents and stands for the human heart. It symbolizes the Jew who at each moment of the day practices and observes מצות

Succos

בין אדם למקום ומצות בין אדם לחבירו, those laws between man and G-d, as well as those that pertain to one's fellow man.

The Midrash says: What does G-d do with all these different types of Jews? He cannot destroy any of them, even those that desecrate and transgress every one of His laws and commandments. Therefore G-d says:

"יוקשרו כולם אגודה אחת והן מכפרין אלו על אלו."

"Let them all be bound together in one bond and these will atone for these."

Thus, we take all four species, the Arba'ah Minim; we hold them together and pronounce one blessing over them. And by so doing, we demonstrate our belief in the concept of *Achdus Yisrael*, the oneness of Israel, the idea that Jews must join forces. They must come together with a unity of purpose and mind.

In fact, the *Ksav Sofer* said that no one single Jew is able to fulfill and observe all the commandments of the Torah. However, when Jews love and respect each other, when they act as one, when they join together as one unit, it is pleasant to Hashem. Then each positive deed, each Mitzvah performed by one person is considered as if it were done by all of Israel. For we are of course responsible for the welfare and well-being of our fellow Jews.

During the Yom Kippur service in the viduy, the specific confessional, we prayed in the plural, not the singular. Our Rabbis explain that this teaches us that whether or not we personally transgressed any specific or particular commandment makes very little difference. The fact of the matter is that even if one Jew transgresses any of the laws of the Torah, it is as if we ourselves performed that iniquity, and we must ask the Almighty for forgiveness. If, on the other hand, each Jew observes some positive deeds, even though he may still be lacking in the overall observance of Jewish tradition, as long as there is love and harmony between Jews, then the Mitzvos of one Jew will be added and linked to that of another. In that way, we will help mark the fulfillment of the *Taryag Mitzvos* by all of Israel.

Thus, what makes Succos so particular and significant is that it alone and no other holiday is considered *Zeman Simchaseinu*, a festival, a holiday, a Yom Tov of rejoicing and celebration. For only when the Jewish people stand together, when we are all brothers and sisters in deed as well as in theory, can Succos truly be a time for happiness.

However, I ask you my friends, has this always been the case? Is there constant harmony and love, closeness and solidarity between Jews the world over? Unfortunately, what we see today is the very opposite. We observe petty squabbles, disputes, and controversies between different groups of our people. And the problem is that we are not the originators of this sin. We are merely repeating our mistakes of the past. Our history is filled with divisiveness, enmity, and strife between Jews.

This began at the dawn of our history. We can point to the dispute of Yosef and his brothers. We observe the rebellion of Korach against Moshe Rabbeinu. We note the dissension between the different Shevatim during the period of the Shoftim. This continued with the friction between the Pharisees and Sadducees and the hatred and animosity between fellow men in the Second Commonwealth of Judea. This led to the destruction of the Temple and the end of Jewish sovereignty in Israel. It continued with the Karaitic schism in the 8th and 9th centuries, the false messiahs—Shabbtai Zvi and Jacob Frank in the 17th and 18th centuries, the Hassidic-Misnagid discord in the 18th and 19th centuries, and the strife between Orthodoxy and Reform Judaism in the 19th century. All these controversies embroiled Jews into conflict which tore apart and threatened the very fabric and inner structure of our faith.

In fact, with very few exceptions, notably the Six Day War, the Yom Kippur War, and the Entebbe rescue, the internal situation in Israel has been almost catastrophic. It has been so difficult to hold dialogues and to unify Israel that it has been said that if the Arab nations would ever sign a peace treaty with Israel and leave her alone, the Jewish state would destroy herself because of internal turmoil.

Do not think for a moment, however, that the divisiveness, severance, and factionalism of Judaism occurs only in the State of Israel. The fact of the matter is that we too in the Diaspora are responsible for our share of incidents which are helping bring about the dismemberment and ultimate undoing of our people. When the major religious Jewish sects resort to ridicule, sarcasm, and name calling instead of dialogue, communication, and interchanging of ideas with each other, then our people are in serious trouble. And even among the Orthodox camp itself, there is absolutely no sense of agreement, concordance, or at the very least an understanding of diverse opinions.

We have Modern Orthodoxy, Centrist Orthodoxy, right wing Orthodoxy, and of course, the scores of Chassidic sects. There are so many Rabbinical and lay organizational bodies within the Orthodox camp that even those in a position of leadership have difficulty identifying the "players without a scorecard." When the two most well-known Chassidic sects clash over ideology to such an extent that one group attacks the other both verbally and physically, we have cause for alarm.

During the Second World War, Jews could not get together and decide upon a common course of action to help our condemned brethren. And partly because of our divisiveness and lack of unity, six million Jews went to their deaths, and the world was deathly silent.

Today, once again, we are confronted by the major problem of being unable to come together and grapple with the real issues of our day. We are fragmented, disjointed, and detached from one another. We are swimming along different currents and moving in opposite directions. This certainly is not the way or the means to help save and perpetuate our faith and tradition. Haven't events of the past years in the United Nations and in other international arenas taught us that the anti-Semite does not differentiate between those who profess loyalty to the State of Israel and those who maintain that its existence serves as an act of heresy against G-d? Did Hitler distinguish between one who was a שומר מצות and one who was a מחלל מצות? Did the infamous Dr. Mengele ask if one was a Zionist, a rich Jew, a Chassid, or a Reform Jew before sending our brethren to the gas chambers and the crematorium? What is required in order to preserve Judaism and all its beauty is our ability to look beyond our own selfish and petty needs. We must see the Jewish people as one large, homogenous group which, despite its diverse opinions, must come together and unite out of love. And while this does not mean a renouncement of our own views and ideas, it does suggest that we must think of the whole of Israel rather than any segment or part of it.

The sainted Rav Avraham Yitzchok Kook זצ"ל, the late chief Rabbi of Israel, once was accused by his opponents of spending too much time with the irreligious and anti-religious Jews, the Kibbutzniks, the intellectuals, etc. His response was classic but also quite characteristic of his personality. He said: "I would rather be guilty of Ahavas Yisroel, love and affection of Israel, then be guilty of Sinas Yisroel, hatred of Israel." For the love of one Jew for another will certainly help and alleviate any and all problems that we face. This then, my friends, is the message of Succos.

When the Jew takes the Four Minim in his hands – the Lulav, the Esrog, the Hadasim, and the Aravos, we are holding together the collective Jewish people – the righteous, the kind, the good and the wicked. When we stand united with love, friendship and affection, then the Midrash relates that the Almighty says: אותה שעה אני מתעלה: "At that moment I am exalted."

Abraham Lincoln said: "A house divided against itself cannot stand." But Dovid HaMelech, *l'havdil*, put it even more beautifully when he composed Psalm 133:

הִנֵּה מַה טּוֹב וּמַה נָּעִים שֶׁבֶת אַחִים גַּם יָחַד.

Behold, how good it is, how pleasant when brethren dwell in unity together.

If we are to truly make Succos the festival of rejoicing and celebration, we must internalize and take to heart its most significant and important message – the unity, love, and harmony of the Jewish people. And then we will certainly bring about the exaltation of the L-rd and a much closer relationship between G-d and His people Israel. Amen.

20. The Universal Succah
Succos
פְּרִי הַחַג

The holiday of Succos, the Festival of Tabernacles, is one, of the most unique of all Jewish celebrations. As in the other biblically ordained holidays, Succos commemorates historical and religious events that occurred to our people thousands of years ago. It is also an agricultural holiday. Succos was the time when the ancient Jewish farmer gathered all his produce from the fields. After many months of working by the sweat of his brow, he was finally about to reap some rewards. He collected his fruits and vegetables, his wheat and barley, and he brought them from the fields to his storage units and warehouses.

On the one hand, Succos shares a great deal of similarity with the other biblical festivals. On each of the Shalosh Regalim, in the recitation of the Kiddush and during the Shemoneh Esrei, we express our thanks to Hashem for all His kindness. We especially show our appreciation to Him for taking us out of Egypt, the Yetzias Mitzrayim, which is the unifying aspect in each of the Yom Tovim. But this is where the resemblance ends. Every celebration and every tradition of the other festivals are specifically geared to the Jews. By performing the various rituals involved, the Jew is to be reminded of the benevolence that the L-rd had for his ancestors.

At the same time, we express our beliefs that it is only through the acts of the Ribono shel Olam that we remain alive. He continually aids and sustains us. He keeps us strong, vibrant, and secure. We are reminded that had there not been a Yetzias Mitzrayim, we would still be עבדים לפרעה. We, our ancestors, and our descendants would remain enslaved both physically and emotionally. This situation would probably never change.

Succos

When the Jew eats Matzah and reads the Haggadah on Pesach, he commemorates the L-rd's taking Israel out of the land of Egypt. He remembers how G-d redeemed his forebears from the yoke of slavery and from the hand of oppression. When the Jew learns the *Tikun Leil Shavuos,* when he studies the entire Torah on the Yom Tov of Shavuos, he recalls G-d's love for Israel. He remembers how the Almighty presented us with the Torah, our way of life, our guide and map for a total and complete existence.

The fact of the matter is that Succos is quite different than the other Yom Tovim. Sukkos is the only one of our festivals which has appeal to non-Jews as well as to Jews. In fact, Succos, in stark contrast to the other Yom Tovim, is universal in nature. On Succos, after the regular daily Korban Tamid was offered in the Beis HaMikdash, a number of additional offerings were brought. Each day of the holiday, a different number of these additional offerings were presented to Hashem. In addition to the regular *Korban Musafin* that the Jews brought during this Yom Tov, they added an additional 70 oxen over the course of the entire Succos festival. These 70 corresponded to the 70 original nations of the world.

Our ancestors brought these sacrifices as atonement for the sins of the world. They also prayed for their well-being, as well as for universal peace and harmony between them. Today, even though there is no longer a Temple, and although animal sacrifice can no longer be brought, we still continue this tradition. In the Torah reading for Succos, we read pesukim which list the different korbanos. We mention various sacrifices brought by our ancestors on behalf of the world community.

This universal appeal of Succos is, in fact, the main theme of the Haftarah for the first day of Succos. There the prophet Zechariah (14:16) foretells:

"It shall come to pass that the remnant of all nations...will go from year to year to bow before the King, the L-rd of hosts to observe the Festival of Succos."

Why, my friends, is Succos so universal in nature, especially in contrast to the other festivals? What significance does Succos have for humanity in general? What is its appeal?

I believe that we can better understand the importance of Succos with an analysis of its position in the Jewish calendar. The Tur, Rabbi Yaakov ben Asher, one of the greatest Jewish commentators and codifiers, offered a most beautiful explanation. He said that the holiday of Succos recalls the wonders and miracles that G-d performed for our ancestors during and immediately after the Exodus from Egypt. Thus, Succos, for all intents and purposes, should be observed in the month of Nissan, around Pesach. However, during the spring season the weather improves, the temperature rises, and one usually moves to a summer home, an outdoor booth. The month of Tishrei however, is the beginning of fall, the onset of the rainy season. Cold and inclement weather often occurs during this month. This is the usual time when people leave their summer homes and return to their permanent abodes. Therefore, when Israel takes up residence in the frail, brittle, and hastily constructed huts during the month of Tishrei, they do so *l'sheim Shamayim,* for the sake of G-d. *The entire world will see and observe that Israel dwells in Succos not for their own comfort.* Rather, they do so to fulfill the decree of the L-rd. And this will in turn be a blessing to the holy Name of the Almighty.

I humbly suggest that the fact that Succos is not observed when it should have logically been celebrated is indeed very significant. Succos is the only biblical holiday that does not commemorate any one specific event. The very nature of this holiday indicates the constant, ongoing, never-ending care and devotion that the Almighty has for Israel and all of mankind. *Chag HaAsif,* the

Festival of Ingathering, *Zeman Simchaseinu*, the celebration of rejoicing makes an overt and public appeal. It calls out to all humanity, to Jew and non-Jew alike. It asks us to see, to observe, and to internalize the benevolence, the kindness, and the beneficence of the L-rd. It calls upon us to raise high the banner of the Almighty. It implores us to make G-d's way of life, our way of life. It begs us to become charitable, forgiving and loving. It requests of us to walk in the path of the *Ribono shel Olam*.

Israel, the nation and the people, both in ancient times and in our present day, have upheld this decree. We have indeed met the challenge. We have always been altruistic and unselfish. We have always forgiven others for wronging and hurting us. We cared not only about ourselves and our destiny, but also about the world around us. In every era, in every generation, the Jew, when allowed to, played an active and vital role in ameliorating the life and times of his contemporaries. However, did the world ever appreciate this fact? Did mankind in general ever acknowledge our acts of kindness? Did the general public ever express their gratitude and thanks for all that we did? They did not do so in the past, nor are they doing so presently.

The Midrash in *Bamidbar Rabbah* describes Israel as bitterly complaining to the L-rd: "Master of the Universe, behold we offer 70 oxen on behalf of the nations of the world. They should have loved us for this. Instead, as a substitute for love and affection or even acceptance, they hate us and afflict us. Nevertheless, we continue to pray for them."

You see my friends, while the Jew has learned and taken to heart the universal and general message of Succos, the non-Jew has not. As he has not yet acknowledged the dominant role played by the Almighty, so too has he failed to recognize the importance and significance of G-d's children, Israel. This has been demonstrated down through the ages in almost every country in the world. This is also the case today.

The Gemara in Avodah Zara (3a) explains that on the ultimate Day of Judgement, the L-rd will rebuke the *Amei Ha'Aretz*, the nations of the world, for not practicing the principles of the Torah. Hashem will say that whoever was involved in and observed the precepts of the Torah should come forth and take their reward. The non-Jews will then claim that all that they have produced, their entire and sophisticated infrastructure, was done for the benefit and for the betterment of the Jews. Hashem will scoff and dismiss this outrageous proclamation. They will then ask for yet another opportunity to prove themselves. They will say that if Hashem would only give them the Torah now, they would certainly observe it. Hashem says: יש לי מצוה קטנה ושמה סוכה. "I have one very small and easy commandment, Succos. Go and perform it." The non-Jews will construct their little huts and will begin dwelling in them. Whereupon G-d will cause a summer heat to beat down, and each one will kick in his Succah.

There are two problems with this text. 1. Of all the holidays, why was Succos alone the one chosen to be given to the non-Jews as a test of loyalty? 2. Why did they fail so miserably?

The non-Jewish world can perhaps understand and even accept a Mitzvah which is purely spiritual such as prayer and repentance on Rosh HaShanah and fasting and the affliction of the soul on Yom Kippur. However, what they cannot comprehend is the concept of sanctifying the physical. They cannot fathom that by residing and eating one's meals in an external abode, a temporarily constructed hut, one fulfills the dictates of the L-rd. Thus, when it is too hot or even too cold, they walk out and kick the Succah with disgust.

The Jew has always been the epitome of the concept of Succah. He has never believed in either total asceticism or epicureanism. Rather, he has always been involved with and enjoyed the pleasures of the world. But he has, at the same time, sanctified the mundane, elevated the physical, and taken hold of that which could bring man to the lowest levels and raised it to the highest degree of holiness. It is this idea that the non-Jewish world cannot accept or even recognize.

These two divergent views are indeed crystalized by the symbol associated with the Jews, the Magen Dovid, and, *l'havdil*, the symbol associated with the Christian world, the cross. Rabbi Akiva Tatz observes that the cross contains a vertical line, which can be conceptualized as representing spirituality, or man's connection to Heaven. The horizontal line of the cross represents man's physical reality. These two lines form a cross, denoting that the paths of spirituality and physicality are in total, opposite directions. Spirituality, in their view, is defined as one who is ascetic, celibate, and removed from the daily affairs of this world. A physical life can in no way be aligned with spirituality.

להבדיל אלף הבדלות, the Magen Dovid represents the Jewish worldview as described above. The six lines of the Magen Dovid represent the six directions: north, south, east, west, up, and down. The Magen Dovid also has lines which represent this earth and man's connection to Heaven. However, instead of leading in opposite directions, these lines interconnect and coalesce into one whole, demonstrating the synthesis of the physical with the spiritual. No Mitzvah symbolizes this interconnectivity more than the Succah.

The Yom Kippur Jew is concerned about his fate and future. He stands with his hat in his hand and begs for forgiveness and mercy. This Jew is accepted by the non-Jewish world as the "genuine and authentic Jew." He is pitied, and consideration is given for his very future. The wandering Jew, the Jew of the *golus*, was, until the Shoah, never completely destroyed. Yet, he was tortured and oppressed. He was made an example for the entire world to see, but he was kept alive. His physical continuity was usually assured.

This was even the case when the State of Israel was established and it began its miraculous road toward industrialization and urbanization. While its future hung in the balance, as long as its Arab neighbors appeared to be stronger and able to destroy her, the non-Jewish world was worried and empathized with the Jewish state. However, as soon as the Yom Kippur Jew gave way to the Succos Jew, everything changed. When the Jew synthesized the physical and the spiritual, the non-Jew was puzzled. When the Jew elevated the mundane into the holy realm, the non-Jewish world was taken aback. On Succos, when the Jews' success and plenty in many different areas of life becomes manifest, the non-Jews' feelings of envy and anger become front and center. Immediately after the glorious Six Day War, Israel, the nation whose demise the world would have mourned with "crocodile tears," suddenly became alienated from the world community, alone and bereft of allies and friends. It stood by itself and was bereft of allies and friends.

Western democracies and the newly emerging nations joined hands and supported the Arab world and the Palestinian cause. They all very conveniently forgot the friendship, comradery, and the assistance that Israel gave to the under-privileged and needy nations. They abandoned her when Israel desperately needed friends.

We are Israel's brothers and sisters. We must at all times be their most fervent defenders. We have to constantly be *mispaleil* to Hashem to keep her safe and secure.

I believe that it was Abba Eban, the great Israeli statesman, who once said, "With peace, Israel will blossom into a wonderful *Gan Eden* of agricultural and industrial productivity. Without peace, it will take somewhat longer. It will however, take place."

If we can indeed internalize this, if we can impart this to the entire world, how much better off would we be. With our help and with the aid and assistance of *HaKadosh Baruch Hu*, we will one day see a peaceful, secure, and prosperous Israel.

Only then will we see all the nations of the world acknowledge that Hashem is the L-rd of Heaven and Earth, and we, the Jewish nation, are His people. We will then truly see the fulfillment of the words of the *Navi Zechariah*:

וְהָיָה כָּל הַנּוֹתָר מִכָּל הַגּוֹיִם הַבָּאִים עַל יְרוּשָׁלָם וְעָלוּ מִדֵּי שָׁנָה בְשָׁנָה לְהִשְׁתַּחֲוֹת לְמֶלֶךְ ה' צְבָקוֹת וְלָחֹג אֶת חַג הַסֻּכּוֹת.

And it shall be that all who survive from all the nations coming against Jerusalem shall go up from year to year to worship the King, the L-rd of Hosts, and celebrate the festival of Succos."

This will truly be the realization of the dream that the Jewish Yom Tov of Succos will one day also become the universal Succos. It will then be observed by all mankind. We will then truly bask in the glory of the Melech HaMoshiach. Let us do what we can to hasten that day. Amen.

21. The Synthesis of the Ancient and the Modern
Succos—Shabbos Chol HaMoed
ברכת שהחיינו

We have no better reminder, my friends, than Succos that the winter season is not far off. The trees begin to lose their leaves, and a chill wind blows through our temporary and hastily constructed huts—our Succos. It gets darker much earlier from week to week. And the slowdown in nature and the curtailment of the earth's productivity reflect the inevitable state in man's life as well.

This unspoken pessimism is characteristically reflected in the Book of Koheles—the Book of Ecclesiastes. If we paid strict attention to it and studied it carefully this morning, we would have realized how dreary and discomforting this work is. King Solomon, the famous Shlomo HaMelech, the builder of the Beis HaMikdash, the wisest of men, reaches the end of his days. He discovers that he really isn't all that wise at all. He really isn't as powerful as he thought. Our Rabbis used their tremendous insight when they chose Succos as the most appropriate time for the reading of Koheles.

In marked contrast, we observe a very different holiday in another season. Pesach is the Yom Tov that celebrates birth and growth, the joy of liberty, and the optimism of freedom. It marks new buds and blossoms on the trees, the growth of new, beautiful, and colorful flowers, a resurgence of nature. Pesach is the holiday which commemorates the Exodus from Egypt, the release from slavery, from oppression, and bondage. Then we read Shir HaShirim, the Song of Songs. It is a story that demonstrates the drawing together of Hashem and *Am Yisrael* as two lovers. This idea is reflected in the parable of a princess who descends from a most noble family and a shepherd.

In these two Biblical books we find the contrast of all the opposites of life. Pesach denotes ambition and resolution; Succos symbolizes frailty and brokenness. This annual cycle of Pesach and Succos, of Shir HaShirim and Koheles, of optimism and pessimism, is the cycle of life. It represents both the life and development of an individual. It also reflects the growth of a country and a nation.

The question to which we must address ourselves today is which of these two moods most clearly reflects the indomitable spirit of the Jew? What are we as Jews? Are we basically optimistic or are we pessimistic? Do we represent the old or the new? I humbly suggest that in the annual reading of these two Megilos, we are provided with a most insightful answer. Judaism is both. Shir HaShirim and Koheles are both integral parts and segments of the same Torah. Judaism seeks to synthesize the old and the new. It tries to reconcile two seemingly incongruous moods by subjecting both to a higher motif, the Holy Torah.

An analysis of one of our most important Tefillos which we recited on the first two days of Succos can give an added dimension to the Jewish synthesis of the new and the old—of Shir HaShirim and Koheles.

On Succos, we take the Lulav and Esrog in our hands; we also make the Kiddush in our Succah. After the traditional blessings for both, we bless the Almighty and we say:

שהחיינו וקיימנו והגיענו לזמן הזה.

Blessed art Though G-d, our G-d, King of the universe, Who has kept us alive and preserved us and made it possible for us to reach the present day.

One can observe that this beracha contains two ideas. The idea of remaining alive and that of attaining the present day. Why are both ideas mentioned? If one remains alive does he not automatically reach to the present day? The concluding words to this beracha are "והגיענו לזמן הזה," "Who caused us to reach the present."

It does not speak merely of living or of living now. It speaks of reaching, being on par with the present age. From this approach we can, I think, obtain some insights into the secret of Jewish existence.

In any analysis of history, we can observe two ways in which nations have successfully retained their identity. The first lies in isolating itself from all other groups. These nations refuse to participate in the life of other nations by withdrawing entirely into a shell and living life exactly as their parents, grandparents, and ancestors to the earliest generation lived theirs. They are well described by the statement of the Torah, "עם לבדד ישכן." They are, in truth, nations which lived entirely by themselves. We can immediately think of several examples of this kind of nation—the Chinese, the Hindus, and certain African countries. These are people who make a religion of adherence to the past. Indeed, the Chinese are noted for their ancestor worship. Any new or modern ideas which come in contact with this type of culture are simply absorbed and integrated, while the culture itself remains exactly as before.

The second way of retaining one's identity is by changing the customs and institutions, or by adapting one's own civilization so that it keeps abreast of the pace of life itself. The end result of such progress is that in the course of time the original culture is completely changed. Good examples are the Greeks and Italians. Both exist from ancient times, both were powerful ancient people, and both are relatively modern countries. Yet how completely different they both are from their ancestors. There is no resemblance to their forebears. The people are different, a product of the mixture of many races; the language is very much changed; the religion is another; the forms of government are different, and the customs are entirely changed.

The first group, the Chinese and the Hindus represent the שהחיינו וקיימנו; they are still living but have no contact with our time. They are living a thousand years back. The second group, the Italians and the Greeks, symbolize the והגיענו לזמן הזה; they have reached our time, they are a part of it, but in the process, have lost their contact with their past. The first is static and stagnant; the second is part of our life but not part of their past.

Herein lies the great lesson to be learned from the blessing of the Shehechiyanu. In the *beracha* we praise Hashem Who has not only kept us alive but has helped us attain to the present time. He has kept us modern and vital. The Jewish people is unique in that it has placed emphasis on both the שהחיינו וקיימנו as well as on the והגיענו לזמן ה־ה. We are not content with a merely stagnant, vegetative existence. We insist on being a dynamic part of the present-day life. We cling to our ancient and beloved homeland, Eretz Yisrael. Millions of Jews have already helped settle and restore it to its ancient fertility. However, the methods used, especially those in warfare, are based on current technology and not the methods of our ancestors. They have been the latest developed by science. That land of ours is indeed ancient, but our techniques are the most modern and up to date. Our G-d is still the G-d of Avraham, Yitzchak and Yaakov. Our Torah is still the Torah of Moshe Rabbeinu. Our Talmud is still the Talmud of Rabbi Akiva, Rabbi Yehudah HaNasi, and Abayey and Rava. Our Shulchan Aruch, is the product of Rabbi Yosef Cairo and the Rema, as well as the Vilna Gaon and the Chofetz Chaim. Our tradition and culture are not the product of yesterday or today. They are centuries upon centuries old. But we are at the same time the most progressive of people. Judaism is and never has been afraid to accept ideas and truths from the outside world. There is, however, one caveat. We must always remain true to our tradition and heritage.

This is the secret of the existence of our people. If the Jew merely kept faith with the faith of his fathers, if he were merely a loyal, blind, unsophisticated follower, then the first breath of worldly wisdom and progress would have swept away all his religious beliefs from him. But the Jew is at the same time a modern man. He lives in the present. He is, however, totally committed to Torah and all aspects of Halacha.

We ourselves must take to heart the lesson placed so concisely in this *beracha*. It is no accident that the blessing of שהחיינו is recited on all important Jewish occasions and festivals. If we desire to keep strong our allegiance to our people and assure its uninterrupted existence, our efforts must be directed toward a fusing of the ancient with the modern; we must keep strong our adherence to the ancient forms and contents of our religion. At the same time, we must acknowledge the advances that modern technology has to offer.

There are many Jews who fail to realize the necessity to fuse these two concepts and instead choose either one or the other. This results in a truncated religion that bears little resemblance to Judaism. Some Jews look at their Judaism as a collection of quaint customs from the past with little or no bearing on their current lifestyles. Judaism for these people consists of eating bagels and lox and gefilte fish. They have been dubbed "culinary Jews." They may say Yizkor and Kaddish, because while they may identify as Jews, they are performing merely perfunctory gestures. Judaism is little more than a cultural museum.

Other Jews take the opposite approach. They have created a new Judaism that is Avant Garde and conforms to that which is politically correct. While they understand that current knowledge must be integrated into Judaism, they fail to accept the necessity of preserving the historical underpinnings of our religion. And yet, there is a third group. They cling tenaciously to our past, historically, sociologically, and theologically. They take almost nothing from the present. They really do not plan for the future. This too does not represent true and authentic Judaism. True Judaism can only exist when one maintains the old while invigorating it with the new. When we synthesize the glory days of the past with the magnificent era that lies before us, then will we truly succeed.

As we march forward, we must hear the call of the ancient prophet Jeremiah:

הֲשִׁיבֵנוּ ה' אֵלֶיךָ וְנָשׁוּבָה חַדֵּשׁ יָמֵינוּ כְּקֶדֶם:

Return us O L-rd unto thee and we will return; renew our days as of old.

With G-d at our side, living by His law, we will march forward to new heights established upon old and ancient foundations. Then this day, my friends, will see the synthesis of Koheles as well as Shir HaShirim, of Succos and Pesach, and will be the שהחיינו וקיימנו as well as the והגיענו לזמן הזה. Amen.

I want to give credit for this sermon to my late uncle and mentor, Rabbi Hyman Tuchman ז"ל. It was his idea that stirred me to develop and expound on this *drasha*.

22. The *Pitom* and the *Oketz*: A Lesson in Jewish Distinctiveness
Shabbos Chol HaMoed Succos

This morning, I wish to discuss the distinctiveness of Succos and its emphasis upon Jews and Jewish tradition. There are those who maintain that Jewish ceremonies and laws are very important parts of our historic past. They were absolutely necessary and imperative in the early years of our people's history. The Mitzvos and customs were required in order to mold our ancestor's character and conduct. Our ancestors, they claim, were primitive and uncultured, unsophisticated and unworldly. They needed a guideline, a roadmap for their early and formative years. This was also true during most of our Golus, our 2,000-year Diaspora.

When we were oppressed and persecuted, harassed and ostracized from the general society, we desperately needed to cling to our tradition and faith. We required an internal stimulant to be strong and courageous in our dealings with the cruel and menacing external world. However, today when we are accepted as part of the general non-Jewish milieu, when we are looked upon as equals and partners in the overall workings of our society, they ask, "Why do we need rituals and laws? What purpose do these diverse and complex commandments serve? Why should our actions be different and distinct from those of the rest of our neighbors and friends? Why should we stand out and apart from the world around us? We needn't any longer fear the anti-Semites. The walls and barriers between Jews and non-Jews have long ago been broken down. We are all one mankind making our unified and manifold contributions to the furtherance and continuity of the human race. Traditions and laws, obligations and observances are mere relics of a past which is light years away and which no longer have a place in our modern and

Succos

sophisticated society." These are not only the arguments of Jews who have abandoned their faith. They are also advocated by the Reform Jew and, to a lesser extent, by Conservative Jews.

To these irreverent and non-observant Jews, the Festival of Succos responds unequivocally. More specifically, the one element of Succos which represents Jewish tradition both in the past as well as in the present—the Esrog—proves the fallaciousness and the unsoundness of their argument.

Judaism teaches us not to be ashamed of our heritage. We ought not hide our faith and our tradition. In fact, everything about our religion indicates in the strongest possible terms how important it is for us to be apart and distinct from the rest of society. We are not, G-d forbid, told to withdraw into our *"Daled Amos"* and stand alone. Rather, we are called upon to be of aid and assistance to the poor and the needy, the hungry and the oppressed throughout the world. However, we are at all times commanded to refrain from excessive socialization and fraternization with those who are not of our faith. This is so that we do not suppress and hide our own religious beliefs and practices and take on the guise and appearance of those around us.

Our tradition tells us that in dealing with the general society, we should maintain our faith and its attendant customs. We have to demonstrate the moral and ethical values which we possess. We will, by our actions, be a beacon of light, an אור לגויים to society. We are to stand up and be counted as members of the human race, but also, as people who are visibly and particularly Jewish. From the earliest commandment of Bris Milah to the laws of Kashrus, from the observance of Shabbos and Yom Tov to our tradition of marrying only within the Jewish fold and to being buried in strictly Jewish cemeteries, we have always stressed this dual approach. The Esrog symbolizes all this and more.

The Esrog, the *Pri Eitz Hadar,* upon which we make a beracha during this Yom Tov, has always intrigued our people. While the blessing that is made is over the Lulav, *al netilas Lulav,* that is because the Lulav is bundled with three of the four species required on this holiday. However, the Esrog is undoubtedly the most sought after of the *Arba'ah Minim.* The Esrog, according to *Chazal,* represents the לב, the heart of the Jew. This symbolizes the Tzadik, the pious individual who is both kind to his fellow man and is מקיים all the Mitzvos between man and Hashem.

The Gemara in Succos (35a) explains why the *Pri Eitz Hadar* is the Esrog and not, perhaps, the pepper. The requirement that it be the fruit of the goodly tree implies a tree whose fruit and wood tastes the same. As such, the pepper should suffice for it meets this criterion. However, the Gemara says: חדא לא מינכרא לקיחתה—one pepper standing amongst other items will be unrecognizable because of its miniscule size. The Esrog, on the other hand, fulfills all the requirements, and it also stands out and is distinguishable. Thus, it, and not the pepper or a like fruit, is utilized.

Thus, what the Esrog teaches us is that only he who does not attempt to hide his particularity and his distinguishing features is accepted as the real and authentic Jew. On the other hand, he who acts like the 19th century Reform Jew will not succeed. These Jews introduced the ludicrous and absurd practice of observing the Sabbath on Sunday in order to mimic and ape their Christian neighbors. They did not represent Judaism and have barely survived. There remains hardly any trace of their children and grandchildren within our religion. Only those of us who are prepared to stand up and be counted and are not ashamed of our uniqueness and individuality are the true heirs of our great tradition. Like the Esrog, we remain apart and distinct from the world around us. And we will thereby be worthy of seeing our children and grandchildren continue observing that which we consider holy and pure.

The Esrog also has another important and equally significant message. It tells us that Judaism is neither archaic nor is it a relic of the past. It is modern, vibrant, and always compatible with the times within the bounds set up by Halacha. The Tur, Rabbeinu Yaakov ben Asher, the great codifier and giant Halachist, explains the various opinions as to what disqualifies an Esrog from use on Succos. He quotes different authorities, specifically R' Yaakov bar Yakar who maintains that if the *pitum* (that which projects from the Esrog and is a remainder of the flower blossom of the Esrog tree) has been removed so that a cavity is visible, the Esrog is posul, it is disqualified from use.

On the other hand, R' Yitzchak HaLevi, opines that the *oketz* (the stem with which the Esrog was attached to the tree) is most important. If it has been removed the Esrog is unfit for the fulfillment of the Mitzvah. The Tur then cites the opinions of the Rif, Rambam and Rosh, who contend that both the *oketz* and the *pitum* are equally important for an Esrog to be used properly on Succos. If either the *oketz* or the entire *pitum* is missing, the Esrog is considered lacking and incomplete. And it is this opinion which is accepted as Halacha and which we follow.

The *pitum* is the part of the Esrog that protrudes as it grows, indicating and representing growth, alertness, and movement. The *oketz* is that which connects the Esrog to the tree, to its past experience. To be devoid of the *oketz* is like one who detaches himself from his roots. One who divorces his present from his past is missing an important and integral part of his life. On the other hand, one who is missing the *pitum*, he who does not face the future and its challenges, lacks vitality, originality and innovation.

Thus, through the symbol of the Esrog, Judaism teaches that we need both the *oketz* and the *pitum*. We require that our tradition and our historical past become a vital part of our present. We need both the sagacity of yesterday and the novelty of today. In order for us to develop and grow as important members of the human race and as complete and practicing Jews, it is necessary for us to join together the *oketz* with the *pitum*. If we wish our Esrog to be kosher, if we desire that our Jewishness remain unique and distinctive, we cannot then afford to either hide or disguise our Jewish beliefs. We can neither eliminate either of the two essential elements of the *Pri Eitz Hadar*.

Only those Jews who are committed to preserve and guarantee authentic and genuine Judaism will succeed. Only those of us who believe wholeheartedly that our G-d is the G-d of Avraham, Yitzchak, and Yaakov, that our Torah is that which was given intact to Moshe Rabbeinu, that our Shulchan Aruch is based upon a tradition stemming directly from Mt. Sinai, only such Jews will survive and maintain their distinctiveness and individuality as Jews. Only if we truly believe that our tradition and culture are not the products of yesterday or today but are centuries upon centuries old will our children's children remain Jewish.

At the same time, though, we are the most progressive of people. The Jews have never been afraid of accepting ideas and innovations from the outside world. This idea presents itself in the beracha that Noach gave his sons: יפת אלקים ליפת וישכון באהלי שם. Yefes—the acculturated non-Jewish world—is indeed beautiful. However, that beauty only achieves its purpose when it is incorporated within the tents of Shem, the Beis HaMikdash and Torah life.

This is the secret of the existence of our people. If the Jew merely kept faith with the past heritage of his ancestors and nothing else, then the very introduction of current and progressive ideas would have caused a cataclysmic effect on his total belief system. But the Jew is not merely a representative of the *oketz*. He is at the same time a *pitum*, a thoroughly forward-thinking man. He not only represents the past – he also lives in the present. He stresses, however, not only secular knowledge but the primacy of Torah. If we desire to keep strong our allegiance to our people and assure its uninterrupted existence, our efforts must be directed toward the linking of the past with the present. We must retain our loyalty and observance of the ancient form of our religion. At the same time, we must acknowledge the opportunities that modern scientific advances have to offer. We must always continue to explore and experiment with new ways of discovering that which is necessary and crucial without abandoning one iota of the past. Only that group of Jews who are committed to preserving the Judaism of the past and are willing at the same time to adopt to the new and modern times will guarantee the survival of both the Esrog and that which it represents to our people.

Fifty and sixty years ago, the non-observant and non-traditional sects of Judaism were writing epitaphs and eulogies for Orthodoxy in America. They said that we were a dying race; we were a people who clung so tenaciously to the past that we had no future. While this may have been possible then, we nevertheless weathered the storms and emerged stronger and more resilient.

Years ago, an article appeared in the New York Times which stated that the Reform and Conservative sects in this country were becoming wary and uneasy over the strength and apparent power of their Orthodox brethren. This has worried them to such an extent that they believe that they would have to eventually merge forces in order to retain their position as the dominant religious group among American Jewry.

Why is Orthodoxy so powerful? Why are the non-traditional sects so alarmed and frightened? The fact of the matter is that the present generation of young people are searching for truth and honesty. They don't want fraud and hypocrisy. If they are to be true and loyal to their faith and tradition, then they desire and need real genuine and authentic Judaism. They do not want a watered down or adulterated version, one that almost totally discards the past for the preservation of the present. They want not only the *pitum*; they want the *oketz* as well.

A visiting professor at the Conservative Jewish Theological Seminary, Dr. Charles Liebman, wrote in the American Jewish Yearbook in 1965: "The only remaining vestige of passion in America resides in the Orthodox community. And it is this passion and dedication, not psychoanalytic studies of divorce, which will stem the tide of intermarriage." Moreover, this will keep Judaism and Jewish values alive.

No matter what the circumstances and what the problems may be, we must retain our commitment to Hashem. Even if we are faced with overwhelming difficulties, we have to remain who we are and what we are. If, G-d forbid, we are faced with life threatening illness, the loss of a loved one, or great emotional and financial stress, we should not ever surrender. We may sometimes be tempted to just throw up our hands and give up. We, however, must have continuous אמונה בה'. We must go forward with a positive attitude as well as with a nostalgic look to the past.

Many years ago, an article appeared in the news about the tragic murder of an Orthodox diamond merchant, Pinchas Yaroslovitz. In the more than a week between his disappearance and the subsequent discovery of his body, his family suffered the anguish and torment of expecting the worst and hoping for the best. Someone saw the slain man's father on Erev Succos on the Lower East Side purchasing a Lulav and Esrog. Mr. Yaroslovitz said, "My heart is not in it, but I must fulfill the Mitzvah. My present agony cannot do away with the observance of a most significant Mitzvah." This, my friends, is the joining of the past to the present, the merging of the ancient with the modern, the harmony of the *oketz* and the *pitum*.

Only he who has a complete Esrog, one which is unique and distinctive and contains all the necessary elements, is kosher and is fit to be used. Only this kind of Jew truly represents our people.

SHEMINI ATZERES – SIMCHAS TORAH

23. Sacred Tasks, Divine Blessings
Shemini Atzeres-Yizkor/Simchas Torah 5738 (1977)

From time immemorial, whenever the Jew has left his all-Jewish environment and entered the domain of the gentiles, he has tried to be accepted as a friend and as an equal with the non-Jew. In Babylon, during the 70-year exile, in Judea upon the arrival of Alexander the Great and his Hellenistic way of life, in Egypt during the reign of the Ptolemies, and in the amphitheaters of the Roman Empire, the Jew has attempted to become something which he was not. He tried to placate and appease first the pagans and then the Christian world.

This attitude has multiplied a thousand-fold since the walls of the European ghettos were opened almost two centuries ago and the Jews were "liberated." In order to give thanks and show our gratitude to the non-Jewish world, many have sacrificed practically all our traditions and customs. We have imitated their lifestyle in the hope of being accepted by them. We have not only helped to undermine our very existence but have invited derision and contempt. By casting away our traditions, by sacrificing our heritage, we have not, by any means, succeeded in befriending those who are not of the Jewish persuasion. They merely ridicule and laugh at us for not being who we are.

A Jew who brings a Christmas Tree into his home to show the Christians that he is one of them is not accepted as one of the boys or one of the "goys." Rather, he is ridiculed and laughed at. The non-Jews become antagonized that someone who is not Christian is encroaching upon their territory. "If you admire our customs so much," they say, "then why not join our ranks, abandon Judaism, and embrace the world's most popular faith. You will not be discriminated against; you will not be spat upon and beaten as a member of an accursed people."

However, no matter how far we stray from Judaism or how much of our tradition we have forsaken, we are Jews. And even if we, G-d forbid, leave the fold and openly convert, we will still be categorized as Jews. Did Hitler ימח שמו make any differentiation between an observant and practicing Jew and one whose parents even accepted Christianity? They were all Jews as far as he was concerned. And they all died in the same inhumane way. Thus, no matter how much we sacrifice to become a member of the club, we will still be considered a member of the Tribe.

For the past seven days, Jews the world over have celebrated the Festival of Succos. The Holiday of Tabernacles indeed represents universalism. During the time of the Beis HaMikdash, our ancestors offered 70 bulls as sacrifices—more so than on any other festival—on behalf of the 70 nations of the world who classically comprised the organized human society. This, our Rabbis tell us, is an indication that we are all part of one humanity. Each nation, while different in its structure and purpose, must act together, in harmony, with the rest of the family of nations. This represents the idealistic form of the United Nations as expressed in the liturgy of the Yomim Noraim:

ויעשו כולם אגודה אחת לעשות רצונך בלבב שלם
And they will all become a unified assembly in order to fulfill Your will with a complete heart.

This does not undermine the individuality of any specific nation. Rather, it points to the particularness of each country whose own contributions to the community of nations will guarantee the success of a world order for all. Thus, on Succos, in days of old with sacrifices and in modern times with prayer, we ask the Almighty to grant health and success upon the nations of the world. However, on the eighth day of the Succos celebration, after we have given of

Shemini Atzeres – Simchas Torah

ourselves to others, we are asked to do something for our own people. After we have contributed to the growth and development of the society around us, marched for equal rights, demonstrated for or against every general cause or concern, we are told, "It is about time that you think of yourselves."

The novelist, Tolstoy, once said to an overzealous reformer: "The trouble with you is that you sweat too much blood for the world; sweat some for yourself first." You cannot bring the kingdom of G-d into this universe until you bring it into your own heart first. להבדיל אלף הבדלות, the great Chofetz Chaim, sage of Radin, one said, "In my early years, I wanted to reform the entire world. When I was middle aged, I wanted to change my community of Radin. Now, in the latter stages of my life, if I could only change myself—what a great feat that would be."

The Midrash in Bamidbar Rabbah says that Shemini Atzeres may be compared to a king who made a festival for seven days, inviting all of the citizens of his country. When the seven days were over, he said to his closest friend: "We have already given all the inhabitants of the country their due share. Let the two of us now relax and partake of some meat, fish, or vegetables." Thus did G-d say to Israel: "On the eight day it shall be an *Atzeres,* a convocation to you. Relax with whatever you find with one ox and one ram."

Thus, the message of Shemini Atzeres tells us that it is good and beneficial to have working and amiable relationships with the non-Jewish world. However, to offer sacrifices for others exclusively, especially at the expense of our Jewish identity and Jewish distinctiveness will guarantee us not love and affection but ultimate destruction and elimination. We must eventually come to the realization that we owe ourselves a sacrifice as well. This idea and concept is brought home ever so clearly in the guise of the Festival of Shemini Atzeres. Shemini Atzeres is a distinct holiday for a very special people.

Shemini Atzeres – Simchas Torah

If this be so, then why do we have yet another holiday during this period? Why on the day following Shemini Atzeres (and in Israel, on the very same day) do we observe Simchas Torah? How did the Yom Tov of Simchas Torah evolve from the observance of Shemini Atzeres?

The advent of Shemini Atzeres according to the Midrashic literature was G-d's method of indicating the degree and intensity of His love and affection for His people. This merely demonstrates one side of the coin. Shemini Atzeres speaks of G-d's feeling for His people. It says nothing of his children's attitude toward their Creator and Father. How do the Jewish people react to the Almighty's request to stay an extra day? Do we just linger on for one more day and eat and be merry? This, of course, is not the Jewish response. Such a reply would indicate a deficiency in the dialogue between G-d and His people.

The natural and proper reaction to G-d's invitation is for us to show our appreciation. We are asked to remain and stay with our host because He is happy with us. In order to reciprocate, we indicate our jubilation and exaltation for the L-rd. We do so by celebrating, and of course observing Hashem's most concrete manifestation of His concern for His people, the Holy Torah.

On Simchas Torah we read the famous verse:

תּוֹרָה צִוָּה לָנוּ מֹשֶׁה מוֹרָשָׁה קְהִלַּת יַעֲקֹב:

Moses charged us with the Torah as the inheritance of the Congregation of Jacob.

No other nation or people has by virtue of their past decisions or actions any portion or inheritance in the Torah. In fact, our Chachamim say that the word should not be מוֹרָשָׁה but rather מְאוֹרָסָה, betrothed. For indeed, the Torah is betrothed to Israel as a wife to her husband. We are to rejoice with the Torah as a groom rejoices with his bride.

During Succos, the other nations have received their portion in the form of the sacrifices and blessings offered by Israel on their behalf. On Shemini Atzeres and then on Simchas Torah, the Children of Israel enter within the confines of the House of G-d. We delight with the joy of the Torah which is our very own inheritance.

Thus, on Simchas Torah, as we rejoice with our Law, we spontaneously respond to G-d's exulting on Shemini Atzeres. We are reciprocating the feeling that Hashem has demonstrated to us. Simchas Torah thus is not superimposed on Shemini Atzeres. Rather, it is the human fulfillment of the Divine call of Shemini Atzeres. If Shemini Atzeres is to be successful then we must make certain that Simchas Torah and all that it represents is successful.

Our actions and deeds during the New Year must indicate that we know who we are and where we are headed. Let us take a few moments out from our daily, hectic, and frenzied activities and take stock of ourselves. Let us determine once and for all that while we are American citizens, while we belong to the community of mankind, while we are for world civilization and human continuity, we are also Jews. We have an obligation and commitment to not only better society, but also to improve Jewish society.

We must see to it that the State of Israel not only physically survives but is also militarily strong and economically vibrant. We must protest and decry every attempt to castigate and malign our people throughout the globe. And we must guarantee that our own brand of Jewishness, authentic and traditional American Orthodox Judaism, will continue to prosper and flourish. We can do this through the development and growth of more Yeshivos and Day Schools and through more widespread observance of Shabbos, Kashrus, and all other Mitzvos.

By becoming distinctively Jewish and doing something about it we will certainly perpetuate the memory of our loved ones whom

Shemini Atzeres – Simchas Torah

we fondly recall today. For Yizkor is a memorial to souls that sacrificed for Jewish life, your Jewish life and your Jewish survival.

Toward the end of the Torah portion which we read tomorrow, the last Sidra, וזאת הברכה, Moshe Rabbeinu concludes his final blessing to the Jewish people before his demise. He says (33:28):

וַיִּשְׁכֹּן יִשְׂרָאֵל בֶּטַח בָּדָד עֵין יַעֲקֹב אֶל אֶרֶץ דָּגָן וְתִירוֹשׁ אַף שָׁמָיו יַעַרְפוּ טָל:

Israel shall dwell in safety, the fountain of Jacob is solitary upon a land of corn and wine, yea his heavens shall drop down dew.

The Netziv, R' Naftali Zvi Yehudah Berlin, comments on this sentence in his classic work העמק דבר. The safety which the Torah refers to is the tranquility of the soul, the love between human beings which is not disturbed by the envy and greed of the other nations of the world. The word "בדד" "alone," refers to the observance against undue mixing either socially or through marriage with the other nations. Rather, the Jewish people are to stand alone and apart, separate and distinct.

We are thus told that physical safety and economic security is not automatically guaranteed. We must avoid unnecessary assimilation as well as aping, mimicking, and imitating the ways and belief of those who are not Jewish. We must remain committed and dedicated to the very traditions of our faith. And only if we do so will we enjoy the promise of living in "A land of corn and wine" where the Heavens of G-d will "drop down dew."

Let us on this very distinctively Jewish holiday do what we can for Yiddishkeit and all that it represents. Let us be ourselves. Let us remember on this day of remembrance that we gain nothing by denying our heritage. We will however, gain everything by adhering to and guaranteeing its continuity and growth. In that way we will survive and the memory of our loved ones will continue to live on. Hashem will be happy and content. We will not only have rejoiced with the Torah, we will have relied only on Hashem. We will have acted in the manner in which Hashem expects of us and in which our loved ones imparted their values to us. For this, Hashem will be satisfied and will bestow upon us His many ברכות: שלום and חיים and success in all our endeavors. Amen.

24. Blessings, Not Curses
Shemini Atzeres—Yizkor
תפילת גשם

Today on Shemini Atzeres, during our *Musaf* service, we will offer the prayer for rain, the *Tefillas Geshem*. This prayer is the first sign of the coming of the winter season, the rainy season in the Holy Land, Eretz Yisrael. From today until the start of Pesach, we add an additional segment to our Shemoneh Esrei. We extol and praise the Almighty as being the מַשִּׁיב הָרוּחַ וּמוֹרִיד הַגֶּשֶׁם, "The One Who blows the wind and brings down the rain."

It is interesting to note, my friends, that the word *ruach*, or wind, has yet another meaning, that of "spirit." The word *geshem*, which is usually interpreted as rain, can also be translated as "material substance." We speak of the material, the physical, the earthly, and the mundane as *gashmios*. Perhaps this is so because the wind, though we can feel it, is abstract and hidden from our sight. Although we do not see the wind, we can observe that which the wind moves, the object of the wind's furious gestures. Rain, on the other hand, can be seen as well as felt. Therefore, the wind is the symbol of the abstract spirit which we can sense but which we cannot observe. The material rain, so essential to the fruitfulness of the earth, to its development and growth, can be clearly seen; hence, it represents the physical as well.

We pray for rain, we beseech the Almighty to grant us that life sustaining source. If, G-d forbid, the winter months in the Land of Israel are not blessed with a sufficient amount of rain and moisture, then drought may set in, and disaster and famine will most certainly follow. We recognize that the Almighty's causing the wind to move clouds is essential to a fruitful and plentiful world. We therefore declare His might and His mastery over the keys of abundance.

Shemini Atzeres – Simchas Torah

I wonder, dear friends, whether this phrases of משיב הרוח ומוריד הגשם – "Who blows the wind and brings down the rain," might not also be translated according to the second definition of these words. If man can be one who stirs his spirit, if he can be one who is conscious of the image of G-d that he represents, then he certainly can arrive at new heights. Then the material, the physical, and the mundane which man is so prone to celebrate, can be lowered to its proper proportions. If man can cause his spiritual being to prevail and reign sovereign over his physical interests, it will be very beneficial. If he can be a "משיב הרוח ומוריד הגשם", one who stirs the spirit and lowers the physical, then man will most definitely reach far greater truths and strive for eternity.

If only our world could be stirred by the spirit of peace, brotherhood, and understanding and stop speaking of and demonstrating prowess and military might, how fortunate we would all be. If only a G-dly spirit could prevail, if only a law of justice for all, as preached by the Torah and called for and demanded by the Nevi'im, could be implemented, we would then have a much better world. If material advance would properly become an avenue of blessing and goodwill instead of serving as a threat of curse, war, and destruction, our society would be one of peace and tranquility.

If the Almighty is the משיב הרוח ומוריד הגשם, if He is the One "Who stirs the wind and brings down the rain," then man can most definitely become the "משיב הרוח ומוריד הגשם", the one who restores the spirit and brings down the material to its just position. This will certainly assure us of great blessings.

Can this realization come to us more clearly than now on this Eighth Day of Succos, on Shemini Atzeres, just before we recite our Yizkor services? At this time, we recall the spiritual significance and enduring contribution made to us by those loved ones who are no longer with us. In recalling our dearly departed and all that their memories invoke within us, we can behold the true value of the

Shemini Atzeres – Simchas Torah

material substance that all too often masters our interests and enslaves us.

Indeed, material advances and scientific progress are most significant. Man reaches into outer space. Man flies outside the earth's atmosphere. Man visits the moon and explores the surface of that celestial body. Yet, all this advance without spiritual guidance and direction is not unlike a powerful vehicle moving without a steering wheel or brakes. This vehicle may move at high speeds; it also may destroy all that stands in its path. The genius of its manufacture may be the source of its very destruction.

At Yizkor, when we remember our loved ones, we ought to be able to judge with greater accuracy the real and significant power of the material and the physical. We then can place it in its proper perspective. We ought not to allow it to dominate our lives. Rather, we should harness it to serve us and our spiritual needs. For in the final analysis, all our material goods and profits that we amass during our lifetimes will all be left behind when we meet our Maker. We go alone, only with our Mitzvos and our *ma'asim tovim.*

How wise were our *Chachamim* when they informed us of the segment of the service where this prayer of משיב הרוח ומוריד הגשם is to be recited. The Mishnah, informs us: מזכירין גבורות גשמים בתחיית המתים, "We mention the might of the rain in the prayer of the resurrection of the dead." Lending our second interpretation to the word "*Geshem*," we may give a new interpretation of this statement. The "prayer of the resurrection of the dead" refers to our mandate to keep alive those who are with us in spirit and in our hearts. It is at that juncture precisely that "We mention the might of the physical and material." In the context of a prayer for our cherished ones who have passed on, one gains the appropriate perspective on how to sublimate the "גבורות גשמים", the apparently powerful physical aspects of life.

This is true, my friends, not only in international relations where it is so very important, but also in our personal lives and in our interpersonal relationships. It is true in the values which we set on material wealth and our spiritual responsibilities toward G-d and our fellow man.

In our performance of the Mitzvah of Tzedakah, let us help the poor, the oppressed, the widowed and the orphaned. Let us contribute to our synagogue and its total and complete development. Let us give as generously as we can to the State of Israel during her time of need. Let us grow in spirit. Let us become stronger in our commitment to Torah observance. Let us internalize all the customs and traditions taught to us by our parents and our dearly departed relatives whom we memorialize presently. Then our material gifts will assume their rightful and proper proportions and bring us all the good that we seek.

If we can be משיב הרוח ומוריד הגשם, if we can stir our spirits and reduce the state of the material, we will have succeeded. If we can be מזכירין גבורות גשמים בתחיית המתים, if we can be among those who mention the might of the physical in the context of the resurrection of the dead, then we can await the fulfillment of G-d's gifts of wind and rain and *Techiyas HaMeisim.* We will then certainly see the fulfillment of our request and plea to the Almighty for "לברכה ולא לקללה", "For blessing and not for curse," and "לחיים ולא למוֶת", "For life and not for death." We will be *zoche* to an era of אהבה ואחוה ושלום ורעות, a time of love and harmony, peace and companionship. Amen.

25. The Three Keys to Life
Shemini Atzeres-Yizkor 5736
October 16, 1976

Today, on Shemini Atzeres, we recite Yizkor. Today we pause for a few moments, we take some time off from our hectic schedules and reflect back upon the memories of our loved ones who have departed from this world. We think of their lives, of their contribution to us personally and to mankind in general. And as we do so, we attempt to recreate those moments that we shared together and which today are just fleeting segments of our historic past.

The Yizkor that we recite today is also said on three other holidays during the Jewish year. We remember our departed on the last day of Pesach, on the second day of Shavuos, and on Yom Kippur.

All those days are certainly appropriate times to pause and reflect upon those who are not with us at the present. Pesach, the *Zman Cheiruseinu*, the season of freedom and independence also evokes memories of the Jew's difficult time in Mitzrayim. Shavuos, the holiday which calls to mind G-d's Revelation of the Torah certainly is a time when we should remember our ancestors to whom the Torah was so dear and precious. And of course, Yom Kippur, a day whose major characteristic is atonement not only for the living but also for the dead. What is puzzling, however, is the addition of the Yizkor prayer on the last day of Succos.

Even though Shemini Atzeres is a "רגל בפני עצמו," a festival which has its own characteristics, it shares the same appellation of Succos, זמן שמחתינו, the Time for Rejoicing. Why then do we recite such a mournful and depressing prayer on this holiday? Anyone who takes this prayer to heart and internalizes its message cannot help but be moved by the memories of those who have passed on to their eternal rest.

Shemini Atzeres – Simchas Torah

There is another interesting custom which we observe today. On the eighth day of Succos, Jews throughout the world pray for rain. We recite the *Tefillas Geshem*. Rain is a most important and indeed very precious commodity. Without it, the earth would become parched, the rivers would dry up, and man would lose his ability to develop, grow, and even to survive. In fact, the Midrash in Bereishis Rabbah says:

אם אין ארץ אין מטר, ואם אין מטר אין ארץ, ואם אין שניהם אין אדם.

"Where there is no land, there is no rain; where there is no rain, there can be no land; and without both, there can be no man."

Thus, today, as we conclude the harvest season, after the Jew has dwelled in his Succah for seven days, after the Jew in ancient times made his way to the Temple for the pilgrimage festival of Succos, we pray for the winter rain. This will water the earth and give us life and sustenance in the months ahead. Therefore, our prayer this morning is geared toward the future—the tomorrow of the coming year.

However, if we carefully pay attention to the Tefillah itself, we will notice that this petition for the future begins with a remembrance of the past. We ask G-d to meet our needs for this winter and supply us with an ample amount of rain—something which is not manufactured by man but whose source and supply rests only with G-d. And before we do so, we ask G-d to remember the deeds of our ancestors. "Please O L-rd, recall the devotion and dedication of Avraham, Yitzchak, and Yaakov. Remember with fondness the loyalty of Moshe and Aharon, and because of their *zechus*, due to their merit, please grant us rain. Provide us with a blessing and not a disaster; give us life and not death; may this year be one of plenty and not of famine." And with the reciting of this prayer we can now understand the significance of the Yizkor service even on this Yom Tov which epitomizes happiness and joy.

Shemini Atzeres – Simchas Torah

The fact of the matter is that Judaism does not believe in reflecting back upon the past merely for its own sake. Rather, we recall the past, we remember our departed relatives so that we can take a page from their book of life. We do that so we can learn a lesson from them, thereby using the past as a link to the future. If we call to mind – not only for G-d but for ourselves as well – the facts and deeds of our forefathers and earliest leaders, they will hopefully serve as an example for us all to follow and emulate. When we think of our parents and grandparents on this day of memorial, we do so with the hope that they serve as a source of inspiration for us in our year ahead.

The link and connection between G-d's power over rainfall and His supreme authority over the resurrection of the dead finds its source in the Talmud. The Gemara in Ta'anis (2a) says:

אמר רבי יוחנן: שלשה מפתחות בידו של הקדוש ברוך הוא שלא נמסרו ביד שליח, ואלו הן: מפתח של גשמים, מפתח של חיה, ומפתח של תחיית המתים.

R' Yochanan said: Three keys are kept in G-d's hands and are never delivered through a messenger. One of them is the key to rain; the second is the key to life; and the third is the key to the resurrection of the dead.

These three keys form a triad that, homiletically, can be explained in a way which is most significant today. The first and third keys, those of *Techiyas HaMeisim* and *Geshem* have a deep connection to Shemini Atzeres. This morning, I wish to demonstrate that the second key of G-d, the key of birth, has a special relevance to this Yom Tov in a most personal way. Only Hashem determines who shall be born and which parents will be the proud beneficiaries of G-d's *berachos*. It is this key which has mystified man from time immemorial. It is most appropriate, I feel, that on this day when we join the keys of rain and *Techiyas HaMeisim* together, that Rivka and I have the merit to complete this three-fold prayer of homage and thanksgiving to G-d with the מפתח של חיה, the key to life, as we name our daughter Frumie.

The third key, that of *Techiyas HaMeisim,* can refer not only to the ultimate resurrection of the dead. It also is concerned with the ability of one who has physically died to remain spiritually alive by the perpetuation of his deeds and actions by his loved ones who remain on this Earth. It is in this spirit that we feel we are helping carry on the link between the past and the future by naming our daughter, our firstborn, for my late mother-in-law, Fruma Fink, הרבנית פרומה בת נח זאב ע"ה. In this way, and hopefully in the kind of home that we will, with the help of Hashem, bring her up in, we will perpetuate the memory of my mother-in-law.

She, unfortunately, did not live a long life. She was ill for many years. However, she was a genuine אשת חיל, a very special person whose אמונה in Hashem and whose righteousness was evident to all who knew her. She was a wonderful עזר כנגדו, a perfect helpmate and partner to my father-in-law. She helped him become the outstanding Rabbi that he is today, an exceptional תלמיד חכם and a leader of the Jewish community.

As a mother, she helped raise four outstanding and very talented children who even today, at a young age, are making their mark on the Jewish world.

By naming our daughter after her we will hopefully help guarantee that her name, her lifestyle, and the true woman of valor that she was will live on and be a blessing for our family and for all of כלל ישראל. Amen.

Postscript

It is now almost 42 years since this drasha was delivered. Our daughter, Frumie, has grown into a beautiful and amazing woman. She certainly has fulfilled all of our dreams and aspirations. She is a true successor to my late mother-in-law, her namesake. Her

Shemini Atzeres – Simchas Torah

observance of the מצות בין אדם למקום as well as the מצות בין אדם לחבירו in her own quiet and unassuming manner have been exceptional and truly inspirational.

Her love, compassion, and closeness to her many dear friends and relatives as well as her acts of chessed are truly amazing and serve as a shining example to all.

For the past 22 years, she has been married to a remarkable, wonderful, and caring Talmid Chacham, Hillel Drebin. Together they have raised a beautiful and magnificent family. Their children, as well as our other grandchildren, continue to give Rivkie and myself much nachas, joy, and happiness. They are truly the pride of our lives.

Frumie, together with Hillel, help support many Torah institutions. They have a well-deserved sterling reputation in their community. They are known as a couple to whom both individuals and communal organizations can count on at all times and in all circumstances.

Mostly, Rivkie and I are so very proud of both Hillel and Frumie as well as our other children, Aryeh and Goldie Gross and Dena and Yaakov Kibel, for fulfilling to the utmost the very important Mitzvah of כיבוד אב ואם, honoring one's parents. In that area, they have no equal. We are truly blessed to have them all as our very precious and amazing children.

My late mother-in-law, Mrs. Fruma Fink ע"ה, would be so very proud of each and every one of them.

CHANUKAH

26. A Beacon of Light in a World of Darkness

One of the greatest potential difficulties that man faces is that of living in a world consisting of complete and total spiritual darkness. Throughout history, few generations have experienced this phenomenon. Among those who did are the barbarians who sacked and ravaged the grandeur of the Roman Empire as well as the Nazis of 20th century Germany. One of the first, however, was Hellenistic Syria. It tried and almost succeeded in destroying the very fiber and substance of Judaism.

The Jewish people are commanded annually to kindle lights for eight days beginning on the 25th day of the month of Kisleiv. Lighting the Menorah commemorates the victory of the Maccabees over the Hellenistic Syrians. However, what does the kindling of lights have to do with the military victory?

Our Chachamim maintain that the remarkable military success of the Maccabean forces was not the reason for the institution of the commandment to kindle lights. The reason rather was to observe and commemorate the miracle performed for the Jews when they entered the holy Temple in Jerusalem following the conclusion of the war. After cleansing the Beis HaMikdash of all the impurities brought there during the Syrian occupation, the Jews attempted to light the sacred Menorah. Much to their dismay, however, the only pure oil to be found which the Syrians had not defiled was only enough to last one day. Miraculously, the oil burned for eight complete days until fresh, pure oil was able to be transported to Jerusalem. It is for this reason, the Gemara says, that we light candles on each of the eight nights of Chanukah.

However, if we carefully analyze all the available historical and narrative literature, we would realize that there is yet another basis for this commandment, namely, the elimination of the influence of Hellenism from Jewish life.

Hellenism, as practiced by the Syrians of old, emphasized depravity, decadence, and corruption, rather than virtue and ethics. It stressed physical prowess and aesthetic beauty over spiritual development, morality, and righteousness.

For the Jews whose lives are symbolized by light, who are taught to be moral and ethical, such a world represented complete and total darkness. But Hellenism, along with its many perverse customs, did attract thousands and thousands of Jews, including many legislative and religious leaders. When this existential danger was over, the Jews celebrated by annually kindling lights.

As a matter of fact, the concept of total spiritual darkness is completely foreign and alien to Judaism. We are symbolized by the radiance of hope and optimism rather than the twilight of despair and pessimism.

At an earlier time in our history, during the last stages of our servitude in Egypt, the Jewish characteristic of light vis a vis the darkness of the surrounding neighbors was most evident. In the book of Shemos (10:21), we are told about the ninth of the 10 Plagues which Hashem inflicted upon the Egyptians.

וַיֹּאמֶר ה' אֶל מֹשֶׁה נְטֵה יָדְךָ עַל הַשָּׁמַיִם וִיהִי חֹשֶׁךְ עַל אֶרֶץ מִצְרָיִם וְיָמֵשׁ חֹשֶׁךְ:
And the L-rd spoke unto Moses, "Stretch out your hand to heaven that there may be darkness over the land of Egypt; darkness which may be felt."

The Seforno is puzzled by the introduction of darkness as a concept by itself. He says that darkness is nothing more than the absence of light. When there is no light, it is dark. This, however, can be changed by simply kindling a flame. The Seforno, therefore, offers a new and novel interpretation. The darkness in Egypt, he maintains, was a phenomenon in its own right. It was so real that it could be felt; it was so powerful that light could not penetrate through it.

Two sentences later (10:23) we are told that the Jews did not experience the same darkness which engulfed their Egyptian neighbors and countrymen. The Torah states:

וּלְכָל בְּנֵי יִשְׂרָאֵל הָיָה אוֹר בְּמוֹשְׁבֹתָם:

... and all the children of Israel had light in their dwelling.

Much of our religious life centers around the symbols of light. The candles of Shabbos, the flame of the Havdalah candle, the yahrzeit memorial lamp and the Chanukah Menorah are all very basic and very important to our faith. Light is the very symbol of hope and optimism.

From time immemorial, it has been the Jew who has helped illuminate the world. Our people in all walks of life have performed acts of kindness to our fellow man. By our living moral and ethical lives, we have helped save the world from falling into an abyss of depravity and oblivion. Jews throughout the centuries have made manifold contributions to the growth and development of civilization. In every profession and in every walk of life, from the Nobel Prize winners to the inventors and innovators of modern society, the Jew has always shed light on a very darkened society.

Today, world Jewry looks to the Jews in America as their beacon of light and their symbol of strength and hope. It is we who have the most influence of all the Jews, and it is we who have the power to help our oppressed brethren throughout the world. However, there is a very real distinction between having power and using it. It is one thing to have the ingredients for fire, but quite another to actively produce the flame. You can have two flintstones, but unless you rub them together very vigorously, there will be no fire. A room can have a light switch, but it will remain dark until the switch is turned on. Yes, we have the ability to light the world, to add illumination, but have we been fulfilling our responsibility?

During the near total blackness of the Hitler era, American Jewry possessed the ingredients to help minimize the total catastrophic effects of the Holocaust. That was, of course, the greatest destruction of our people in all of Jewish history. However, because of our own fears and our own internal conflicts, we did not produce the torch which could have and should have radiated throughout the world. Instead, we managed to ignite only a spark which was barely visible to our government, and not seen at all in the darkness of Europe.

For 12 years, between 1933 and 1945, we studied the events in Europe and composed some of the most eloquent and brilliant resolutions. However, although we attempted to act on behalf of our condemned brethren, we were far more successful in our attempts at studying the situation and at the writing of flowery statements than we were at saving fellow Jews. Had we but acted forcefully and with strength and determination, perhaps Hitler's diabolical plan would have been significantly mitigated. If we only tried more forcefully, we might have been able to influence our governments to act to save our brethren.

We have thus seen that the Jewish mission of adding light to the world will not be fulfilled by those Jews whose sole concern is themselves. It will be carried out only by those who are actively involved in continually providing relief for their brethren the world over.

We must not allow history to repeat itself again. We must not disappoint the different groups of Jews who live throughout the world in fear and trepidation. We should on this Chanukah, the festival of lights and commitment, rededicate ourselves to the concerns of all our fellow Jews wherever they may find themselves. We must not disappoint our coreligionists throughout the world.

We observe our brothers and sisters throughout the European

continent being subjected to continuous anti-Semitic invectives and even physical attacks. The millions of Muslims who have moved to so many of these countries in Europe are causing our brethren to be both concerned for their safety and for their very future in Europe.

Our fellow Jews in the state of Israel need our support financially, morally, and politically. The world continues to apply pressure to give up "land for peace." They are urging our brethren to complete a peace agreement with the Palestinians. They are trying to convince them in the strongest possible language to give up so many of our holy and sacred memorials: the Kotel, Me'aras HaMachpeilah, Kever Rachel, and others. Only this, they are told, will ensure that the Palestinians will agree to a genuine and authentic peace agreement. They say that after 50 years, it is so important to finally give a country of their own to the "poor, oppressed, and maltreated Palestinians."

We have to make certain that the words of the Torah apply to all Jews throughout the world –

וּלְכָל בְּנֵי יִשְׂרָאֵל הָיָה אוֹר בְּמוֹשְׁבֹתָם:

– that all the children of Israel have light in their dwelling.

Let us resolve on this Chanukah to take our individual candles which we light and place them all together with those of our fellow Jews. By combining these flickering lights, we will then turn it into a great and glorious torch. This will certainly illuminate a darkened world and bring hope and freedom to all our people throughout the world.

A happy and meaningful Chanukah to all. Amen.

Addendum

The question put forth in this essay was how the military defeat of the Greeks is commemorated through the lighting of the

Menorah. The answer, in essence, is that the light of the Menorah overcame the darkness which the Greeks represented.

This theme can, perhaps, explain the enigmatic viewpoint of Beis Shamai regarding the method of lighting the Menorah. Beis Shamai is of the opinion that one lights eight lights on the first night of Chanukah, seven lights on the second, and so on until the last night of Chanukah when one lights only one candle. The first reason for this opinion will be explored in the next essay. However, the Gemara offers a second explanation for this opinion. Just as the sacrificial bulls on Succos were offered in decreasing order, so too are the Chanukah lights lit in a descending order. This is troublesome, for how do the Succos sacrifices relate to the method of lighting our Menorah?

As discussed at length in earlier essays (Chapters 20 and 23), the 70 bulls were offered as protection for the 70 nations of the world. In addition, the prophet foretells how the gentiles will ascend to the Beis HaMikdash in the times of Moshiach to celebrate the festival of Succos (see Chapter 20). Thus, we see that the first seven days of Succos are partly dedicated to bestowing the light of Torah and Judaism upon the world. On the eighth day, Shemini Atzeres, only one bull is offered. That is the day where G-d devotes His time, so to speak, exclusively to the Jewish people in an intimate setting.

Beis Shamai views the eight days of Chanukah in a similar vein. As discussed, the lighting of the Menorah represents the shining of the light of Torah onto the world, fulfilling our role as an אור לגוים—a light unto the nations. This fulfills the same role as the bulls on Succos. In Beis Shamai's reckoning, the dénouement of Chanukah is on the eighth day with the lighting of merely one, single candle. This parallels the final day of Succos, Shemini Atzeres, which is a day dedicated solely to the unique relationship between G-d and the Jewish people. The first seven days of Chanukah, however, recall the influence of the light of Torah on the nations of the world.

When one counts the number of candles lit according to the order of Beis Shamai, there is a startling observation. If one lights eight candles on the first day, seven on the second, and so on, then after seven days, one will have lit 35 candles. These 35 candles are lit in the humble home of each Jew, shedding light on the darkness of the world around him. The nations of the world who then see this light, in turn, reflect the light of the Chanukah candles, dissipating the darkness of Greece completely. When 35 candles are reflected on the outside world, these 35 turn into 70—representing the 70 nations of the world. We can therefore see that Beis Shamai's comparison of lighting the Menorah to the bulls offered on Succos is indeed appropriate and exact.

27. Chanukah: Facing the Enemy Within and Without
בית שמאי ובית הלל

In Parshas Vayishlach, the Torah discusses Yaakov Avinu's return to the land of Canaan. He prepares to meet his brother and archenemy, Eisav, after a lapse of 34 years. When Yaakov was told that Eisav was approaching him with an army of more than 400 men, he became very concerned and very much afraid. Rashi says that he immediately prepared himself for three different approaches and scenarios:
1. Appeasement through the presentation of gifts.
2. Preparation for battle.
3. Prayer to G-d.

Yaakov's actions are questioned by our rabbis. If a Jew prays, what else is necessary? Second, if the prayer does not help, how will the other areas be of assistance to him? The explanation is that Yaakov prayed that his gift be accepted by Eisav. If it would not be accepted and he would have to go to war, he prayed to G-d that he should prevail. This, we are taught, is the way of the righteous. They do not to rely on miracles. Rather, they do all that is possible and then pray to G-d that their efforts succeed.

The second area that I would like to discuss deals with the holiday that we will celebrate next week – the holiday of Chanukah. The hallmark of this festival is the kindling of the eight-branched candelabra, the Menorah. We follow the time hallowed tradition of kindling one light on the first night and an additional one for each successive evening.

In the Talmud in the tractate of Shabbos, a dispute is brought down between the schools of Shammai and Hillel. Beis Shammai says that on the first night we light eight candles, and on each night after that we subtract one. The reason for this, they say, is that the candles represent the days yet ahead in the holiday. Beis Hillel maintains that on the first night we kindle one light, and on each successive night we add a candle. Beis Hillel maintains that the candles correspond to the days which have passed. The Gemara then gives another reason for their way of thinking which will not be discussed here.

It has, however, been suggested that each school understood the specific miracle of Chanukah on a different level. In essence, Chanukah commemorates a twofold victory. One is the victory of the Maccabees over the Syrian forces from without. Secondly, it was a victory over the Hellenistic Jews, those who made up the fifth column. They were the ones who sympathized with the Greek way of life, who forsook Judaism and embraced paganism.

To Beis Shammai, the miracle of Chanukah commemorates the victory over the forces from without. At first there were many enemies bent upon destroying our people. However, as time went on, their numbers grew smaller and smaller. Thus, Beis Shamai's position in regards to lighting the Menorah.

To Beis Hillel, the *neis* of Chanukah occurred in the spiritual victory over the opposing forces from within. At first there were very few dedicated and committed Jews who were ready to stand up courageously and valiantly for the principles of their faith. However, as time passed, they reaffirmed their faith in G-d and Israel and slowly, gradually, added their strength to the cause of Jewish independence. They abandoned their former assimilated policies and helped to mold Torah-true Judaism.

As noble as was the position of Beis Shammai, we nevertheless follow and practice the position promulgated by Beis Hillel. The great achievement of the Maccabees was not necessarily in their military victory. Rather, it was in their defense of the sacred ideals, traditions, and laws of the Torah. As significant and important as is the defeat of our external enemies, those bent upon our total destruction and annihilation, it plays a secondary role to our fighting for and attempting to preserve our unique quality of Jewish life.

Jews today are faced with enemies around the world who wish to see us disappear and be wiped off the face of the earth both as a people and as a nation. Our brothers and sisters in the State of Israel are continuously threatened by the mullahs and leaders of Iran. They boldly proclaim that they will strike the land of Israel with their long-range missiles and their developing nuclear arsenal. We face the subhuman terrorists of Hamas from the south and Hezbollah in the north. We also have to be seriously concerned about the strengthening of ISIS. They are implanted in Syria and Iraq and are attempting to wreak havoc in the Middle East and around the world. We have to be on the lookout daily and protect ourselves from the Palestinian terrorists who try to enter Israel both legally and illegally and want to maim and kill Israeli citizens.

Jews in Europe today are extremely fearful for their lives. The influx of millions and millions of Muslims into all European countries has caused them to be quite concerned. The Jews today are more worried about their very future than in the last 70 years. Be it in France, Germany, Great Britain and numerous other countries, anti-Semitic attacks and threats have continually increased and occur with more intensity from year to year.

Even here in the United States of America, the land of the free and the home of the brave, perhaps the greatest democracy and the most welcoming country that the Jews have ever lived in, we are beginning to see some rumblings of latent anti-Semitism. The white supremacists, the Ku Klux Klan, and other radical groups are beginning to flex their muscles. They are beginning to talk and to blog about killing Jews among other minorities. Even though they are fringe groups and are not part of mainstream America, we dare not ignore them or their very potential danger.

However, as serious as is this problem of the Jewish physical survival worldwide, we have a tradition that we have always cheated the Angel of Death. We have done so in the past and we will do so again in the future. What concerns us equally is our battle with the forces from within – those Jews who have given up their tradition and their faith. These individuals have found a haven and feel quite comfortable within the non-Jewish world. They have completely assimilated into American society and have left Judaism in its rearview mirror.

There is more assimilation and intermarriage among Jews today, both in this country and throughout the world, than perhaps ever before. While real, genuine and authentic Judaism is growing by leaps and bounds, that is not enough. Even though the *ba'al Teshuvah* movement has transformed thousands of Jews and brought them back to Yiddishkeit, we continue to see a diminution among our ranks. The rate of those leaving the fold as well as those who have already gone and given up their traditions is increasing in record numbers.

The evangelical groups, the "Jewish" missionaries and other such organizations are unfortunately making tremendous inroads. They target our most vulnerable people, just as Amaleik did when they attacked the Bnei Yisrael in the desert. They target the elderly, the poor, the feeble, and the infirm. They especially go after the many new Jewish immigrants who have come here in the past 25-30 years from the former Soviet Union. These individuals who were denied the study and the observance of Jewish law for almost 70 years are the most vulnerable and easily persuaded of our people. The approach of these missionaries is much subtler and more sophisticated than in prior times. They purport to teach these very uneducated Jews about Judaism. They present them with money, food, and shelter. However, their ultimate goal, their purpose and their endgame is first to take the Jews away from authentic and traditional Judaism. They then attempt to convince them to completely abandon their Judaism and to accept Christianity as their religion.

I ask you, my friends, how do we bring these people back? How do we once again make Judaism relevant and significant for this lost generation? How do we also get back our brothers and sisters, men and women from all spectrums of Orthodoxy, who have completely abandoned and thrown away their tradition, faith, and heritage? I believe that we can only succeed if we follow the advice given to us by Yaakov Avinu. First, we must give gifts. We give of ourselves physically, emotionally, and materially to help our institutions survive, grow, and flourish. They must take the lead in combating this terrible and destructive disease. Second, we must, like our father Yaakov, prepare for war. We must always be on the alert. We must always be ready to battle with those who attempt to subvert our religion and destroy our faith. We must be prepared to defend to the utmost the faith of our parents and the traditions of our forebears. Third, we must enhance and develop our *Tefillos*. We must continually daven and pray to Hashem for His guidance, counsel, and help in defeating this very difficult and life-threatening enemy.

We have to do battle with the current and modern day Eisav, the 21st century Antiochus as well as the current Hellenists who want to destroy Judaism. Perhaps, in that way, we will do our share in increasing the candles and the light in our present-day Menorah. We have to work and fight until they burn ever so brightly. It then will transform all of the darkness of despair, ignorance, and hatred of the world into a blazing torch of light, knowledge, and love. This will certainly illuminate all of mankind and will never, G-d willing, ever again be extinguished, Amen.

Purim

28. Always Remember - Never Forget
פרשת זכור

This week we observe the second in a series of four special Shabbosim which precede Pesach. The first Shabbos, which was celebrated two weeks ago, was called Parshas Shekalim. Next week we will observe Parshas Parah, followed the next week by Parshas HaChodesh. Today, the Shabbos before Purim, is entitled "Parshas Zachor," "the Sabbath of Remembrance." In addition to the regular weekly portion of the Torah, we read a special section from the book of Devarim in Parshas Ki Seitzei:

זָכוֹר אֵת אֲשֶׁר עָשָׂה לְךָ עֲמָלֵק בַּדֶּרֶךְ בְּצֵאתְכֶם מִמִּצְרָיִם: אֲשֶׁר קָרְךָ בַּדֶּרֶךְ וַיְזַנֵּב בְּךָ כָּל הַנֶּחֱשָׁלִים אַחֲרֶיךָ וְאַתָּה עָיֵף וְיָגֵעַ וְלֹא יָרֵא אֱלֹקִים: וְהָיָה בְּהָנִיחַ ה' אֱלֹקֶיךָ לְךָ מִכָּל אֹיְבֶיךָ מִסָּבִיב בָּאָרֶץ אֲשֶׁר ה' אֱלֹקֶיךָ נֹתֵן לְךָ נַחֲלָה לְרִשְׁתָּהּ תִּמְחֶה אֶת זֵכֶר עֲמָלֵק מִתַּחַת הַשָּׁמָיִם לֹא תִּשְׁכָּח:

Remember what Amaleik did to you by the way when you went out of Egypt. How he met you by the way and smote the stragglers at your rear when you were faint and weary, and he did not fear G-d. Therefore, it shall be when the L-rd, your G-d will give you rest from all your enemies around you in the land which G-d will give you for an inheritance, that you shall wipe away the remembrance of Amaleik from under the heavens. You shall not forget.

As we read this section, we are confronted with two significant questions. First, what was the importance and the significance of this battle that it warranted a special Shabbos to be set aside? Second, why do we read this portion about war and killings on the Shabbos before Purim, our most joyous and festive holiday?

On the surface, the significance of this battle lies in the fact that it marked the first time that the Jews were attacked after *Yetzias Mitzrayim*. This victory over the Amalekites boosted the Jews'

Purim

morale and gave them a feeling of pride in defeating a well-armed and trained army. However, this certainly was not the most decisive battle in Jewish history. In fact, the Jews did not completely decimate and destroy Amalek. They repulsed the attack and prevented them from inflicting harm on the Jewish people. The Torah however, does not mention that any territory was captured, as in the wars of Joshua and the Maccabees, nor does it indicate how many Amalekites were killed. However, if we examine the broader context within which this battle occurred, we may derive an everlasting message from this encounter and why the Jews are commanded never to forget this incident.

  The attack of the Amalekites on the Jews set a precedent which has been continuing for nearly 4,000 years. The Jews were attacked for no apparent reason or motive. They had just been redeemed from over 200 years of slavery and oppression. They were tired and weary, beaten and downtrodden. Although, when they left Egypt, the Jews had already attained the status of the "Chosen Nation," the עם הנבחר, they had not yet been given the Torah at this point. They had also not received the exalted titles of עם סגולה, ממלכת כהנים וגוי קדוש: "a treasured people, a kingdom of priests, and a holy nation." In fact, our rabbis tell us that while enslaved in Egypt, the Jews almost sank to the same level of immorality as the Egyptians. *Chazal* say that had the Bnei Yisrael stayed even a moment longer in Egypt, they would have reached the nadir, the 50th level of *tumah*. Their actions were so base and degrading that four-fifths of the nation died during *Makas Choshech*, the plague of darkness. These Jews argued against leaving Egypt, indicating the moral affinity they had with the Egyptians.

  Chazal also tell us that at the Yam Suf, there was a *kitrug*, a serious prosecution, against the Bnei Yisrael. The *Malachim* complained to Hashem, "Why are you rescuing the Jewish people and killing the Egyptians? הללו עובדי עבודה זרה והללו עובדי עבודה זרה.

Both the Egyptians as well as the Jews are idolaters. There is, in essence, no difference between them."

In addition, the Torah tells us that the attack by Amalek occurred at Refidim. Rashi explains that the word רפידים derives from the word רפה, indicating that the Jews loosened their hold on the few Mitzvos that they possessed. These were the people that Amalek attacked.

We see from all of these sources that the Jews were drawn into battle *in spite* of their religious beliefs – not because of it. Amalek attacked the Jews for one basic reason – that they were Jews. This has been the model that anti-Semites have emulated ever since. Jews have been subjected to attacks, persecutions, and killings because they were Jewish. This has occurred throughout the centuries, time and time again.

Unfortunately, even today, many Jews believe that by imitating the non-Jews, the hatred of the anti-Semites will diminish and perhaps even disappear. History, however, has taught us just the opposite. We learn this lesson from the Amalek attack on the nearly assimilated Jews. We also learn it from the story of Purim.

In the Purim narrative, Mordechai and Esther rose to prominence in the Persian Empire. Together, they convinced King Achashveirosh to mitigate the desires of his wicked prime minister, Haman, who had planned to murder all the Jews.

In this story, as well, we must examine the religious observance of the Jews at that time. Our rabbis tell us that the Jews residing in Persia wanted very much to become assimilated into Persian society. They attempted every possible method of winning the respect and the admiration of their Persian countrymen.

Chazal tell us that Achashveirosh threw a huge party in which he celebrated (based on his faulty calculations) the dashed hopes of Jewish national revival and the failed wish to rebuild the Beis HaMikdash. Among all the different nationalities who were invited to this feast, the Jews throughout the kingdom were also extended an invitation. Unbelievably, the Jews accepted the invitation en masse. The fact that the Jews accepted an invitation, attended, and participated in a party celebrating their demise as a nation shows how far the Jewish population had deteriorated.

The Jews, over the 70 years of exile in Babylon and then Persia, gradually adapted to the mores of their host country. Their attachment to the pagan way of life ran so deep, as demonstrated by their bowing to Nevuchadnezzar's idol and to Haman. This need to acculturate was so strong that the Jews could attend Achashveirosh's party, drink the non-kosher wine, and actually toast their own public humiliation. The Jews of that era obviously forgot the Biblical decree:

זָכוֹר אֵת אֲשֶׁר עָשָׂה לְךָ עֲמָלֵק

Remember what Amalek did to you.

They forgot that assimilation and emulation do not work. Therefore, they were subject to the wrath of Haman, a descendent of Amalek.

There is a very strong connection between Shabbos Zachor and Purim. Assimilation, or attempting to conceal one's religious beliefs, will not help the Jew hide from the clutches of the anti-Semites of the world. We have seen this most tragically in our own times in Nazi Germany. The first Jews that Hitler persecuted and killed were not the traditional Jews of Poland, Russia, and Hungary. They were the Jews of Germany and Austria, some of the most assimilated Jews in the world. So many of these Jews considered themselves 100% German and 0% Jewish. They were appalled and shocked when they were isolated from the rest of their fellow Germans and discriminated against as Jews.

We read this portion about Amalek on the Shabbos before Purim because the underlying themes of both Purim and Parshas Zachor are similar. The Jews are commanded not to forget that by giving up their religion and trying to win over the anti-Semite, they will only succeed in fooling themselves. The way to end hatred of the Jew for all time is not to emulate the non-Jew; it is, instead, to walk in the path of Hashem and obey His Torah and all of the Mitzvos.

By being proud and identifiable Jews, we will win the honor and respect from the nations of the world. By living an ethical Jewish life, we will set an example for our non-Jewish friends. Perhaps by our actions, all mankind will accept and practice some aspects of the principles of the Torah. Instead of war and hatred, we will be blessed with peace and love. Let us try to make that day occur soon, במהרה בימינו. Have a happy and joyful Purim.

Purim

29. Fasting and Feasting
Purim

Of all the Yom Tovim on the Jewish calendar, the observance of the festival of Purim is most perplexing. Purim, as well as Chanukah, are not mentioned at all in the Torah. Both fall under the realm of Mitzvos which the Rambam terms, "Divrei Sofrim," i.e., Rabbinical enactments. If we would compare the observance of Purim to that of Chanukah, we would find that in the general, non-Orthodox Jewish community, the festival of lights is much more widely observed than the holiday of lots. Why, my friends, is this so?

This problem of the non-observance of Purim is especially difficult to comprehend when we read about some of its other laws and customs. For instance, Jewish children traditionally dress up and masquerade as the heroes or villains of the Purim story. We send gifts to our friends and neighbors. Yet, if we would inquire as to the number of Jews who exchange gifts, or the number of people who partake in the Purim meal, we would be extremely disappointed.

In fact, studies have shown that even less of our non-observant coreligionists attend shul to hear and be inspired by the mandatory reading of Megillas Esther.

I believe that Chanukah is much more widely observed than Purim by the non-traditional Jews for one specific reason. Most of these individuals live, associate with, and even socialize and break bread with non-Jews. They may be totally integrated and assimilated into the Christian world. Some, unfortunately, have abandoned all aspects and characteristics of *Yahadus*. However, the vast majority of Conservative, Reform, and even unaffiliated Jews still crave and desire some manifestation of Jewish life. They see their non-Jewish neighbors and friends celebrating their festivals which fall out during the same season. Thus, the greater observance of Chanukah over Purim is primarily a calendarial association.

Purim has no non-Jewish holiday competing with it. Therefore, for those who pick and choose which rituals they want to observe, Purim is not even on their radar. Even though Purim has such significance and has so much historical meaning, it is almost completely forgotten by those people.

We can also add another reason. Our *Chachamim* maintain that the holiday of Purim is perhaps more difficult to observe than even the holiest day of the year, Yom Kippur. On Yom Kippur, the Day of Atonement, the Jew is commanded to fast and abstain from food and drink for 25 hours. He must repent for his sins and supplicate Hashem to forgive him for his past deeds. Although it is considered a major Yom Tov, Yom Kippur is undoubtedly the most solemn day in our calendar. It is not too difficult for one to put aside a single day during the year and refrain from enjoying any physical pleasures. We instead concentrate on spiritually perfecting ourselves. It is perhaps for this reason that Yom Kippur is the most widely observed of all our holidays.

Purim, on the other hand, is a holiday when we must approach G-d both on a spiritual as well as on a physical level. We are told to eat, drink, and be merry, but we are also commanded to remember those less fortunate. We are told to make noise in the shul when the name of Haman is mentioned, but we must be perfectly quiet and listen to every word of the Megillas Esther. We are not only allowed to eat on Purim, but are commanded to partake in a special Purim meal—*Seudas Purim.* It is also customary to be merry and to drink wine so that we cannot even recognize the difference between Haman and Mordechai. We must accompany this meal and our merriment by sanctifying Hashem and acknowledging His role in history. Purim, therefore, is a very difficult holiday to observe to the fullest and to truly understand its most significant message.

Purim

This distinction between the physical aspects of Purim and the spiritual aspects of the other holidays is brought out with greater clarity by a comment of the Gerrer Rebbe. He offers a reason as to why a special feast was ordained for Purim but not for Chanukah. On Purim, he says, we celebrate the annulment of the royal decree aimed at the physical destruction of the Jewish people. The Jewish people were saved from a potential Holocaust and disaster. We therefore partake in an enjoyable meal in order to provide ourselves with physical pleasure. In doing so, we also recall the miraculous nature of our survival as a people and as a nation.

On Chanukah, however, our people were rescued from a decree which would have destroyed the spiritual fiber of Judaism. We therefore chant the Hallel, recite *Tefillos* of thanksgiving, and light the Chanukah Menorah. We do this to be spiritually and religiously uplifted. We are not commanded to partake in any festive meal, for this holiday does not commemorate an escape from physical annihilation.

The non-observant Jews have a difficult time relating to and accepting the Jewish principle of sanctifying the mundane, elevating the physical, and taking hold of that which could bring man to the lowest levels and raising it to the highest degree of holiness. For this reason, the more spiritually focused holidays of Yom Kippur and Chanukah are more widely practiced by non-observant Jews than the more physically focused holiday of Purim.

It is my hope and prayer that Jews the world over, of all persuasions, will once again understand and appreciate the true essence and importance of Purim. They will then participate in this most beautiful and religiously inspiring Yom Tov. They will observe and commemorate it as it should be done.

Perhaps, one day the words found in Megillas Esther may be said about the Jews of our generation:

לַיְּהוּדִים הָיְתָה אוֹרָה וְשִׂמְחָה וְשָׂשׂן וִיקָר:

"The Jews had light and joy, bliss and dignity." I pray that this great day will soon be here.

Pesach

30. Freedom and Tenacity
זרוע וביצה

    Pesach, more than any other of our holidays, is filled with many traditions and customs, celebrations and symbols. We clean our homes, and we remove all traces of chametz. We join with our families and celebrate the Seder. We partake of the marror, the bitter herbs which remind us of the bitterness which the Egyptians inflicted upon our ancestors. We eat the matzah, the bread of affliction, as did the enslaved Jewish people. The matzah also reminds us of the haste with which our ancestors left Egypt on the 15th day of Nisan. Saltwater placed on the Seder plate recalls the oceans and seas of tears shared by the suffering and agony undergone by our people. The *charoses* reminds us of the bricks and mortar which our forebears were forced to manufacture in Egypt.

    There are however, two foods which, on the surface, appear quite problematic. We refer to the *zeroa*, the roasted shank bone, and the *beitzah*, the roasted egg. What is their significance and importance? What is their purpose on the Seder plate? If we make a thorough examination, we will find that they are extraordinarily essential elements of this Yom Tov. Through a spiritual lens, they represent the concepts of freedom and independence, perseverance and tenacity.

    The *beitzah*, the roasted egg on the Seder plate, is placed there to symbolize our remembrance of the *Korban Chagigah* which was offered in the Beis HaMikdash on every Yom Tov. The Mishnah Berurah notes that this *minhag* has evolved to the point where nowadays, everyone at the Seder is served a hard-boiled egg dipped into saltwater at the *Shulchan Oreich* segment of the Seder.

While the most oft-cited reason for the egg relates to the *Korban Chagigah,* there is another symbolization of the egg that goes beyond recollecting days gone by or yearnings for the future. There is a message in the egg that is relevant to us today, 2000 years after the cessation of Korbanos. The egg, more than any other food, represents the Jew and Judaism. The *beitzah* is the only food that the more it is cooked, the harder and the more secure it becomes. So has this been with our people down through the ages. The more difficult times we were forced to endure, the more severe the persecutions, the harsher the decree and the more brutal the oppression, the greater was our resolve to remain committed, dedicated, and devoted to Hashem and His Torah,

Whether it was at the banks of Babylon, the amphitheaters of Rome, the ghettos of medieval Europe, the ports of Spain and Portugal, the wastelands of Siberia, or the ovens and gas chambers of Auschwitz, we proclaimed with an egg-like strength, "*Ani Ma'amin,*" "I believe." "I believe in the destiny of my people. I believe in the swift coming of the Moshiach." And while it is true that many of our coreligionists could not withstand the difficulties, sufferings, and tortures and gave up their religion, the vast majority of Jews in every country and in every era tenaciously and stubbornly clung to their religion and to their faith. Millions gave their lives to assure and guarantee the future and the very survival of Judaism.

I believe that when all the anti-Semites down through the ages have attempted to annihilate the Jewish people, it was the totality of Judaism that they wished to eradicate. It was not just the physical Jewish people; rather it was the Jewish way of life. When we are steadfast in our observance of the Mitzvos, when we pledge to retain the continuity of Jewish values and the very essence of Yiddishkeit, we are actualizing an egg-like quality which truly represents real and authentic Judaism.

Pesach

The second food, the *zeroa*, the shank bone, demonstrates another important message of Pesach. We see within it the concept of freedom and independence. Before the Jews were redeemed from their servitude and oppression, before they were transformed from a group of slaves into a holy nation, Hashem searched for *zechusim*, merits, with which He would be able to redeem them. The mitzvah of partaking in the ceremony of the Korban Pesach, the slaughtering and consuming of the lamb, is what transformed this group of slaves into *Am Yisrael*.

According to the Midrash, the lamb was chosen because it was the deity of their Egyptian Masters. By dragging it through the streets in full view of the Egyptians, by keeping it tied to their beds for four days and then slaughtering the Egyptian god and dedicating it to Hashem, our ancestors indicated that they were servants to no one but Hashem. With this act of courage, they began their march to freedom, independence, and nationhood.

The Torah's passage dealing with the *Korban Pesach* is most informative, and its message is quite instructive. The lamb was to be eaten in a carefully prescribed manner (Shemos 12:11):

וְכָכָה תֹּאכְלוּ אֹתוֹ מָתְנֵיכֶם חֲגֻרִים בְּרַגְלֵיכֶם וּמַקֶּלְכֶם בְּיֶדְכֶם וַאֲכַלְתֶּם אֹתוֹ בְּחִפָּזוֹן פֶּסַח הוּא לַה׳:

You shall eat it in the following manner: your loins should be girded, your shoes should be on your feet, and your staffs in your hands, and it shall be eaten in haste—it is a Passover offering to Hashem.

If these directives are observed, then, as the Torah says (12:23):

וְלֹא יִתֵּן הַמַּשְׁחִית לָבֹא אֶל בָּתֵּיכֶם לִנְגֹּף:

And G-d will not permit the destroyer to come to your houses to strike.

In these rather cryptic words, we have a prescription for the attainment and the realization of freedom for Jews throughout history. How shall we make certain that there be no plague amongst us? We must stand with our belt tied and our shoes on. We should stand straight and ready with our walking staffs. Finally, we should eat the Korban Pesach in haste.

The first requirement of מָתְנֵיכֶם חֲגֻרִים – "your loins should be girded," means that we must be ready for battle. In different eras and through the ages, Jews employed different tactics for survival.

One of the most important personalities in Jewish history was the *Shtadlan*. He was the Jew who used his influence whenever and wherever it was necessary. He attempted to lobby against laws and promulgations which were devised against the Jewish community. When a difficult situation arose, this *Shtadlan* hastily arranged an appointment or meeting with the king, the emperor, the lord, or the local bureaucrat. Various means were employed including pleading, persuading, and more often through "contributions," the bribing via large sums of money. This often succeeded in preventing the implementation of the specific decrees.

There were times where other efforts were called for. The Jews utilized some of their great thinkers and intellectuals who often publicly debated the local theologians on various topics in the Bible. Instances of this include the famous debate of the Ramban in 13th century Barcelona and the many articles penned by rabbis worldwide in defense of Mendel Beilis at the beginning of the 20th century.

Finally, when these approaches may have failed, the Jews were forced to engage in battle or warfare. Obviously, most of them were ill-equipped or ill-trained. When unable to stand up to their more powerful foes, as, for example, when facing the marauding and merciless Crusaders, the Jews galvanized their strength and killed themselves rather than be forced to kneel before the cross.

The second characteristic is נַעֲלֵיכֶם בְּרַגְלֵיכֶם; we were bidden to eat the Korban Pesach in Egypt with our shoes on our feet. In contrast, when the Jews of antiquity came to the Beis HaMikdash to offer the Korban Pesach, they were required to *remove* their shoes since they were walking on holy and sacred ground. The Jews in Mitzrayim, however, found themselves in a place of *tumah* – complete and total spiritual impurity and defilement. They had to be completely aware of that fact. Keeping our shoes on is a reminder that we are not dwelling on our own sacred land. We pray:

השתא הכא לשנה הבא בארעא דישראל.

Now we may be in exile; next year we will be in our holy land of Israel.

The third aspect is וּמַקֶּלְכֶם בְּיֶדְכֶם – "Your staffs shall be in your hands." That is another lesson for *golus*. While at times we must gird our loins and defend ourselves and our loved ones, at other times we have to uphold our walking stick and realize that we are truly in exile. We have to once again become the wandering Jew, forced to flee from our various cities and countries and resettle in new and different locales.

However, this too can be a message of freedom and independence. The Gemara in Tractate Sanhedrin (20b) says that originally, the great Shlomo HaMelech ruled over both the upper and lower spheres. However, his dominion gradually weakened until Ashmadai, king of the demons, dethroned Shlomo. At that point, he ruled over only his walking staff.

Rabbi Chaim Shmuelevitz, the former Mirer Rosh Yeshivah, explained that the Gemara is teaching us a most important and instructive lesson. While Shlomo's only subject was his staff, he nevertheless was king over it. In other words, Shlomo never completely lost his sense of royalty and nobility. This, my friends, is also the message of Pesach in exile. We might question our *Zman Cheiruseinu* while observing the Seder in *golus*. However, we are reminded by Shlomo HaMelech that even if the nations of the world reduce our belongings to nothing more than a walking staff, we can still be and feel royal and free over that staff.

The final requirement for the Korban Pesach is that it be eaten בְּחִפָּזוֹן, in haste and in a hurried manner. This is a most significant ingredient in attaining independence. Freedom comes to those who do not put off until tomorrow what can and should be accomplished today. What should we do? What should we be accomplishing today? If the moment calls for certain actions, if the lives of our people require important and significant deeds, then the Torah tells us that we must not procrastinate; we must not put it off. Rather, we must act immediately. The Kabbalists tell us that had the Jews tarried even a moment longer in Egypt then they would have sunk to the lowest level of impurity and would have no longer been able or been fit to leave Egypt. This meant that even though the dough of their bread was not yet ready to rise, they took advantage of the appropriate moment and left Egypt.

These manifold lessons of the Korban Pesach are all symbolized by the humble and too often ignored shank bone that rests on the Seder plate. It teaches us the true meaning of freedom alongside the *beitzah*, the hard-boiled egg which reminds us of the tenacity and perseverance and the freedom of the Jew.

There is an old and all too often accurate saying that history repeats itself. For most of Jewish history, because of circumstances beyond our control, historical developments repeated themselves time and time again. Willful or otherwise, we did not learn from the lessons of the past. We were unable to internalize the message of both the *Zeroa* and the *beitzah*. However, for the past 70 years, one segment of our people has learned this message and has incorporated it into their lifestyle. Because of their attitudes, we in the United States and elsewhere have begun to follow suit.

Our brethren in the State of Israel were hardened by the brutal and catastrophic events in Europe during the Hitler era in the 1930s and 1940s. They were influenced by the atrocities perpetuated not only by the Nazis but by the callous and indifferent attitudes of those who aided and abetted them. These include not only the citizens of the countries which the Nazis occupied, but also the governments of England, the United States and the other so-called enlightened Allied powers. The Israelis realized that in order to survive, they must become hard-boiled, strong as a rock, able to endure invectives, and able to withstand threats of annihilation. In addition, they also had to emulate some of the characteristics of the *Zeroa*.

The State of Israel came into being on May 14, 1948, just before the onset of Shabbos. It is to the great credit and courage of its leaders who said that the moment had arrived. They shrugged off all advice from the United States and other countries who advised delaying the proclamation announcing its Statehood so that the Arab countries may be convinced not to attack. In the face of the greatest possible odds and threats of annihilation, the modern Jewish State of Israel was brought into being. After consultation with a number of rabbinic leaders, they made their decision. The hour was right. It was time for independence. It was the moment to eat and enjoy the modern-day symbol of the Korban Pesach.

Our brethren in Israel have maintained their freedom and independence ever since, all the while surrounded by a world of hostility. They constantly have faced nations near and far who wish for only one thing – to see the total destruction and annihilation of the Jewish State of Israel. However, Israel has constantly said "No" to the world's desire that we be eliminated from the community of nations. The former non-combatants, the untrained and weaponless Jews have been transformed. We today possess an army that has been forced to fight at least eight wars in the 70 years of our existence against forces that have outnumbered us by 50 to 1. We have been successful each and every time, thanks to the aid and assistance of *HaKadosh Baruch Hu*.

Pesach

The main characteristic of our Israeli brethren is that they have shown the world that a Jew must stand up with his loins girded, with his shoes on his feet, and with his staff in his hand. He must act when he must and do so with haste and in a very hurried fashion. Israel has taught us this most significant lesson of Pesach – that of freedom and independence, tenacity and perseverance. May she continue doing so for many more years and may we continue to learn these lessons and incorporate them into our lives. We hope and pray that the persistence of the Jew, as symbolized by the *beitzah,* and the boldness and strength of our people, as exemplified by the *zeroa,* will continue to inspire Jews the world over. We pray that one day soon the world will experience the coming of the Messianic era where peace will reign and Hashem will be recognized for Who He is and we, His people, will finally be able to fulfill our real and true destiny as an אור לגויים, a light onto the world. במהרה בימינו אמן.

31. Dayeinu: Appreciating What G-d Has Given Us

Pesach 5776 (2016)

The Pesach Haggadah, next to the Torah and Siddur, is perhaps the most popular and widely read Jewish text. It contains within it the order of the Seder, including the laws, traditions, as well as historical events that led up to *Yetzias Mitzrayim*, the Exodus from Egypt, and beyond. In addition, there are within it various texts from the Mishnah and Gemara which elucidate the essence of this special Yom Tov. The interpretation of these paragraphs is most instructive. Even those sections which, from a cursory glance, appear to be no more than popular and lyrical hymns, can, in fact, shed light on the underlying theme of the Seder night. One of the most popular of these poetic songs is *Dayeinu*. Scores of commentaries have questioned the meaning behind this song and have given many diversified and significant interpretations.

In order to truly understand this song, we must go back to the Torah in Parshas Vaeira. There Hashem told Moshe to approach the Bnei Yisrael and inform them that the time had arrived for their emancipation from slavery and oppression. In these words, Moshe relates four expressions of redemption (Shemos 6:6-7):

לָכֵן אֱמֹר לִבְנֵי יִשְׂרָאֵל אֲנִי ה' וְהוֹצֵאתִי אֶתְכֶם מִתַּחַת סִבְלֹת מִצְרַיִם וְהִצַּלְתִּי אֶתְכֶם מֵעֲבֹדָתָם וְגָאַלְתִּי אֶתְכֶם בִּזְרוֹעַ נְטוּיָה וּבִשְׁפָטִים גְּדֹלִים: וְלָקַחְתִּי אֶתְכֶם לִי לְעָם וְהָיִיתִי לָכֶם לֵאלֹקִים וגו'.

Say to the children of Israel, I am the L-rd, (1) and I will bring you out from under the burdens of the Egyptians. (2) I will deliver you out of this service. (3) I will redeem you with an outstretched arm, and with great judgments. (4) And I will take you to Me for a people, and I will be to you a G-d.

Pesach

[Our Chachamim in the Talmud Yerushalmi explain that the reason we have four cups of wine at the Seder is based on these four expressions.]

Moshe thought that after proclaiming this to the Jewish people, they would be comforted and happy. However, instead of the mood of the Hebrews turning from gloom and despair to happiness and exaltation over the pledge of Hashem, the people's attitude remained the same. The Torah tells us (Shemos 6:9):

וְלֹא שָׁמְעוּ אֶל מֹשֶׁה מִקֹּצֶר רוּחַ וּמֵעֲבֹדָה קָשָׁה:

They did not listen to the words of Moshe because of the anguish of this spirit and through very hard work.

Evidently, their inhumane workload, their oppression, and their tortured souls had become so embittered, their spirit so broken that they were unable to see beyond the moment.

Their depression appeared to be quite contagious. It was immediately felt even by Moshe, the idealist and the optimist. His mood and way of thinking began to resemble the oppressed Jews. Hashem told Moshe to appear before Pharaoh and instruct him to send the children of Israel out of his land. Moshe's response is similar to that of the Jews. He says:

הֵן בְּנֵי יִשְׂרָאֵל לֹא שָׁמְעוּ אֵלַי וְאֵיךְ יִשְׁמָעֵנִי פַרְעֹה וַאֲנִי עֲרַל שְׂפָתָיִם:

Behold the Children of Israel refused to listen to me; how will Pharaoh even give me an audience, I who am tongue tied.

Hashem's reaction was one of sternness tempered with tenderness. He demanded that Moshe perform His will (Shemos 7:1). It is as if Hashem was saying, "You may very well be afraid, Moshe. Total and complete desperation, however, is unacceptable. You may not know how the Jewish people will be redeemed, but you cannot give up. Do not be pessimistic. You must look not just at the present but towards the future as well. You must project a sense of optimism and hope to the Jewish people."

Pesach

Today, my friends, we may be very tempted to emulate the behavior of Moshe and the Jewish people. Not since the 1940s, during the Holocaust, has there been a period where Jews living in Europe have been as frightened and in despair over the future as they are now.

It seems like yesterday that the Jewish people were one of the most elite groups in the United States in terms of culture and prestige. It was also just a short time ago that the State of Israel represented the epitome of honor and glory. Its military was heralded. Its development and growth were envied by the world. Today, however, we observe pessimism and despondency over the future of the Jewish community.

We also are concerned whether and for how long the United States, our greatest and strongest ally, will continue to support the State of Israel in the halls of world opinion. Will our current president (Obama) help Israel in its fight for survival, or will he continue his "Carteresque" approach? Will he realize that Israel is as important for America as America is for Israel, or will he continue to curry favor with the Moslem world at the expense of the Jewish state?

Our despair today also concerns itself with the political and economic isolation of Israel. We are gravely worried over the worldwide economic boycott against her, the B.D.S.

If our survival over the millennia has taught us anything at all, it is that we cannot despair and we cannot give up hope. Our existence is based not on the rational nor on the logical. The fact that we are here today while all the other ancient nations have long since disappeared is evidence that we are not just an accident of history. Rather, all that we experience and endure is part of the השגחה פרטית, G-d's Divine Plan.

It almost seems as if there are no solutions to our countless and numerous problems. However, somehow, we Jews have become experts in the art of survival in the face of supposedly overwhelming odds. For Jews, from time immemorial, the belief in the survival of our people has been a basic and elementary article of faith.

I ask you, my friends, are our problems today of a greater magnitude than those that faced the Jewish exiles who found themselves on the Babylonian riverbanks? There, bereft of homeland and independence, they could have given up, they could have been מייאש. Instead, they wept but also sang to Hashem:

אִם אֶשְׁכָּחֵךְ יְרוּשָׁלָם תִּשְׁכַּח יְמִינִי:

If I forget thee Jerusalem, may my right hand forget its cunning.

Cry they did, but despair – certainly not. The tears were of hope and optimism. They did not look only at the current moment; they thought of the great and glorious future that would one day arrive.

Are our problems today more severe than those facing Rabbi Yochanan ben Zakkai and his generation in the year 70 CE? They witnessed the destruction of the Second Beis HaMikdash and the loss of Jewish sovereignty and independence. They observed the wholesale slaughter of over one million of their coreligionists. They saw the Romans taking thousands upon thousands of Jews as prisoners to Rome. They cried and wept, but they planned for the future. With Jerusalem demolished and leveled to the ground, Rabbi Yochanan succeeded in convincing the Roman leaders to allow the Jews to continue their religious life in Yavneh. With that act of heroism, optimism, and foresight, he saved the very future of Judaism, both physically and spiritually.

Are our problems today more serious than those that faced the Jews of Spain at the end of the 15th century? They had to make the agonizing choice of either becoming baptized or be forced to flee their homeland, and, oftentimes, even to face death.

Can we seriously claim that our future looks bleaker than that of our fellow Jews who languished in the purgatory of the Nazi

Pesach

concentration camps? They faced almost certain death day in and day out. However, by and large, they did not despair, and they did not give up hope. In fact, thousands and thousands of these holy martyrs marched into the gas chambers with the full knowledge that their physical death was only moments away. Despite that awareness, they sang the אני מאמין, "I believe with perfect faith that the Messiah will come, and even though he may tarry, I still wait every day for his arrival." That, my friends, was true heroism and optimism.

In a number of concentration camps, such as Buchenwald, Landsberg, Bergen-Belsen and others, Pesach was celebrated with Matzah, the Seder, and the reciting of the Haggadah. These Jews were experiencing life and death struggles and were thus exempt from observing the Mitzvos of Pesach. Nevertheless, many refused to eat Chametz and celebrated the holiday as best as they could.

An incredible episode occurred in the Landsberg concentration camp in 1945 as they conducted their Seder. Upon reciting the verse, "Now we are slaves, next year we will be free," – לשנה הבאה בני חורין, a pale young man suddenly began shouting, "Brothers! We cannot wait for next year! Not 'לשנה הבאה'; rather, 'לשנה הזאת', *this* year we will be free!'" And indeed, one month later, on April 20, 1945, the day designated as Pesach Sheini, the Landsberg concentration camp was liberated by the United States Army. Just as their ancestors were freed over 3,000 years ago, so were these enslaved prisoners freed.

If we just remember all that our ancestors have endured down through the ages, and yet still did not give up hope, we will more than be able to overcome our difficult and traumatic times. Without faith in our ability to endure, we would simply drown in our own fears. A truly strong, proud, and secure people gains strength and resolve in their moments of crisis. They also take an inventory of that which they do have and express gratitude to Hashem for what He has given them.

This idea is depicted in one of the most popular songs of the Haggadah – *Dayeinu*. This prayer consists of 14 stanzas of a series of loving kindnesses which Hashem wrought for His people from the time of the Exodus through their entry into the Land of Israel and the building of the Beis HaMikdash. The gratitude of the Jew is evident by his stressing each degree of benevolence and viewing the succeeding kindness as lavishly redundant. It, therefore, is an added measure of G-d's love and affection for Bnei Yisrael. I believe that in light of our times of difficulty, it would do us well to understand the meaning of the word "*Dayeinu*." In essence, it means, "It would have been enough for us." "Had G-d brought us out of Egypt and not executed judgment on the Egyptians, it would have been enough for us." And we go on and on. The message of *Dayeinu* is that we should express our gratitude and thanks to Hashem for what we *presently* possess. *Dayeinu* tells us to take a good and hard look at where we are and what we have. It behooves us to count how many of these blessings we have and which are truly essential.

An example of one of the stanzas in *Dayeinu* illustrates that while what we have currently might not seem sufficient, we still can find ways to show gratitude. In the *Dayeinu* we recite:

אלו קרבנו לפני הר סיני ולא נתן לנו את התורה דינו.

If You, Hashem, had only brought us to Mount Sinai and did not give us the Torah, that would have been enough.

Many commentaries are bewildered by this statement. What would have been the purpose and the value of Bnei Yisrael coming to Mount Sinai and leaving without receiving the Torah?

Rav Avraham Pam *zt"l* gives a beautiful explanation in the name of the *Nachalas Yaakov*. He says that when the Jews came and stood in front of Mount Sinai, the mountain was covered with Hashem's *Shechinah*. The *tumah*, the impurity, that the *Nachash*, the infamous primordial snake had implanted in Chavah and all her descendants as a result of eating from the *Eitz HaDa'as*, was now removed. All of the Bnei Yisrael returned back to the high level of *kedusha*, spiritual purity, that was the state in which both Adam HaRishon and Chava enjoyed at their creation. For this alone, says Rav Pam, just standing at Har Sinai and absorbing its *kedusha* would have been enough.

Rav Pam cites the Midrash Shocher Tov on Mishlei which gives another reason. It discusses a person who enters a perfume store. Even if he does not buy anything, the fragrances alone that engulfs the store will attach itself to his body and his clothing. When he departs from the store, he remains with a very pleasant aroma. Likewise, the mere stay at Har Sinai, even had the Jews not accepted the Torah, would have had a profound influence for the good upon the Jewish people.

Therefore, says Rav Pam, *Dayeinu* teaches us that people are greatly affected by their surroundings, whether it be positive or negative. When one lives amongst Tzadikim, holy and righteous people, he will be influenced by them in a very positive way. Correspondingly, when one resides amongst the wicked, he will also be influenced by them.

Rav Soloveitchik *zt"*l adds a slightly different interpretation to this stanza of *Dayeinu*. The Rav said that the main purpose of *Ma'amad Har Sinai* was to implant in the hearts of each and every Jew true *Yiras Shamayim,* fear of G-d. Therefore, he says, even if Hashem would have not given the Torah to the Jewish people, merely standing at Har Sinai would still have benefited us by implanting *Yiras Shamayim* into our hearts. Thus, by standing in unison at the foot of this holy mountain, we were transformed from a motley group of freed slaves into a holy and sacred nation—all prior to the actual acceptance of the Torah. Our mere presence at that *Makom Kadosh*

Pesach

changed the Jewish nation forever. For that alone, said the Rav, we must say *Dayeinu*.

This is an integral and an internal message for us. Had the Torah not been given, the world would have reverted to תהו ובהו. Nevertheless, the preface to the giving of the Torah alone, however we interpret it, would necessitate the expression of eternal gratitude to Hashem.

My friends, if we were to scrutinize all that we are lucky enough to own, how much of it is truly beyond our basic needs? Usually, we say, "If only I had this or that," or, "If I had more wealth, better health, and more happiness, I would be satisfied. *Dayeinu*."

In truth, however, we should reverse the order. Why should we wait until we lose something in order to appreciate what we once had? Let us count our blessings now. Let us enumerate our joys and our happiness and say, "Dear *Ribono shel Olam*, we truly have enough. We need nothing else. *Dayeinu!*"

Look at the present situation in which world Jewry finds itself today. We can be pessimistic and gloomy over our future. That, however, is not the Jewish approach. We would, by acting in such a manner, be forgetting the message of Pesach and the Haggadah. No matter how many of our forebears went to their deaths as martyrs, we are, and have always been, indestructible. We will never be destroyed. Those individuals or countries who teach and practice hatred and destruction, even if today they appear to be strong and powerful, eventually will also be destroyed. They will, in the future, be long forgotten. We, however, will survive. We will be here for eternity.

Israel today, the people, the nation, and the land – continues to grow and flourish. History has taught us to choose life and resistance, tenacity and hope. We will continue to survive with both distinction and distinctiveness until the dream of the prophecy of total and complete peace is fulfilled.

Pesach

At that time, we will all be able to say in unison, "Thank You, Hashem, for all that You have done for us and for all that You have given us. We certainly have more than our share. *Dayeinu.*"

We certainly are grateful and appreciative. We pray for that day to be here soon. Until then, we must think positively and optimistically. Let us not for one moment ever despair or give up. Rather, we should be hopeful and joyous for the tomorrow, for the future which will soon be here. We must always remember: עם ישראל חי and נצח ישראל לא ישקר. Amen.

32. Transforming Bitterness and Sorrow into Happiness and Joy
Pesach 5777 (2017)
פסח-מצה-מרור

    Pesach certainly ranks as one of the most fascinating and interesting of our Jewish festivals. Its preparation alone is unique in that more time is invested in the days leading up to the festival than any other holiday. There is a plethora of laws, customs, and traditions which the Jew is obligated to familiarize himself with. In the Code of Jewish Law, the Shulchan Aruch, the laws of Pesach occupy more space than any other holiday. The Seder night, the highlight of this holiday, is replete with numerous symbolic foods and practices. Perhaps one of the most perplexing aspect of the Seder is that it is highlighted by questions and answers. The Haggadah, the basic text of our festival, actually begins with a series of questions asked by young children. We then read the questions posed by the four very different and distinct Jewish sons. Our commentators ask: why is this the case with Passover and with no other Yom Tov? We can answer this question by truly understanding and internalizing the theme of Pesach.

    On most other holidays, there is basically only one theme, one focal point which we commemorate and observe. All our *Tefillos* and Mitzvos of the high holy days for example, revolve around *Teshuvah*, repentance. On Chanukah, the lighting of the Menorah and the various prayers we recite all recall the Maccabean victory over the Hellenistic Syrians in 165 B.C.E. On Purim, the reading of the Megillah, the *Shalach Manos*, and the sending of gifts to the poor all celebrate and commemorate the defeat of Haman, the archenemy of the Jews.

Pesach

Pesach, however, is different than all our other holidays. At the Passover Seder, we find side-by-side two central themes which are diametrically opposite one another. We eat the Matzah and the Marror which are reminders of slavery. We also partake in the aristocratic and emancipated form of dipping food in appetizers and reclining like free people.

Only on Passover are we introduced at the very same time to the concept of liberation, redemption, and salvation as well as to imprisonment, incarceration and detention. Thus, the child, who in essence represents the future of our people, is bewildered, perplexed, and mystified. He responds in the only way he knows how – by asking questions. מה נשתנה הלילה הזה מכל הלילות?!– *Why is this night different than all other nights?*

We have heard these questions asked of us year in and year out—but have we ever truly thought about their answer? These questions should not be viewed as mere childish inquisitiveness, for as the Talmud (Pesachim 116a) teaches, sometimes one must even ask himself the *Mah Nishtana.* These contrasting symbols and concepts are indeed quite puzzling. What is their purpose? Why do we include both simultaneously at our Seder and in our Pesach observance?

Each of these themes plays a most important role in the development of the Jew. The Passover Seder recalls a night of unparalleled human drama. During the first half of the night of the 15th day of Nisan, 3,330 years ago, our ancestors were still enslaved. We, their descendants, commemorate that fact with our eating of the Marror and Matzah. However, at the stroke of midnight ויהי בחצי הלילה – they became free, independent, and respected people of G-d. They became an עם קדוש לה'. Thus, we also partake of the foods and observe the customs which are common to all emancipated people.

This has always been the fate of our people down through the ages. We have always initially experienced the darkness of night and

235

then the brightness of day. However, we are unlike other nations or other people. The non-Jewish world perpetuates the great and magnificent events of their past. However, they skip over and almost completely ignore and disregard the less fortunate times in their history. They do this in an attempt to erase them completely from their memory.

The Jewish people, on the other hand, are quite unique. We stress both the good and the bad, the happy and the sad, the glorious and the ignominious. We do this by designating special days in the year as fast days with prayers of supplication and petition. Likewise, we do the same on Pesach, the festival of liberation. We partake of Matzah, the poor man's bread and Marror, the food of affliction, which symbolizes Israel's years of torture and enslavement in Egypt.

We do this in order to illustrate to our descendants that our present and our very future is dependent upon a thorough understanding of our past. This dual message may be behind the fact that the first night of Pesach always falls out on the same night of the week as the night of Tisha B'Av. We tie the apex of our history with the nadir of our existence, for we can only appreciate what we presently possess by remembering the bitterness of yesterday. We can only go forward if we recall all aspects of our history.

It is therefore most instructive that the בעל הגדה says that the most significant aspect of the Seder is the dictum stated by Rabban Gamliel:

רבן גמליאל היה אומר כל שלא אמר שלשה דברים אלו בפסח לא יצא ידי חובתו ואלו הן פסח מצה ומרור.

"Rabban Gamliel said, 'Whoever has not explained these three concepts on Pesach has not fulfilled his duty, namely: Pesach (the pascal sacrifice), Matzah, and Marror.'"

Our rabbis were quite puzzled by this statement. Why, they ask, does Rabban Gamliel list both Matzah and Marror as symbols of our emancipation? We have, in fact, already established that these two foods represent our enslavement and affliction. They seem not to belong here?

The fact of the matter is that both Matzah and Marror contain within them a dual role. They were indeed the very symbols of our enslavement in Egypt. They were the bread of affliction and the bitter herbs of detention and persecution. While it is understood how the Korban Pesach is a most essential element of our redemption, Matzah too is a symbol of our *Geulah*. This was the food which Bnai Yisrael consumed during their very hurried deliverance from Egypt. What is most puzzling, however, is the role of the Marror. What is it about this vegetable that it is also included in the list of symbols of redemption? The Chabad Haggadah explains that it was the intense suffering of Bnai Yisrael that hastened the Exodus.

The Egyptian servitude was to last for 400 years. In Beraishis Hashem told Avraham:

וַיֹּאמֶר לְאַבְרָם יָדֹעַ תֵּדַע כִּי גֵר יִהְיֶה זַרְעֲךָ בְּאֶרֶץ לֹא לָהֶם וַעֲבָדוּם וְעִנּוּ אֹתָם אַרְבַּע מֵאוֹת שָׁנָה:

Know of a surety that your descendants shall be a stranger in a land that is not theirs and they shall serve them and they shall afflict them for 400 years.

Due to the intense bitterness and severity to which Israel was subjected, G-d reduced the servitude to 210 years. However, if this be the case, why is Marror placed last on Rabban Gamliel's list of items which helped bring about the *Geulah*; it should have been listed first?

Rav Bunim of Peshischa explains that one cannot truly appreciate the intense suffering that he is encountering until after he has been freed from his incarceration. My friends, ask any of the survivors of the Holocaust and they will tell you that it was only after they were liberated from their nightmare and hell that they were able to really feel the intensity of their suffering. Therefore, Rabban Gamliel's order makes perfect sense.

Pesach

We begin with the *Korban Pesach*, which in itself represents a two-fold concept of freedom. It first represented the spiritual freedom of the Jews from the idolatry of Egyptian society. It then represented the physical freedom of the Jews. On the tenth day of Nissan, the Jews took the lamb, which was the Egyptian deity. They dragged it through the streets of Egypt in full view of their former taskmasters. This represented the spiritual freedom of the Jews. They then slaughtered it and placed its blood on their doorposts. By doing so, they were physically rescued from the traumatic and catastrophic effects of מכת בכורות.

We then list Matzah which the commentators call "the bread of free men," commemorating the speedy redemption wrought by Hashem. Unlike the לחם עוני, poor man's bread, this Matzah could only be eaten by freemen and only when the hour of liberation and emancipation arrived.

Finally, Rabban Gamliel lists Marror. We must on this night of Pesach remember the bitterness of our enslavement in Egypt. Only when we will have first experienced real and genuine חירות, can we look back. We will then realize that the bitterness that our ancestors experienced was in essence for their benefits. The discord between Yosef and his brothers is what initially led to the descent of the Jews to Egypt. It was precisely the bitterness that the Bnei Yisrael experienced in Mitzrayim that forged them into a single, cohesive unit, thereby rectifying the sin of Yaakov's children. They were then willing and able to follow the command of Hashem as one indivisible nation.

In fact, the Abarbanel, the great 16th century commentator and leader of Spanish Jewry, uses the dual theme of slavery and redemption to explain the questions of the *Mah Nishtana*. He says that these two stages are a reflection of Jewish history and is, in essence, the story of our existence. The Mishnah in Pesachim teaches that the Haggadah must be organized in a fashion of מתחיל בגנות ומסיים

בשבה. We depict the Jewish experience as beginning in the state of bitterness and deprivation which then developed into happiness, joy, and independence. At first, our future looked bleak and foreboding. Eventually, however, we experienced salvation, sunshine, and brightness. That, says the Abarbanel, has been the Jewish fate for 2,000 years.

We are however, a very positive and forward-thinking people. We have an optimistic point of view. The Jewish ideal was never to be sad and depressed. Rather, he who is cheerful and optimistic, he who looks at the future with happiness and has a zest for life has achieved the ideal. He who has a *Simchas HaChaim*, a happy and positive approach, is to be admired and serves as our ideal.

After 2,000 years of darkness and dreariness, after being pulled and shoved from pillar to post, after being exiled and discriminated against by the nations of the world, we might understand the negative attitude of many of our coreligionists. After living through the nightmarish years of the Shoah, we could naturally look towards the future with pessimism and with jaundiced eyes. However, that is not who we are nor is this our present attitude and state of mind.

We live today in one of the most fascinating and exciting times in our history. Yes, we are still living in *golus* and are awaiting the coming of the Moshiach. We do not yet have the third and final *Beis HaMikdash*. However, we are today a most fortunate and grateful people. We have seen, over the past 70 years, the tremendous growth and development of the State of Israel. It has made a remarkable effect on the world in terms of scientific and technological advances. Its prestige as a major industrial and economic country is truly amazing. Religiously, we have seen tremendous strides and progress in the country. There are more yeshivos and seminaries, more learning and more spirituality emanating from all areas of Israel than ever before.

We, in the United States and throughout the Western world, can also be proud of our accomplishments and our development. We too have seen a tremendous emergence of religious life, of Torah learning and Torah living throughout this country. There is not one state in the union that does not have at least one Chabad center. They have attracted thousands of Jews who are being taught the basic rudiments and fundamentals of Yiddishkeit, real and genuine Judaism.

Jews here and throughout the Western world are able to and do participate in every area of life. We have risen to the top positions in government, commerce, business, medicine, science, and academia. Oftentimes, we feel that the sky is the limit . . . or perhaps not. We cannot forget the heroic Ilan Ramon, one of the Israeli air force pilots who participated in the bombing of the Osiraq nuclear reactor in Iraq. He was the first Israeli to fly for NASA and was killed as the Space Shuttle Columbia exploded during reentry in 2003. He flew to space declaring, "I feel I am representing all Jews and all Israelis." He ate only kosher during that tragic flight and attempted to keep Shabbos despite the perplexities of doing so while in orbit.

We are certainly thankful for all of these achievements. We have tremendous הודאה to Hashem for allowing us to live in this wonderful and Democratic country. We are so very thankful for all the freedoms and opportunities that we have. However, with all the good that we have, with all the positive signs pointing to a bright and glorious future, we are beginning to see possible and potential clouds of darkness which can have an adverse effect on our people. Internally, within the Jewish community, we have seen some major problems. With all the learning and the return to traditional life, we are still witnessing an overwhelming disrespect for Torah traditions and Torah laws.

Pesach

Unfortunately, there are more than 70% of Jews in the United States who lack even a basic and rudimentary Jewish education and any knowledge of Jewish laws and traditions. The non-Orthodox community is experiencing a wave of assimilation and non-affiliation with any religious or even Jewish causes or organizations. The rate of intermarriage among these groups is reaching epidemic proportions. It is frightening indeed to read the studies which have shown that within at most two generations the halachic Jewish population (those who are born to a Jewish mother or who convert to Judaism according to strict halachic standards) will only number 1-2 million people (as opposed to the 5 ½ million Jews who comprise the current American Jewish community). The rest will be, G-d forbid, lost to our faith, perhaps, forever. The situation of European Jewry is even more alarming with a rate of intermarriage that is even greater than here in the United States.

In addition, we are seeing some trends, mostly in Europe but also in isolated areas of the United States, that give us cause to worry. It appears that anti-Semitism is once again rearing its ugly head. There was a recent story in the Wall Street Journal which was quite disturbing. It reported that there is a new wave of anti-Semitic attacks that have occurred in Germany (I ask you, my friends, why am I not surprised?). Even though we are two generations post-Holocaust, there are still individuals in Germany who harbor hatred for Jews. The paper reports that "Prejudice and stereotypes harbored by recent migrants from largely Muslim countries have added to an existing undercurrent of anti-Semitism among some Germans and older migrant communities from Eastern Europe, resulting in an increasingly threatening environment."

It was most disturbing to read of a recent ghastly murder of an elderly Holocaust survivor in Paris, France, by her own Muslim neighbor. This murder has been declared an anti-Semitic attack by authorities. This has fueled a perception that "anti-Jewish acts, from casual insults to brutal violence, are on the rise across Europe and that the governments appear unable to do much about it."

However, my friends, let us not be fearful or dismayed. For while there may be some dark clouds hovering over us, while we see some signs that are ominous both internally and externally, we will, in the final analysis, prevail and be victorious. The holiday of Pesach reminds us that before we can see the light of day, we experience the darkness of night.

In the *Pesikta Rabbasi*, Rabbi Yitzchok says that in the year when the Moshiach will arrive, when redemption will come to our people, all the world's rulers will quarrel with one another. The nations themselves will fall into tumult and terror. Israel too will be in a similar state. She will openly wonder whether she will even survive. G-d will then reply to His people: "My children, be not dismayed. The days of your redemption are at hand, and this latter redemption is unlike any of the earlier ones. Following the earlier redemptions there were hardships and enslavement by other nations. However, after the present redemption you will never again suffer either hardship, enslavement, or oppression."

Passover, the holiday of freedom and liberation, is not only a festival of the past; it is also a celebration of the future. The great Navi Micha prophesied (7:15):

כִּימֵי צֵאתְךָ מֵאֶרֶץ מִצְרָיִם אַרְאֶנּוּ נִפְלָאוֹת:

As in the days of your Exodus from Egypt I will show them my wonders.

We too, in the not too distant future, will see all of our problems disappear. We will be witness to the coming of the Moshiach. With his arrival, he will usher in an era of peace and joy, happiness and exultation.

We pray that this deliverance shall soon be here. Amen.

33. Demonstrating Our Uniqueness

Pesach

חייב אדם לראות את עצמו כאילו הוא יצא ממצרים

[This drasha was delivered on the second day of Pesach, 1978. While some of the specific events alluded to may no longer be relevant, its message and its impact on the Jewish world remains as important today as it did when it was first given (RHG).]

Pesach, the Yom Tov of freedom and liberty, independence and self-determination, commemorates one very specific event in our history. On the night of the 15th of Nisan, we recall how Hashem redeemed and emancipated our ancestors in Egypt. For more than 200 years, they were enslaved and oppressed. On that night, He brought them out of the land of their bondage. He transformed them from a group of disparate slaves into one free and homogeneous people, dedicated and committed to Hashem and to His Will.

In the early years of our history, especially during the years prior to and during *Bayis Rishon*, the celebration of Pesach was limited to the offering of the Korban Pesach and certain other observances. During the days of the Second Beis HaMikdash, the holiday of Pesach took on added meaning and significance. In this era, and specifically the centuries of persecution at the hands of the Syrians and the Romans, the situation of the Jews became quite similar to that of the Egyptian servitude. The celebration of Pesach during these times gave our forebears an appreciation and understanding that what they were enduring was not unique only to them. It was not only they who were suffering and oppressed. This had already occurred in their history. Similarly, just as their ancestors were liberated and freed after undergoing periods of travail and hardship, they too would one day become free, independent, and dedicated עבדי ה', servants only to the *Ribono shel Olam* and no one else.

This concept was magnified a thousand-fold with the destruction of the Beis HaMikdash in Jerusalem in the year 70 C.E. With it, the end of Jewish political sovereignty occurred as well as the forced exile of most of the Jewish community. They were taken into a Diaspora which has lasted for 2,000 years. From that point on, no matter where the Jew has found himself, regardless of the difficulties he has experienced, he has always stressed and emphasized the holiday of freedom and independence. He hoped that one day, he too would be allowed to live his life and worship his religion without any outside interference.

Rabbi Yehudah ben Betzalel Lowe, one of the greatest Jewish thinkers of the 16th century, more commonly known as the Maharal of Prague, remarked that every enslavement of the Jews is entitled "Egypt," while every enslaver of the Jewish people is called "Pharaoh." However, while these states of slavery have indeed continued throughout the exile, they are on a different plane than that which we endured in Egypt.

When G-d redeemed our ancestors from Egypt, He implanted within them the seed of "Eternal Freedom," חירות עולם. The Jews would never again be completely enslaved. Even in the spiritual darkness of all our sufferings, in the depths of our hearts, we have always remained completely free. Our bodies and our minds may become enslaved to a new Pharaoh, but our spirits and souls will remain eternally free. This freedom endures precisely because of our remembrance of the first Exodus from Egypt.

Despite being scattered over the four corners of the earth, our faithful grasp of זכירת יציאת מצרים, the recollection of the Exodus, has enabled our nation to persist for 3,300 years. We have survived against all odds in the face of onslaughts both by individual anti-Semites as well as entire nations, generation after generation, who have risen up against us and attempted to obliterate the Jewish people. Hashem, in His infinite kindness and devotion, has protected us from this potential catastrophic destruction.

As we reach the conclusion of *Maggid,* we make a declaration which, at first glance, may appear enigmatic.

בכל דור ודור חייב אדם לראות את עצמו כאילו הוא יצא ממצרים.

In every generation it is obligatory for each individual to see himself as having participated personally in the Exodus from Egypt.

What is the reasoning behind this statement? How can we view ourselves as having left Egypt if we were not actually there? However, in light of the Maharal's aforementioned statement, it is understood. In each generation, we have suffered through another Pharaoh and another Mitzrayim. Just as the Jews saw G-d's outstretched arm redeem them in the original Exodus, we must perceive ourselves as having been redeemed by G-d from our present Pharaoh and Egyptian taskmasters. We survived the ovens of Auschwitz. We escaped from Hezbollah's rockets. We too have been redeemed from Egypt.

However, even when we view ourselves as having been redeemed, we have only participated in the Exodus on an intellectual level. No action on our part is required. Nevertheless, even this is difficult to fulfill for those of us who live in free and democratic countries where we are granted every right and are equal members of our society. We have the possibility and the freedom to potentially become either Prime Ministers or Presidents of our individual nations. It is thus an abstract task to think of our slavery and oppression. While ever grateful to Hashem for easing our situation in our current exile, it remains a yeoman's task to intellectually identify with our ancestor's plight and predicament in Egypt. How can we discharge our obligation to feel that we too just received our emancipation and freedom?

Upon examination of the Rambam's variant reading of the relevant passage of the Haggadah, we may come to a solution. In his נוסח it states:

בכל דור ודור חייב אדם להראות את עצמו כאילו הוא יצא ממצרים.

According to this reading, we are required to actively show and demonstrate in an outward fashion and manner our identification with the Exodus. Rav Soloveitchik explains that by drinking the four cups of wine while leaning, we are actively exhibiting our newfound status as free men. The Rambam indicates that by doing something physical, instead of merely thinking and trying to put ourselves in that place and at that time, we can fulfill this most important Mitzvah most effectively. We then will be able to associate and empathize with the pain and suffering which our ancestors were forced to endure. In order to be free from the present-day Pharaoh's as well, we must do something or act in some manner which will show our independence and demonstrate our freedom.

Unfortunately, not all Jews are blessed with the same ability to exhibit this sense of liberty and freedom as we. There are and have always been millions of our brethren who are oppressed and downtrodden. They cannot worship and live as they wish to. While they cannot truly and completely identify in every sense of the word with the liberation of our forebears in Egypt, they too eagerly look to the day when they will be able to say:

עבדים היינו לפרעה במצרים ויוציאנו ה' אלקינו משם ביד חזקה ובזרוע נטויה

"We were slaves to Pharaoh in Egypt, but G-d took us out with a strong hand and an outstretched arm."

Until that time occurs we must try in a very concrete manner to demonstrate our redemption. We must identify with their present enslavement. We must feel their pain and suffering. We must put ourselves as if we are in their shoes. They were indeed redeemed together with us from Egypt. Yet, while we are blessed with liberty

Pesach

and freedom, they are again forced to endure the yoke of bondage. My friends, being in a state of deliverance, redemption, and freedom imposes certain obligations on each of us. Unless we demonstrate our concern for the enslavement of our coreligionists, we will not be able to completely appreciate our own freedom. Freedom is meaningless unless we use it להראות – to ensure liberation and independence for all our people.

Pesach, thus, is the embodiment of the Jewish vision concerning our emancipation, rescue, and liberation. Thus, even in times when we were poor, enslaved and exploited, we hallowed and extolled freedom and liberty. No person is free unless he has cast off the yoke of man and accepted upon himself the kingdom of Hashem. At the time of the Exodus, G-d made His presence rest over us. He commanded us to be a holy and sanctified people, an עם קדוש לה'. We were given the duty to illuminate the world with the light of the holy Torah and with its Mitzvos. However, before we can go out and shine our radiance and educate the nations of the world, we must not, nor can we ever forget about our own oppressed and downtrodden brethren throughout the world. Thus, in each and every generation, it is incumbent upon us all to alter our behavior and to demonstrate that the concept of enslavement (at least in our hearts and minds) was totally eradicated at the time of יציאת מצרים.

Therefore, while we may have suffered over these 2,000 years in exile and for many years before the חורבן הבית, we always considered ourselves as free men and women. Even during the very dark and dreary days of the Shoah, the Jewish prisoners went to great efforts to observe Pesach, Chanukah, the *Yomim Noraim,* Shabbos, Tefillin, and many others Mitzvos. These were acts of free men who were really עבדים only to Hashem and to no one else. We, who are truly free and independent, cannot passively sit by silently while our brothers and sisters remain oppressed. It is thus the dictum of the Rambam that on this holiday of emancipation it is demanded of us that we demonstrate our freedom to help deliver others from their enslavement.

It is with this thought in mind that we might resolve a problem which has perplexed our scholars for many years. We have a Halachic principle in יורה דעה that if something not kosher is mixed together with food that is kosher, under usual circumstances, if the kosher food is 60 times the volume of the non-kosher substance, then the *treifa* food loses its characteristic and is nullified in the kosher. At that time, the entire mixture is fit for consumption. This is the principle known as ביטול בששים. On Pesach, in the laws of Chametz and Matzah, this principle is not applicable. Rather, we invoke the rule of אסור במשהו. This means that if even a tiny, insignificant particle of chametz is mixed in with food that is kosher for Passover, even if the non-chametz food is 1,000 times the volume of the chametz, the entire quantity is still forbidden.

On Pesach, as opposed to the rest of the year, even a small crumb of chametz will disqualify an entire pot of food. The question our rabbis ask is: why is this so? Why the change in laws that apply throughout the year?

The fact of the matter is that Pesach is distinct and separate from the rest of the Jewish year. Therefore, it requires different laws and customs. Pesach, as we stated previously, is the holiday of freedom and emancipation. It is a time when all Jews should be able to rejoice with the words: עתה בני חורין, "Now we are free and independent." However, if that hoped-for, utopian goal is not achieved, if even a משהו, if even one of our brethren is denied his basic human rights, if he is not allowed to properly worship and uphold his traditions and laws, then the joy and happiness of our festival is diminished and marred. If even one Jew is impoverished and has not what to eat, how can we be so serene?

Therefore, the Rambam tells us that if we want to properly appreciate and commemorate the Festival of freedom and emancipation, then we cannot do so by sitting down and remaining passive in the face of world events. We must go out of our way to demonstrate and show that we care and are concerned for every משהו, every individual Jew wherever he may be and in whatever condition he may find himself.

We must do so not only by seeing ourselves as having participated in יציאת מצרים; we must do much more. We must personally identify with enslavement, harassment, and oppression. We must do what we can in order to help bring the great final and complete Exodus, the גאולה שלימה of all our people throughout the world.

There is a story told about Rabbi Yisrael Salanter, the great 19th century founder of the Mussar movement. In the city of Kovno, where he served as chief Rabbi, there was a house set aside for the indigent, the poor, and the homeless. There they were sheltered and given food. After a number of years of neglect, the house became dilapidated and required a tremendous amount of repair. Rabbi Yisrael saw this condition and attempted to alleviate the plight of these less fortunate Jews. He often attempted to get people to contribute to its upkeep. However, no matter how hard he tried, all too few people contributed funds. The condition of the building deteriorated and became progressively worse.

One year on the first night of Pesach, before the onset of the Seder, Rabbi Yisrael left his own home and disappeared for a number of hours. When he did not return home, his frantic wife contacted many people to help her find her husband. The Jewish inhabitants of Kovno searched throughout the city, house by house, but they could not find the great Rabbi. Finally, they located him in the poorhouse.

To their horror, their beloved and world-renowned rabbi was lying flat on the floor, next to the impoverished Jews of the city. The beds of the poorhouse were broken, so the inhabitants had no choice but to sleep amidst the dirt and squalor. The people begged Rabbi

Yisrael to leave this dilapidated building and return to the comfort of his own home. However, he adamantly refused.

"But Rabbi," they pleaded, "This is no place for you on the night of Pesach. Please come home." However, Rabbi Yisrael was adamant. He refused to return home until commitments were made to have the house repaired and made fit for people to live in. "Are these people," he asked, "any worse than us?" His words and actions made a very deep impact on the Jewish community. Within a few days after Yom Tov, the entire Jewish community of Kovno donated enough money to repair the building. They transformed it into a decent and comfortable living space.

We, of course, might ask ourselves what we can do to help change the course of human events. First of all, we should begin to educate ourselves about the problems facing our brethren throughout the world. We cannot sit home with our arms folded and allow others to work for us. If we do more than just worry about the plight of our brethren, if we act out and demonstrate our love of freedom and emancipation, if we will prove to ourselves and to our fellow Jews and to the world at large that we really and truly care, we will have done our job. We will help guarantee that one day, in the not too distant future, not even a מִשֶּׁהוּ, not even the smallest segment of the Jewish community will be enslaved or oppressed. Then we will have truly fulfilled the dictum of the Haggadah that we internalize and take to heart the message and meaning of *Yetzias Mitzrayim*. We will then have made a significant contribution to Hashem and to our people.

On this Pesach, let us not only see ourselves as having participated in *Yetzias Mitzrayim*. Let us, by our actions, go one step further. Let us demonstrate the relevance of the Exodus both in the past as well as in the future. Let us make manifest that we too were actually redeemed. In that way, we will help bring the Moshiach closer. Then, the entire world will experience a life of peace and

Pesach

tranquility, serenity and conciliation. We hope and pray for that day to soon arrive במהרה בימינו אמן.

34. Who Knows Four: How, When, and Why

Pesach

ארבע כוסות

One of the most interesting and fascinating Mitzvos associated with the holiday of Pesach requires some clarification and explanation. Every adult Jew, male and female, whether wealthy or poor, is commanded to consume four cups of wine at the Seder. For us to truly understand this unique Rabbinic decree fully and completely is to internalize the theme of Pesach and the very message of Judaism.

We are told to drink wine, a beverage which has the capacity to lower man to the basest form of animal life. On the other hand, wine has the ability to raise man to great spiritual and lofty heights. Indeed, in a departure from normative *halachic* practice, we are instructed to make a new *beracha* on each of the four cups of wine, despite all being drunk in the same sitting. The blessing of G-d each time we lift the cup of wine and bring it to our lips clearly demonstrates that we are engaged in an act which, instead of degrading ourselves, actually sanctifies God and with that, the entire universe.

There are, I believe, two basic questions facing us:

1. If wine has such a potentially deleterious effect on man, why did our Sages choose this as an expression of our freedom?
2. In addition, why are we commanded to express this freedom four times with this beverage on the night of the Seder? What sources have the Rabbis given us for this Mitzvah?

Pesach

The late, great HaRav Shlomo Zalman Auerbach *zt"l* offers a most fascinating interpretation. He wonders why wine has to be the vehicle which best expresses the idea of freedom and emancipation? Why could this four-fold ceremony not be performed by using four fruits or perhaps even four Matzos? These choices would be just as effective in arousing the curiosity of our children, who are the focus of the Seder, to ask about this apparently different and strange custom.

Rav Auerbach cites the Talmud Yerushalmi which bases this Mitzvah on the four different expressions of salvation. When Hashem informed the Bnei Yisrael that the time of redemption and emancipation was fast approaching, He informed Moshe (Shemos 6:6-7):

לָכֵן אֱמֹר לִבְנֵי יִשְׂרָאֵל אֲנִי ה' וְהוֹצֵאתִי אֶתְכֶם מִתַּחַת סִבְלֹת מִצְרַיִם וְהִצַּלְתִּי אֶתְכֶם מֵעֲבֹדָתָם וְגָאַלְתִּי אֶתְכֶם בִּזְרוֹעַ נְטוּיָה וּבִשְׁפָטִים גְּדֹלִים: וְלָקַחְתִּי אֶתְכֶם לִי לְעָם וְהָיִיתִי לָכֶם לֵאלֹקִים וִידַעְתֶּם כִּי אֲנִי ה' אֱלֹקֵיכֶם הַמּוֹצִיא אֶתְכֶם מִתַּחַת סִבְלוֹת מִצְרָיִם:

Say to the children of Israel, I am the L-rd and I will bring you out from under the burdens of the Egyptians. I will deliver you out of this service. I will redeem you with an outstretched arm and with great judgments. And I will take you to me for people and I will be to you a God...

HaRav Shlomo Zalman says that the four לשונות of גאולה are not merely repetitive variations on the concept of freedom. Each statement creates a higher degree and an additional level of joy and happiness. The first expression, "והוצאתי", represents the respite the Jews had from the physical labor that they had to endure. "והצלתי" indicates the complete end of the servitude in Egypt. The third expression, "וגאלתי", refers to Hashem's physically removing Bnei Yisrael from Egypt. Finally, "ולקחתי", the fourth לשון of גאולה indicates the spiritual elevation of the Jewish nation, their transformation into the עם קדוש and the עם הנבחר, the holy and the chosen people.

Each expression builds on the effects of the previous one, intensifying the process of redemption. It is to underscore their correlation and successive levels of redemption that the *Chachamim* instituted the mitzvah of imbibing four cups of wine specifically. Had they used either fruit, Matzah or any other food, the effect on each person after consuming each individual component would have remained the same. The first fruit or Matzah would taste the same as the three subsequent ones. However, in regard to the drinking of wine, the effect of the four cups is cumulative. Each cup intensifies the feelings of happiness, joy and exhilaration. Therefore, it is wine specifically which serves as an apt parallel to the four-step process of redemption.

While initially, wine can be looked upon as a medium which brings about the downfall of man, when taken in the context of *Kadesh*, holiness, it can achieve the opposite effect. Instead of sinking lower and lower to one's animalistic state, the drinking of the four cups actually raises us spiritually. As we celebrate the transformation of a slave-nation into a holy nation, we demonstrate the ability to take the mundane and physical and transform it into holiness and sanctity.

The *Shelah HaKadosh*, HaRav Yeshayah Horowitz, the saintly 16th century author of the שני לוחות הברית, suggests a novel symbolism for the Mitzvah of the ארבע כוסות, an important message upon which I would like to dwell. In the *Shnei Luchos HaBris* [*Meseches Pesachim, Matzah Ashirah, Drush Rishon*] he writes that on the night when we celebrate the birth of *Am Yisrael* as a free and independent nation and people, we read in the Haggadah about our forefathers, Avraham, Yitzchak and Yaakov. However, it seems that we completely ignore the contributions of the ארבע אמהות, our four matriarchs, toward the development and growth of Klal Yisrael.

Pesach

This, says the *Shelah*, is a mistake, for we do, in fact, recall their influence throughout the Seder night, as each cup of wine which we consume corresponds to one of the *Imahos*.

Avraham and Sarah chose converts from amongst the nations of the world, bringing them into Hashem's spiritual sphere. In a similar vein, Hashem chose us from amongst the nations of the world. In the Kiddush for Yom Tov we say: אשר בחר בנו מכל עם. When we recall out gratitude for choosing us as His people, we recall the righteousness of Sarah who acted in a like manner.

We drink the second cup after we have told the story of the birth of our nation, after the *Maggid* section of the Seder. We read how our nation had originally come from idol worshipers and heathens. We speak about how we gradually progressed and grew in holiness and in spirituality. Our mother Rivkah's life paralleled our own progress and development. She too grew up in a home of idolatry and depravity. She too developed and grew into a holy and pious woman. She, like us, her children, was: מתחיל בגנות ומסיים בשבח, starting with very humble beginnings and eventually becoming great. She had the *zechus* to be the mother of the progenitor of *Am Yisrael*, the saintly Tzadik, Yaakov Avinu. Therefore, the second cup of wine recalls her merit.

After the *Shulchan Oreich* section of the Seder we say the *Birchas HaMazon*. We then drink the third cup of wine, which is the כוס של ברכה, the cup of blessing. *Bracha,* says the *Shelah*, comes to one's home due to the merit of one's wife. Rachel was the עקרת הבית, Yaakov's main wife. She thus brought great blessing to his home. In addition, she was the mother of Yosef HaTzadik. He was the one who sustained his family and the entire country of Egypt during the years of the great famine. Therefore, it is most appropriate that we honor the mother of the one who sustained the nation after we have completed our own *seudah*.

Pesach

Finally, the fourth cup is drunk after we complete the *Hallel*, our praise to Hashem. Mother Leah, after the birth of her fourth son, named him Yehudah. She said: הפעם אודה את ה': "This time I shall thank Hashem." Our *Chachamim* ask: Why did she wait until she had a fourth son to give שבח and הודאה to Hashem? *Chazal explain* that Leah knew that Yaakov was destined to have 12 sons from his four wives. When she gave birth to her fourth son, she realized that she was actually given more than her share in the growth of the family which was eventually to become *Am Yisrael*. While she certainly was gratified for the birth of all of her children, she now knew that she was given something very special. Therefore, it was only after the birth of Yehudah that Leah gave an extra הודאה to Hashem. In addition, Leah was the progenitor of Dovid HaMelech, the "sweet singer of Israel." Thus, at the point of the Seder when we recite the *Hallel*, we remember Leah who taught the Jewish people how and when to give proper thanks to Hashem.

In fact, my friends, from the very beginning of our history, women have played a very vital and significant role in our development and growth. This *pshat* of the *Shelah* is very much in consonance with the Gemara in Meseches Sotah (11b):

דרש רב עוירא: בשכר נשים צדקניות שהיו באותו הדור - נגאלו ישראל ממצרים

Rav Avira taught: It was in the merit of the righteous women of that generation that our forefathers were redeemed from Egypt.

Their husbands were oppressed and downtrodden, nearly giving up all hope of ever being redeemed and freed. As such, they did not want to bring any more children into a world of slavery and darkness. The women, however, gave them hope for the future. Their faith, their *bitachon* in Hashem and in His ultimate redemption of His children gave them the optimism and the wherewithal to give birth and raise their families. Because of their comfort and love, the

Pesach

husbands had new hope for the future. Family life continued, and the children of Israel, the Bnei Yisrael grew exponentially.

In addition, during their sojourn in the *Midbar*, the women played a very pivotal and positive role in the development of the nation. When the *Mishkan* was being constructed, the women donated the mirrors which they had used in Egypt to beautify themselves for their husbands. Hashem informed Moshe that these mirrors, because of their previous use in giving hope and courage to the men of Israel, were the most cherished of all of Israel's contributions. These mirrors were used to build the copper basin and its pedestal from which the Kohanim purified themselves before doing the *Avodah* in the *Mishkan*.

At the foot of Har Sinai, the children of Israel built and worshiped the golden calf, the עגל הזהב. Not only did the women refuse to participate in the worship of that abomination, they also utterly refused to contribute to its formation. While the men outdid each other in contributing their jewelry, the women completely abstained and eschewed the wishes of their husbands and fathers. Because of their extraordinary behavior, the *Da'as Zekainim* says that they were rewarded with Rosh Chodesh being designated as their particular Yom Tov.

Down through the ages, in every era of our history, women have played an extremely important role in our development and growth. Whether it was Yocheved and Miriam in Egypt, Devorah the prophetess in the days of the *Shoftim*, or Esther HaMalkah in Persia, these heroines were key figures in the salvation of the Jewish people. Moreover, there have been millions of women who demonstrated the courage and determination to uphold our faith and pass down our *Mesorah* to the next generation, whatever the cost.

In modern times, especially during the Holocaust, many women became active leaders or were members of various resistance groups inside and outside the ghettos and even in some of the concentration camps. There were also women who were part of groups seeking to rescue Jews from the clutches of the Nazis or even just to bring them aid, assistance, and sustenance. Many women were also part of the Jewish partisans who attacked the Nazis from deep inside the forests in Poland, Lithuania, Latvia and many other countries under Nazi control.

Some of the more well-known women fighters were Haika Grossman of the Bialystok ghetto, Zivia Lubetkem of the Warsaw ghetto, and Vitka Kempner-Kovner of the Vilna ghetto. Gisi Fleischmann was an integral member of the rescue efforts in Slovakia led by HaRav Michael Ber Weismandel. Recha Sternbuch also played a major role in *hatzalah* work out of Switzerland.

One of the most famous women rescuers during the Holocaust was Hannah Senesch. She emigrated to Palestine from Hungary in 1939. During the war, she became a paratrooper and volunteered to return to Europe. Her goal was to rescue as many Jews as possible from the Nazi clutches. Shortly after her entry into Hungary, however, she was betrayed, captured, and was eventually tried. Although she was tortured, she refused to give her captors any information about her fellow rescuers as well as the object of their mission. She was subsequently killed. Her body was later brought back to Israel where she was buried with full honors on Mount Zion. She has been regarded for all these years as a national heroine.

However, my friends, we need not look only at the Holocaust and other tragic times to find great and courageous women. We can see examples of these heroines in everyday life.

We can point to the millions of Jewish mothers and wives who, down through the ages, have sacrificed their comfort and their personal future for the betterment of their families. They worked long hours and at different and difficult jobs to make certain that their husbands and sons would be able to learn Torah and develop into

Pesach

Talmidei Chachamim. This may be less dramatic and not as historic, but it is also heroism at its very best.

There is a very instructive story about Rabbi Yaakov Levin. Rabbi Levin was the son of the great tzaddik of Yerushalayim, Rabbi Aryeh Levin, and the father of my classmate and friend Rabbi Benjy Levin. HaRav Yaakov was the very distinguished and beloved chief Rabbi of Pardes Channah. In 1977 he was asked to run for the chief rabbinate of Jerusalem. His opponent was to be the great *Talmid Chacham,* Rabbi Betzalel Zolty. A short time after declaring his candidacy, Rabbi Levin withdrew his name from the running. When asked for an explanation, Rabbi Levin replied that he had just discovered that when Rav Zolty was a young boy, his mother worked at two difficult and menial daily jobs. She did this only so that her son could learn full-time with ease and hopefully become a great *Talmid Chacham.* Rav Levin said that this woman, who sacrificed so much and dedicated so much of her life to make certain that her son become a *Gadol B'Yisrael* is a real and genuine heroine. As such, she deserves the *Nachas* of having her son become the Chief Rabbi of Jerusalem. It was for that reason alone that Rabbi Levin withdrew from the race which he was almost certain to win.

Therefore, my friends, in addition to the classical and traditional reasons given for the mitzvah of the ארבע כוסות, the approach of the *Shelah* is very significant. There is, indeed, recognition given at the Pesach Seder to our אמהות, our matriarchs, for their monumental role in helping to develop and shape the Jewish nation. As we gather at the Pesach Seder with our families, we recall how they in turn passed down their very special כחות to the countless generations which followed them. In their זכות and in the merit of all the many heroic women of each generation, we hope and pray that we can all emulate their lives and their manifold contributions to the Jewish people and to יהדות. In addition, we hope that we too will have the merit to pass down our *Mesorah* to the generations which follow us. If this can be done, we will certainly have fulfilled the expectations of our Father in Heaven for the night of Pesach and we will merit that our final request of the Seder, that we be פדויים לציון ברנה – redeemed to Zion with glad song – will be fulfilled speedily in our days, Amen

35. The Dawn of a New Tomorrow
Pesach
מעשה בבני ברק

Pesach is the holiday of liberty, the festival of freedom. Today we commemorate an event of unparalleled grandeur and unqualified drama. G-d, in His infinite wisdom and Divine mercy, redeemed our people from the clutches of their enemy. He alone, not through an angel, not by the means of a messenger, but *HaKadosh Baruch Hu*, בכבודו ובעצמו, freed Israel from the degradation of slavery in Egypt. He rescued them from oppression and hardship. And in so doing, He transformed a motley, heterogeneous mixture of 12 diversified tribes into a holy and sanctified nation. We became unified and united and were dedicated to G-d and His will. That night, 3,300 years ago, which began on the 15th day of the month of Nissan, is described by the Torah as a "ליל שימורים," a night of watching unto the L-rd for bringing our ancestors out of the land of Egypt. The verse reads:

לֵיל שִׁמֻּרִים הוּא לַה' לְהוֹצִיאָם מֵאֶרֶץ מִצְרָיִם הוּא הַלַּיְלָה הַזֶּה לַה' שִׁמֻּרִים לְכָל בְּנֵי יִשְׂרָאֵל לְדֹרֹתָם:

The *Ba'al HaTurim* notes that the verse uses the term שִׁמֻּרִים twice; in fact, he continues, these are the only two times in *Tanach* this term is used. He explains the significance of this as follows:

שחלק הקדוש ברוך הוא ליל ט"ו לשנים, חציו לגאולת מצרים וחציו השני לגאולה לעתיד לבא (מכילתא):

G-d divided the night of the 15th of Nissan into two segments. The first half was dedicated to the Exodus, the redemption of the Jews from their Egyptian servitude. The second half is reserved for the complete salvation of Israel which will occur in the future.

Therefore, Judaism sees a close link, a direct union of the glorious past together with the anticipated grandeur of the future.

However, it is often quite difficult to contemplate the future, especially when one's present is so filled with difficulties and burdens. Yet, our faith has taught us that primarily when we are experiencing moments of depression, when our present world appears dark and foreboding, we believe that the future will indeed be much brighter. The sun of tomorrow will certainly shine with full force and intensity. During such times we are told to think about the miraculous deliverance of our forebears from their Egyptian servitude. This memory of liberation and freedom will help us through all the sorrows and difficulties of the present. It will comfort us and bring us joy in anticipation of the redemption that will truly follow.

The Gemara in Makos (24) describes an incident in which Rabbi Akiva and his colleagues, Rabbi Elazar ben Azaryah, Rabbi Yehoshua, and Rabban Gamliel, were passing the ruins of the Beis HaMikdash. Suddenly, a fox darted out and entered the *Kodesh HaKodashim*, the holy of holies. His colleagues began to cry and moan over the fate of Israel, which now must suffer the sight of an unclean animal trampling over its most sacred site. Rabbi Akiva, however, did not weep; he began to laugh. When asked what prompted this jovial response, he explained as follows: We find an enigmatic verse from the Navi Yeshayahu (8:2):

וְאָעִידָה לִּי עֵדִים נֶאֱמָנִים אֵת אוּרִיָּה הַכֹּהֵן וְאֶת זְכַרְיָהוּ בֶּן יְבֶרֶכְיָהוּ:
And I will have two trustworthy witnesses testify for you: Uriah the Kohen and Zecharyahu ben Yeverechyahu.

This prophesy is perplexing. How could Uriah and Zechariah be joint witnesses if Uriah lived during the times of the First Beis HaMikdash while Zechariah lived during the times of the Second Beis HaMikdash? The explanation, rather, is that their two prophesies are interdependent. Uriah foretold (Micha 3:12):

לָכֵן בִּגְלַלְכֶם צִיּוֹן שָׂדֶה תֵחָרֵשׁ וִירוּשָׁלַםִ עִיִּין תִּהְיֶה וְהַר הַבַּיִת לְבָמוֹת יָעַר:
And so, because of you shall Zion be plowed as a field, and Jerusalem will be turned into piles of stones, and the Temple Mount will become as the stumps of a forest.

[See Tosafos for why Rabbi Akiva attributed this prophesy to Uriah if he cited a verse in Micha.]

Zechariah foretold a message that was diametrically opposite of Uriah's depressing news. He stated (Zechariah 8:4):

כֹּה אָמַר ה' צְבָאוֹת עֹד יֵשְׁבוּ זְקֵנִים וּזְקֵנוֹת בִּרְחֹבוֹת יְרוּשָׁלָם וְאִישׁ מִשְׁעַנְתּוֹ בְּיָדוֹ מֵרֹב יָמִים:

Thus said the L-rd of Hosts, 'There shall yet be old men and old women that sit in the broad places of Jerusalem, and a man will require a staff in his hand due to old age.'

Yeshayahu was saying that the sorrowful news of Uriah is intertwined with the hopeful news of Zechariah. Rabbi Akiva told his colleagues, "So long as the prophecy of Uriah had not been fulfilled, I was fearful that Zechariah's message of hope would not come true either. Now, however, that Uriah's prophecy has literally come true, there is no doubt that Zechariah's prophecy of hope for the future will be fulfilled in all its detail."

Rabbi Akiva truly believed that as bad as were the times in which he lived, which included the failed Bar Kochba rebellion and its brutal aftermath, Judaism's hope lay in the future with the Dawn of a new tomorrow.

In this vein, the *Sefas Emes* gives an interpretation for the custom of hiding the Afikoman until the time for its consumption. The reason, says the great Rebbe of Ger, is that the Exodus, *Yetzias Mitzrayim,* was only the beginning of the process of redemption, not its sum total; the remainder is still *Tzafun,* hidden from full view. That is why we partake of the Afikoman at the start of the second half of the Seder, the segment of the Seder which is dedicated to the future redemption of our people. We are thus instructed:

אין מפטירין אחר הפסח אפיקומן.

"We should eat nothing following the consumption of the *Korban Pesach/Afikoman.*" The reason for this is so that its taste, which represents freedom and independence, should remain in our mouth for the rest of this night of exile and dispersion.

It is of great note that all of our customs and traditions have always called to mind our past history with reverence while at the same time demonstrated belief in a glorious future. We have, from time immemorial, been the supreme advocates of an optimistic future. When we were down and out, when we stood with our backs to the wall with our necks bared to the sword, with enemies facing us on every front, we knew that both personally, collectively, and nationally, we would survive. Judaism has always remained alive. It has developed and grown for 3,300 years by not merely looking nostalgically at the past. Rather, we have made it to this day by holding and grasping onto the future. When we realize that we will survive against all odds and live to see the light of tomorrow, then the oppression and humiliating exile of today loses much of its sting and severity. We can endure the present because we know that we will reach the future. This is Jewish belief. This is Judaism at its best.

Perhaps this is the reason that so many of our coreligionists during the Holocaust did not attempt to fight back in any form or fashion against the Nazi beast. Instead, they went to their deaths passively, quietly, and almost without a whimper. While there are rationales and excuses offered by historians and philosophers, such as the fact that the Jews possessed no weapons and that they were untrained in warfare, I would humbly suggest another explanation. So many of these martyrs were steeped in Jewish tradition and values. They were buoyed by the hope and attitude that had served us so well over the past 2,000 years, that גם זה יעבור, "This too shall pass." They were absolutely certain that they would be able to withstand all the tortures and all the torments of their Nazi oppressors. They could not, nor could anyone for that matter, fathom the idea that in the 20th century, a highly civilized and cultured nation would proceed on a

Pesach

course of action whose ultimate goal was genocide, the destruction of an entire people.

Indeed, Judaism preaches hope and promise for the future, not despair and desperation. Our motto is:

וחי בהם – ולא שימות בהם.

We are confident that the future will be a great deal more productive and certainly less harsh than that of the present. We try to endure any and all invectives, acts of persecution, and even sadistic and inhuman behavior

There are those today who are forever decrying the times in which we live and say that all is not as good as we presently claim. They declare that the notion that we are living in "The Golden Age of American Jewry" is a fabrication and a distortion of the truth. "Look at the facts," they say. "There are very few numbers of Jews in this country and abroad who observe the Mitzvos of the Torah. We are," they say, "witnessing the highest percentage of intermarriage and assimilation that the Jewish community has ever experienced. In addition, there is an overwhelmingly large segment of the Jewish community who is ignorant of even the basic ingredients of our faith. And when we look to the State of Israel, we see a small, isolated country, struggling internally, friendless, and beset by enemies bent upon her complete destruction and extermination. With these vast and complex problems can we really even think of the future? Our only salvation is to crawl into our little shell and concentrate our thoughts on the good old days of the past. Then everything was simple, and we were not traumatized by so many major problems." My friends, if this be our response, we cannot claim credit for its originality; the Pesach Haggadah already related such a sentiment along with its refutation.

There is a famous episode in which Rabbi Akiva, Rabbi Elazar ben Azariah, Rabbi Tarfon, and Rabbi Yehoshua were spending Passover together in Bnai Brak, the city of the *Gadol HaDor*, Rabbi

Akiva. Why is it important for the Haggadah to relate the location of this grand Seder?

These great scholars, and the Jewish people whom they led, were despondent and depressed. Judaism had just witnessed the most severe tragedy, second only to the fall of their political independence and the destruction of the holy Temple. This was the fall of Beitar, the crushing loss of the Bar Kochba revolt to the mighty Roman legions. All hope for the future of a Jewish independent state were lost, at least for the immediate future.

Our forebears were now witness to the cruel and oppressive rule of Rome. They were forbidden from studying Torah. They were not allowed to observe the Shabbos. They could not practice circumcision. There was in essence, not a great deal of hope for the future.

These rabbis, however, knew that their colleague and role model, Rabbi Akiva, could bring light to this state of despair. As they had seen when passing by the ruins of the Temple in the episode discussed above, Rabbi Akiva knew how to see light where there was darkness. It was therefore specifically in Bnei Brak, in the presence of Rabbi Akiva, that these Sages sought to spend their Pesach.

In *The Holocaust Haggadah* by Rabbi Gershon Weiss, he explains what these Sages experienced at this Seder:

> It is entirely possible that Rabbi Akiva's optimistic outlook—seeing in the depths of *golus* signs of the coming *geulah*—is the reason why his mentors and colleagues gathered around him for the Seder. In this tragic time, they could still celebrate the Yom Tov in its proper spirit with Rabbi Akiva. Moreover, since Pesach is the time that G-d makes available to us the *kedusha* of the *Geulah* just as it was on the night of the Exodus, now is the appropriate time to

delve into the Exodus in order to discover ways to bring Klal Yisrael closer to *Geulah*.

Perhaps these Sages saw their situation as similar to the situation in Egypt when Moshe came in the name of G-d and afterwards, unexpectedly, the situation only grew much worse. However, this worsening and torturous situation was only a prelude to the miraculous salvation which commenced six months later. We know, of course, that the Sages maintained and practiced trust in G-d, which indicated that even though the Beis HaMikdash was destroyed, Jewry must trust G-d's promises and be optimistic about its future. The Vilna Gaon states, 'The period before the redemption from *golus* will be more difficult than the entire *golus*.'

After this night full of hope, the Sages indeed received a signal to affirm their newfound optimism. As the day dawned, these great rabbis saw their students, a new generation of Jews who would remain alive and carry on the tradition. The students reminded their teachers that they could look forward to a glorious future. They should recite the Shema of the morning of tomorrow, of a bright new and hopeful future. With the Shema comes the prayer of אמת ויציב, the *Tefillah* which exclaims that G-d's assistance is clearly evident and is very close.

Thus, my friends, we must remember the past, observe the present, and go forward eagerly and optimistically towards the future.

Therefore, while the present may not look very promising, while the night of our dispersion appears to be everlasting, we are, I believe, standing on the threshold of the dawn of a new tomorrow. This is the message of Pesach. This is the ideology of Judaism. We must remember that יציאת מצרים fulfilled only half of Hashem's promise of ליל שימורים. Although we commemorate our triumphs and our victories of the past, nevertheless, the best of times will be in the

Pesach

future. We will then truly celebrate not only our miraculous survival for over 2,000 years of *golus,* but we will also be able to go forward toward our glorious future. We will witness the true and complete redemption, the גאולה שלימה of all our people. Amen.

36. Why Bother with Traditions?
Pesach
כנגד ארבעה בנים דברה תורה

One of the most perplexing as well as intriguing discussions of the Pesach Haggadah is the segment of the ארבעה בנים, the four sons alluded to by the Torah. These include the חכם, the רשע, the תם and the שאינו יודע לשאול – the wise son, the wicked son, the simple son, and the one who does not even know how to ask a question. They all pose various questions on this night.

This section of the Haggadah is introduced by the lyrical verse:

ברוך המקום ברוך הוא, ברוך שנתן תורה לעמו ישראל, ברוך הוא.

Praise to the Ever-present, praised be He; praise the One Who has given the Torah to His people Israel, praised be He.

The commentators observe that this statement includes the word "ברוך" four times, alluding to the fact that the Jewish nation consists of four types of people. Our *Chachamim* direct us to retell the story of יציאת מצרים to our children. However, this retelling must be tailor-made for each of these unique types of individuals, taking into account both their personalities and levels of intelligence.

The first son we meet in the Haggadah is the חכם, the child with a high degree of intelligence. He has the successful combination of wisdom and an unquenchable search for truth, making him receptive towards Hashem's commands and His manifold requirements.

The תם faithfully adheres to the principles of Judaism, but only on a superficial level. He mimics the religious practices of his parents and grandparents, although he has no understanding of why he is doing so. He is capable of asking merely one basic question: "מה זאת" – "What is this?"

Pesach

The fourth son is the one who does not even know how to ask, the שאינו יודע לשאול. He is the newcomer to Judaism, either due to his young age or life circumstance. He does not know where to begin and merely sits at the Seder, silently and expectantly.

The רשע, the wicked son, is one who lives his entire life philosophically opposed to the major components of Judaism, the Torah and the Mitzvos.

Of all these different types of Jews, the רשע appears to be the most enigmatic and perplexing. He presents us with perhaps the greatest problem. Why is he called the רשע? What has he done to cast himself as the wicked son, the stepson of Judaism? Why does he merit being told that had he been in Egypt at the time of the Exodus, he would not have been redeemed? The truth is that he is not that far removed from his family and his faith, as evidenced by the fact that he doesn't even forget the Pesach Seder; he sits at the table with his entire family. What then is his crime? Why does he receive this dishonorable appellation?

The truth of the matter is that while the רשע joins his family at the Seder and participates in the rituals, he nevertheless does not believe in them. He looks at this night simply as another opportunity to spend some quality time with his family. While he may go through the motions in order not to aggravate his parents, he sees nothing significant in their observance.

The רשע refuses to believe in the future of Yiddishkeit. This indicates in no uncertain terms that had he been alive at the time of the Exodus, he would not have been redeemed. He, like 4/5 of the Jewish people, would have been killed during the ninth plague of חשך. This רשע, like so many of those who perished during this most devastating מכה, wanted freedom without any restrictions. They merely wanted to be physically redeemed. They wanted to have the shackles of imprisonment removed. They were not however, interested in accepting Hashem as their G-d and their protector. They did not offer their allegiance to Him and to his Torah. Thus, while the רשע attends his family Seder, he does not buy into the system of the Mitzvos of G-d; thus, he is considered wicked.

In order to understand this more fully, we must analyze the questions that the רשע asks. He says: מה העבודה הזאת לכם. "What is all this ritual to you?" He is rebelling from an intellectual point of view. His thoughts are not in consonance with the principles of Judaism. Because he has used the term לכם, "to you," he seems to have excluded himself from the observance of Torah, Mitzvos, and a firm commitment to G-d. However, my friends, why should we draw this conclusion? Did not the חכם, the wise son, also ask his question in the same manner? He asked:

מה העדות והחקים והמשפטים אשר צוה ה' אלקינו אתכם.

"What are the testimonies, the statutes, and laws that the Eternal One, our G-d, has commanded you?" He ends with the same word – "you" – as does the רשע, thus appearing to exclude himself as well. Yet, we bestow the greatest honor and respect upon him and categorize him as the scholar, the *Tzadik*, a leader of Jews. We point to his lifestyle and say we should try to emulate and follow him. Wherein lies the difference between the two?

A proper understanding comes from a focus on the content of the חכם's question. The wise son strives for further understanding and knowledge. He knows enough about Judaism to be totally and unequivocally committed to it as a system and as a way of life. However, he is also searching to discover that wisdom in each specific area of our faith. As such, his question is authentic, fundamental, and legitimate. He wants to know what the rules of Pesach are. "What are the principles of freedom, emancipation and independence as presented by the Torah?" These are enacted in the drama of the Haggadah and are practiced daily by the halachic Jew. Once he accumulates all the necessary information, he begins to understand all the principles of Pesach.

In regards to the word אתכם, "to you," which appears to put the חכם in the same category as the רשע, Rashi gives a most comprehensive answer. He says that the fundamental difference in the חכם's question is his phraseology of "אשר צוה ה' אלקינו" – "that which *our* G-d has commanded us." His inclusive use of the word "אלקינו" demonstrates that the word אתכם — "to you" is not meant to be exclusionary.

The reason the Haggadah harps on the רשע's phraseology so much is due to the fact that he is not really asking a question at all; he is, instead, merely offering his own opinion. He has no need for questions. He is the kind of person who knows it all, who has all the answers. He does not begin with the "what" of Judaism. "What must I do to be a good, committed, and authentic Jew?" No. He begins with the "why." He doesn't understand, nor does he care to comprehend, all the elements of our tradition. In a condescending manner he asks: "Why? Why all the need? Why all the fuss?" His "why" is not a request for information; it is, rather, a challenge to authority. מה העבודה הזאת לכם – "What use is this service?" "Why do you need these rituals?" he asks. "What difference does it make to G-d whether or not we observe the customs and traditions? Why must we observe all the practices, all the Mitzvos? Is it not enough to be a good Jew at heart without practicing the cumbersome and often very intricate and complicated laws and traditions?"

The חכם, on the other hand, wants to learn. He wants to comprehend. He wishes to understand before he judges and before he presents his opinions. Only in that manner will his conclusions be informed and knowledgeable.

This distinction can be clearly seen in the *pesukim* from which the statements of these four sons originate. In Devarim 6:20, we find the question of the חכם:

Pesach

כִּי יִשְׁאָלְךָ בִנְךָ מָחָר לֵאמֹר מָה הָעֵדֹת וְהַחֻקִּים וְהַמִּשְׁפָּטִים אֲשֶׁר צִוָּה ה' אֱלֹקֵינוּ אֶתְכֶם:

*When your son shall **ask** you tomorrow saying, "What are these statutes..."*

In Shemos 13:14, the question of the תם reads:

וְהָיָה כִּי יִשְׁאָלְךָ בִנְךָ מָחָר לֵאמֹר מַה זֹּאת...

*And it will be when your son **asks** you tomorrow saying, 'What is this?'*

In each of these verses, the Torah states clearly that the son is asking a question. However, when we get to the posuk of the רשע, we see a clear disparity in how his statement is presented. In Shemos 12:26 it reads:

וְהָיָה כִּי יֹאמְרוּ אֲלֵיכֶם בְּנֵיכֶם מָה הָעֲבֹדָה הַזֹּאת לָכֶם:

*And it will be when your children **say** to you, "What is this service to you?"*

Unlike the questions of the חכם and תם, where the terms "יִשְׁאָלְךָ" "he will ask you" are used, when it comes to the רשע, the statement is prefaced by the expression "כי יאמרו אליכם בניכם" – "when your children will **say** to you." This underscores the abovementioned explanation. The רשע is not asking a question but is simply placing his own agenda on the Seder table. [Of course, the term יִשְׁאָלְךָ is not used by the שאינו יודע לשאול either (Shemos 13:8), as he is certainly not offering any question or statement whatsoever.]

The question – or, more accurately – the statement of the רשע seems to have a very modern ring about it. Many today, especially young people, are asking the very same questions. "Why all this ritual? Why all the details and practices? Let us instead emphasize the ideals of our religion, the ethical and moral values of Judaism. Let us concentrate on faith in G-d and love of man. What is so essential about Shabbos, Kashrus, Tefillin, and other Mitzvos? They are all merely relics of the past which disappeared hundreds of years ago and are no longer needed or relevant."

These questions cannot simply be pushed aside. These issues beg our attention, especially on this holiday of Pesach. Is it really necessary to wear ourselves out cleaning, koshering, and changing the house over from chametz to matzah? Do we need to do all this in order to celebrate and commemorate the struggle for freedom and independence? If one, for argument's sake, cannot partake of matzah or marror, does it mean that he cherishes freedom any less? Does it mean that he wishes to be counted out of the people of Israel?

The problem with these questions is that they are not Jewish questions. While these problems may have a certain degree of validity, they do not even begin when viewing matters from a Jewish frame of reference. Judaism, my friends, while stressing ethics and morality, is not just a religion of creed. It is, rather, mostly a religion of deed, a religion of law. The heart and soul of our faith has not been only through ideals. In fact, the way in which we were able to perpetuate our religion through all forms of persecution and torturous times and survive as a people has been through the practice of our faith, through the observance and the fulfillment of the Mitzvos.

My friends, without our "Constitution," without our Mitzvos, we would be no different than any other nation on earth. Hashem chose us as His firstborn. We are not like any other people. We must strive to be an עם קדוש and an עם נבחר, a holy and chosen people. The only way that this can be achieved is through our observance and our performance of the Mitzvos.

The language of Judaism is not expressed in abstract ethics but in מצוות מעשיות, the practice of our commandments. Rabbi Dr. Norman Lamm, the former president of Yeshiva University and one of the most eloquent spokesmen for Orthodox Jewry in the last century, wrote:

Pesach

      All Jewish organizations that taught that Judaism as a religion is dead and is a relic of the past and that the Jew can actually live today without the word of G-d have all proven to be bankrupt. The only component of Judaism which is alive, vibrant, and which will lead us into the future is Torah-true *Yahadus*. Only a Judaism based on Torah and Mitzvos will preserve our faith.

One example of a Jewish movement which was founded on non-Torah values was the political Zionist movement. Political Zionism began in the 19th century as a substitute for religion and, to a great degree, remains so even today. Most of the leadership of the Zionist movement, with some rare exceptions, were and are non-observant Jews. Their attachment to the soil, the land of Israel, is not based on religious principles and history. Rather, the political Zionists approach Zionism as a substitute for the observance of the laws and traditions of the Torah.

      This, of course, is not the philosophy and rationale of the religious Zionists. They truly believe in the Mitzvah of ישוב ארץ ישראל, and that its very safety and security enhances and helps our people to further their Yiddishkeit. They base themselves on the Halachic position that through settling the land will we be capable of fulfilling the many Mitzvos that we cannot observe in חוץ לארץ. This enables us to better serve הקדוש ברוך הוא. Thus, it serves as a great assistance in the growth and development of a Torah-true life.

      Another example of non-Mitzvah based Judaism are the two major non-observant Jewish groups, namely, the Conservative and Reform movements. The philosophies of these factions have watered down and even disregarded the most basic elements of *Yahadus* and, as a result, find themselves almost totally Jewishly bankrupt.

      Isaac Mayer Wise, the founder of American Reform Jewry during the 19th century, took the words of the רשע and made it the rationale for a new religion. He chose to discard most of the laws and commandments of the Torah. He embraced a religion that is focused solely on ethical and moral teachings.

The leaders of Reform Judaism believed – falsely – that they were following in the path of the prophets of old. They challenged conformity and wanted to bring a new "light" into a world of darkness. They embraced working in partnership with those of other faiths. They welcomed to the fold any and all Jews who converted by choice, regardless of their educational beliefs or commitments to Judaism.

Conservative Judaism has maintained many of the Halachos of the Torah. However, their total abandonment of some of our essential laws have placed themselves completely outside the fold. These branches of Judaism have been a colossal and unmitigated failure.

Before World War II, we witnessed the rise and fall of the Haskalah in Europe. Originally founded by Moses Mendelsohn, he adversely influenced thousands of Jews to leave traditional Judaism and accept in its place his warped philosophy with the goal of being accepted by the non-Jewish world.

The fallacy of Mendelsohn's ideals hit home directly. While Mendelsohn himself was an observant Jew, the results of his outlook led to his own daughter converting to Christianity. Shockingly, his great-grandson became a member of the Nazi party. This is the sad legacy of one who attempts to break away from the protective force of Torah and Mitzvos.

The goals of these movements have been to make Judaism more attractive to the masses. The results of these efforts have been the removal of almost all vestiges of our faith. These attempts, as can be clearly seen today in 2018, have ended in complete failure. Their longstanding status as comprising two-thirds of American

Jewry appears to be coming to a close. They are gasping for air merely to survive, and their end is certainly within sight

Instead of attracting more adherents and more participants to their temples and synagogues, the opposite has occurred. The rate of assimilation and intermarriage among these groups is approaching record numbers. The average young Jewish American is turned off by this artificial brand of Judaism. Those who are searching for real and genuine religion are turning to Orthodoxy. They see it as truly representing Judaism at its finest.

Unfortunately, today we have a new nemesis. We are facing a group of Jews who, in my opinion, are far more dangerous to the survival of Torah-true Judaism than even those from the Conservative and Reform camps. I am referring to the Open Orthodoxy movement. They claim that they are working within the guidelines of Halacha. These claims are bolstered by the unfortunate fact that many of their organizers studied and received *Semicha* from very reputable Yeshivos. As a result, many in the Jewish community see these "Rabbis" and their congregations as real and authentic representatives of Orthodox Judaism. However, the innovations and changes that they have made go against all areas of our Mesorah. As a result, they are threatening the very fiber and soul of traditional, authentic, and Torah-based *Yahadus*.

They have chosen to ordain women as congregational rabbis and decisors of halacha. They join together with Conservative and Reform as well as some non-Jewish sects for ecumenical services throughout the year. These and many more Halachic violations go against the decision made a few years ago by some of today's leading Rabbis and major Roshei Yeshiva. It certainly is against everything that the Rav, Rabbi Soloveitchik *zt"l*, advocated. It is sad and disgraceful that some of the leaders and founders of the Open Orthodoxy movement were students of the Rav and continually quote him and his *Piskei Halacha* out of context and in a distorted manner.

Pesach

All of these groups, through preaching the abandonment of Mitzvos, reveal through their actions that they are nothing less than the רשע of the Haggadah. This רשע is an impetuous, self-hating, and rebellious Jew. He is one who first abandons the practices and customs of his faith. The next and inevitable step is to become so worldly, so concerned with the downtrodden and the oppressed of the world community, that he completely forgets his own people. Their needs and concerns are of no importance to him. The final step, as history has shown us, is the leaving of our fold completely and embracing either another faith or becoming an agnostic or an atheist. Worse still, he may even become a hater and an enemy of religious Jews, and ultimately, of the Jewish people as a whole.

The Yom Tov of Pesach is the time when one's pride in Judaism should supersede all doubts and dispel all illusions. The effects of the Mitzvos of Pesach upon Jews over the ages should convince even the greatest sceptics of the value of practice over theory, of the benefit of positive minded Mitzvos over abstract ideas. The transformation of the home, the fascination of the young, the reuniting of generations, certainly should impress even the "part-time Jew" of the importance of Judaism as an omnipresent and ongoing force in one's life.

The Torah tells us that 3,300 years ago, in the month of Nissan, an enslaved people and an idolatrous nation was redeemed and molded into an עם קדוש לה', a holy and dedicated nation onto G-d. In a future Nissan, say *Chazal,* we will once again be redeemed. Moshiach will come, and all Jews, no matter what stripe or affiliation, will return to a life of Torah and Mitzvos. Even the רשע at that time will see the foolishness of his ways and return back to tradition. He will finally realize that Judaism without the performance of Mitzvos is meaningless and bankrupt, a mere cultural and historic exercise with no lasting significance. At that time, these Jews and their children and grandchildren will join together with us and become yet

Pesach

another link in our great chain of the Mesorah. May that day come soon – במהרה בימינו אמן.

37. To be Tempted, or to be Threatened: Two Threats to our Survival
Pesach
מרור: תחילתו רך וסופו קשה

    The Pesach Seder is replete with many foods, observances, and commemorations of שעבוד מצרים as well as יציאת מצרים. Each of these aspects is extremely important. Perhaps most important is the statement of Rabban Gamliel. He says that the key elements of our commemoration lie in our discussion of "Pesach, Matzah, and Marror." The significance of Matzah and the Korban Pesach have been explored in earlier essays. I would like, at this point, to review the third element – Marror. It alone represents the bitterness and hardship of שעבוד מצרים. Jewish life in Egypt was not only difficult and degrading but oppressive and discouraging as well. The Jewish people were not only being destroyed physically; their adherence to morals and ethics were slowly being extinguished. This is truly represented by the bitterness of Marror.

    Marror, however, is not only eaten to recall the bitterness of our past Egyptian exile. It also serves to warn us about the salient and varied aspects of future exiles. The Gemara in Pesachim (39a), commenting on the *posuk* (Shemos 1:14) of וַיְמָרְרוּ אֶת חַיֵּיהֶם states:
ואמר רבי שמואל בר נחמני אמר רבי יונתן: למה נמשלו מצריים כמרור - לומר לך: מה מרור זה שתחילתו רך וסופו קשה, אף מצריים - תחילתן רכה וסופן קשה.

R' Shmuel bar Nachmeini says in the name of R' Yonason: Why are the Egyptians compared to Marror? When first eating Marror, its taste is mild and bland; upon additional consumption, its taste becomes difficult and bitter. So too with the Egyptian servitude. Initially, its effect upon the Jewish nation was minimal. As time progressed, it became more and more unbearable until our forebears were on the verge of destruction.

This is the reason that many, in fulfilling this Mitzvah of eating Marror, use romaine lettuce. This is done because initially, its taste is sweet and pleasant. Only with the passage of time is its true bitterness felt.

The *Da'as Zekainim* of the *Ba'alei Tosafos* depicts for us Pharaoh's ingenious plan of enticing and ensnaring the Jews. He initially, like the Marror, spoke softly and gently to them. On a specific day he proclaimed a "national day of labor." He personally began to manufacture bricks and asked his countrymen to join him. The Jews, eager to prove their loyalty and patriotism, responded enthusiastically by working exhaustingly and devoting all their energies to this "great project." At the end of the day, after producing enormous numbers of bricks, Pharaoh appointed taskmasters who imposed upon the Jews the production of the same number of bricks each day. Henceforth, they pounced upon the unsuspecting Jews and gradually but surely transformed them from equals in Egyptian society into the lowest class of slaves and serfs.

The Jews now became the pariahs of Egyptian society. This submission and slavery nearly destroyed the Jewish nation before it was even formally founded.

This pattern of persecution, unfortunately, has always been our lot in exile. We have constantly been duped, deceived, and misled. We have allowed ourselves to be ensnared and trapped by the supposed friendliness of the nations of the world.

We were taken in by their superficial invitations to be equal citizens with full rights and benefits. In addition, we were promised that we would be completely accepted into their society. Unfortunately, when we fell for their bait, when we let down our guard, when we believed these words of falsehood and insincerity, we found out that we were the victims of a cruel and inhumane joke.

However, at that time it was too late. We were either subjugated and oppressed by the nations in whose lands we resided or we had by then lost so much of our heritage and tradition in order to be accepted by our fellow countrymen. At that time, we had nowhere to go and no one to turn to for help.

In Tehillim 118, which we read in Hallel this morning as well as at the Seder last night, Dovid HaMelech offers the same kind of warning. He says (in verses 10-12):

כָּל גּוֹיִם סְבָבוּנִי בְּשֵׁם יְקֹוָק כִּי אֲמִילַם: סַבּוּנִי גַם סְבָבוּנִי בְּשֵׁם יְקֹוָק כִּי אֲמִילַם: סַבּוּנִי כִדְבוֹרִים דֹּעֲכוּ כְּאֵשׁ קוֹצִים בְּשֵׁם יְקֹוָק כִּי אֲמִילַם:

10. All the nations who surround me (סְבָבוּנִי), in the name of G-d I cut them down. 11. They encircle me (סַבּוּנִי), they swarm about me (סְבָבוּנִי), in the name of G-d I cut them down. 12. They swarm about me (סַבּוּנִי) like bees, but they are extinguished like a fire of thorns, in the name of G-d I cut them down.

Our rabbis explain the interchanging in the Psalm of the two words סַבּוּנִי and סְבָבוּנִי. Both, they say, refer in actuality to the attempt on the part of our enemies to destroy and annihilate us. However, each one represents a different tactic, combining to form a diversified approach.

The method of "סַבּוּנִי" is one in which our enemies have attempted to preach brotherhood and the unity of man. They have, in essence, formed a universal circle and asked us to join them as equals and partners. They have approached us and offered us honey and sweetness. Underlying these sweet overtones, however, lies their primary aim and goal – the spiritual elimination of the people of Israel.

The plan of the advocates of "סְבָבוּנִי" has been to surround and encircle the Jews. They attempt to isolate us from the rest of society. They wish to single us out for attack economically, socially, and ultimately, physically.

Pesach

Throughout much of our history, our enemies have displayed wrath and fury towards our people. We have endured Amaleik in the desert, Haman in Persia, and Hitler ימח שמו וזכרו, in Germany. Their only goal was את כל היהודים להשמיד להרוג ולאבד–סְבָבוּנִי – to destroy, kill and obliterate every Jewish man, woman and child. They wanted to see the complete annihilation of the Jewish people and the end of the "Jewish problem" once and for all. They, in the words of the Psalmist, drew a circle and placed the Jew in the middle. He in turn became the scapegoat, the fall guy for all the ills and misfortunes that befell their particular society.

The other type of enemy is personified by the more subtle, cunning, and sly anti-Semite. As discussed, Pharaoh was the initial prototype for this approach, but he had many imitators. Antiochus Epiphanes of the Syrian-Greeks, the Roman emperors during the Second Temple era, Lenin and Stalin at the beginning of communism, and the leaders and proponents of the enlightenment movement in the 18th and 19th centuries in Europe are perhaps the most well-known representatives of this type of approach. While their ultimate vision for the Jews was the termination and elimination of Judaism as a religion and as a way of life, the method utilized was much more intelligent and successful. They proclaimed belief in the universality of man. All men are equal, and there should be no distinction, no differences between them.

These individuals represent the approach of "סַבּוּנִי", they drew a line and extended the hand of friendship for us to join with them. "Together," they proclaimed, "we will bring about the betterment of society." They, however, added one stipulation. "If you wish to be accepted as equals and partners, you must eliminate any distinguishing features that separate Jew from gentile. Forgo Bris Milah, do away with the observance of Shabbos and Yom Tov and with all the other Mitzvos which are ancient and archaic. Join our circle." They said "סַבּוּנִי", "Become assimilated with us and then you will be accepted by all."

Like the Marror which is mild and pleasant at first but later becomes sharp and biting, so too with these attempts at destroying the distinctiveness and the uniqueness of Judaism and the Jewish people. While some of our coreligionists were misled into thinking that the future would be bright and rosy, they were eventually jolted out of their sense of false illusion. They realized, often too late, that these attempts at friendship were not valid and legitimate. They were made merely to throw the Jew off guard and to be unprepared for the coming troubles.

The problem, my friends, is that we absolutely refuse to learn from the mistakes that our forebears committed. We study history and internalize our tradition. However, when we are faced with the same set of circumstances, we forget all the errors that those before us made. We then act in the same careless manner as did our ancestors

Many of the Jews living in Hellenistic Israel during the second Jewish Commonwealth abandoned their faith for the purpose of universal acceptance. They were, at the end of the day, truly disappointed by the results of their efforts. Western European Jewry in the 18th and 19th century accepted hook, line, and sinker every promise given to them by the so-called enlightened leaders of France and Germany. However, when a scapegoat was required, Colonel Alfred Dreyfus, a totally secular and assimilated Jew, was brought to trial simply because of his religion. And of course, all too many of the Jews of Germany in the early part of the 20th century considered themselves 100% German. They were totally dedicated to the Fatherland, quite often at the expense of their Jewishness. However, all this patriotism and loyalty did not help save them from Hitler's madness. In fact, the first Jews discriminated against and persecuted were the over 600,000 Jews living in Germany and Austria.

Pesach

Today, many of us living in the United States believe that with the open society, with the great opportunities that this wonderful country provides for us, we have nothing to fear. We have complete equality and total freedom. There is a mindset that we no longer have any need for our religion and our heritage. While it is true that we very rarely find Jews who formally renounce their Judaism and openly embrace Christianity or Islam, that is because this is not required to be accepted in the United States today. One may retain the religion of his birth and continue to be a part of the great American milieu. He can be accepted in the highest social circles. He can be appointed to important government positions. But this is often done with one proviso. It may not necessarily be explicit, but it certainly is implicit that the Jew not practice his faith religiously. Unfortunately, this idea is mushrooming across this country and throughout the world. It is as if the non-Jewish world is saying to us: "סַבּוּנִי" – join our circle, take our hand, and become one of us. And we naïvely follow suit.

Why must we wait for another catastrophe or another threat to our faith, either spiritually or physically, for us to see the light? Why must we forget our past and all the experiences therein? No, my friends, the message of Pesach and the Seder in particular is to remember the past and not repeat the same mistakes. We will be prepared for the future which will be glorious and wonderful. We will then be living in the era of the Moshiach.

If we come to the realization that our only salvation, our only real ישועה will come through our complete and total faith in Hashem, we will succeed. Thus, instead of being influenced by the סַבּוּנִי or being fearful of the סְבָבוּנִי, by those who tempt us and by those who threaten us, we should take to heart and internalize the words of the Haggadah: והיא שעמדה לאבותינו ולנו – "And it is this that has stood by our fathers and us." The commentators tell us that the word "והיא" is an allusion to the Torah, both the written and the oral law, the תורה שבכתב and תורה שבעל פה.

If we abide by the Torah, if we dedicate ourselves and are committed to the continuity of our faith, we need fear no antagonists, for Hashem will protect us and will guarantee that we will survive, grow, and flourish. We will defeat all the Pharaohs, the Hitlers, and the Antiochuses of the future. May that day soon be here, Amen.

I want to give my sincere thanks to my late father-in-law, Rabbi Samuel Fink zt"l, for his inspiration in the writing of this chapter.

38. Silent Gratitude vs. Exuberant Shirah

Seventh Day of Pesach

This morning, we read one of the most dramatic and fascinating episodes in all of Jewish history. It had been a mere six days since the Jews had been released from their long, difficult, and torturous servitude in Egypt. Now, Pharaoh seemingly had a change of heart. He regretted his decision to allow the Jews to leave, so he gathered a large force and pursued them. When the Jews saw the Egyptians approaching they became frightened and begged Moshe to take some affirmative action. Moshe began doing what he knew best – he turned to Hashem and prayed for divine intervention. However, Hashem said to Moshe, "The time is inappropriate for prayer and contemplation; that will follow later. Right now, speak to the children of Israel that they shall go forward."

The people adhered to the advice of Hashem. They entered the waters, and the sea miraculously split apart. This allowed them to cross on dry land, enabling them to escape forever from the oncoming Egyptians. These former taskmasters were subsequently swallowed up in the onrushing waters. Following this, the final chapter in their emancipation from their servitude and oppression in Egypt, our ancestors offered their thanks to G-d. Led by Moshe and his sister Miriam, they sang the *Shirah,* the great praise to Hashem.

Our rabbis, while commenting on the singing of the *Shirah* at the Red Sea, are both puzzled and amazed. They say that it was proper and correct and indeed most appropriate for our ancestors to sing praises to G-d after He completely obliterated their enemies at the Red Sea. However, they sang no song of thanks, nor did they offer any acclaim to Hashem when they left Egypt just six days before. Wasn't their delivery from 210 years of enslavement and tyranny reason enough for the Jews to express their appreciation and thankfulness to G-d? Why was the gratitude to the L-rd first expressed at the Red Sea and not before?

This question has also been asked concerning two other events in Jewish history. In the book of Shoftim, Judges, we are told of the great military victory of the Jews led by the prophetess Devorah and her Chief of Staff, Barack, over the Canaanites in the early days of ancient Israel. Following their resounding triumph over an enemy far more numerous and certainly better prepared for battle, our ancestors thanked G-d. Led by Devorah and Barack, they gave praise to Hashem by singing yet another *Shirah*.

Many years later, the Assyrian hordes were besieging the capital of Israel, Jerusalem. They were planning for one final thrust against the City of David. Inside the walls, King Chizkiyahu and his subjects were panic-stricken. They truly anticipated the worst. However, the night before the final assault was to occur, a *Malach*, an Angel of Hashem descended upon the Assyrian camp and wrought havoc in its midst. Hundreds of thousands of Sancherev's soldiers were killed. After witnessing this miraculous victory over his enemies, however, King Chizkiyahu was deathly silent. He offered no verbal thanks to G-d.

What is the difference between these two incidents? In both episodes, a great and miraculous victory was had. Nevertheless, the responses to these events were diametrically opposed. Why did Devorah feel the need to sing *Shirah* while Chizkiyahu did not? Our Rabbis tell us that Devorah, Barack and their followers played an active and key role in their decisive victory over the Canaanites. Following their phenomenal and prodigious triumph over great odds, they were exultant and expressed a great appreciation to Hashem.

King Chizkiyahu and his supporters, on the other hand, took no active role in the battle with the Assyrians. They put their absolute trust and faith in Hashem. They conducted themselves in accordance with His divine promise to keep, protect, and defend the Jewish

Pesach

people. They henceforth played a completely passive role and did not participate at all in the war. They did not experience any of the sorrows and casualties of battle. Thus, while the enemy was completely vanquished and their success was assured, the Jews did not publicly thank G-d. They remained completely silent.

This difference between active and passive participation in victory can shed light on the disparity in the response of the Jews on the first day of the Exodus and the seventh. When our ancestors left Egypt, they too were not instrumental in overthrowing their autocratic and despotic oppressors. They passively stood by as mere spectators. They observed as the Almighty destroyed the very backbone and total hierarchy of the Egyptian nation. Thus, following the Exodus, the Jews did not sing praises or offer public thanks unto Hashem. However, at the Red Sea, just one week later, the miracle of the splitting of the waters did not occur until the Jews actively became involved. Only when they went forward and personally jumped into the waters and put their lives on the line in order to follow G-d's command did the Red Sea split for them. Since this salvation occurred after their personal and direct involvement, they now jubilantly expressed their thanks and appreciation to G-d.

While this understanding helps us understand Chizkiyahu's silence, his decision had terrible ramifications. Our Sages, who in regard to every other facet of his life had the highest praise for Chizkiyahu, now were most critical of his apparent lack of הכרת הטוב and acknowledgment of the work of Hashem. In fact, the Talmud in Tractate Sanhedrin proclaims that Chizkiyahu was originally designated by Hashem to become Moshiach. He was supposed to lead the Jewish people into an age and era of peace, tranquility, and harmony. However, because he chose not to sing praises and give thanks to Hashem, he lost this possibility forever.

This, however, leads us to a problem. Why is King Chizkiyahu castigated and maligned for not expressing thanksgiving whereas we see no criticism leveled at the Bnei Yisrael for not singing *Shirah* at *Yetzias Mitzrayim*? If Chizkiyahu was expected to verbalize his thanks upon witnessing the total defeat of the mighty Assyrian army, why was there no such expectation when the Bnei Yisrael left Egypt with much fanfare, pomp, and circumstance?

We have to appreciate that when Chizkiyahu did not sing *Shirah*, this was not due to any lack of gratitude on his part. The same is true for the Jews in Mitzrayim. However, having not participated in the miracle, they did not feel worthy enough to sing Shirah. Shirah is not merely a song of gratitude. As Chazal say, "All the songs in the Tanach are holy; the Song of Songs is the holiest of the holy." The singing of Shirah is a spiritual experience and can serve as the ultimate form of gratitude to G-d. One who is not on the proper spiritual plane has no right to sing the Shirah. This idea can, perhaps, be better understood by the following Chassidic legend, as related by Rabbi Dr. Abraham J. Twerski (*Four Chassidic Masters, pp. 11-12*):

> *Rebbe Yisrael of Rizhin related that when the Baal Shem Tov saw that misfortune was threatening to befall Klal Yisrael, he would go to a particular place in the woods to meditate. He lit a candle and said prayers with certain kabbalistic kavannos [meditations], and the misfortune was averted.*
>
> *Later, the Baal Shem Tov's successor, Rebbe Dov Ber, the Maggid of Mezeritch,* (my very illustrious ancestor—R.H.G.) *had occasion to intercede in heaven to abrogate an unfavorable decree. He would go to the same place in the woods and say, "Ribono shel Olam [Master of the Universe], I can light the candle and say a prayer, but I do not know the kavannos." This, too, averted the decree.*
>
> *Later yet, Rebbe Moshe Leib of Sassov said, "Ribono shel Olam, I do not know the prayer, but I know the place, and I can*

light a candle there. May the merit of the tzaddikim who prayed here arouse Your mercy on Your people."

The Rebbe of Rizhin would say, "Ribono shel Olam, I do not know the prayer, I do not know the kavannos, and I do not even know the place. All I can do is to relate what these tzaddikim did, and may their merit bring us salvation."

Although all four of these holy Rebbes wrought salvation through their efforts, it would appear astonishing, at first glance, that as the generations progressed, their efforts diminished. Wouldn't their efforts need to increase as their spiritual powers lessened? The lesson of this story is that when one is on a higher spiritual plane, he can put forth more effort without losing sight that the salvation is entirely from G-d and not due to his own merits. As the generations progressed, each successive Rebbe felt that in order to attribute such miraculous salvation entirely to G-d, some measure of spiritual input must be withheld by his own part to forestall any haughty thoughts.

In this light, we can understand the various responses when it came to singing Shirah. Singing *Shirah* is recognition of a miraculous event which occurred. If the Jews would have sung the *Shirah* immediately upon their Exodus, they would have felt that this miraculous experience was something that they deserved. While they were certainly grateful, they had to remain silent to demonstrate to G-d their recognition that they were completely unworthy of this miraculous salvation. This was underscored by the fact that they had no participation in the miraculous escape.

Seven days later, however, the Jews were on a completely different spiritual plane. The miracle came about only through their own initiative. As they crossed the sea, they reached tremendous spiritual heights, rivaling that of the future prophet Yechezkel. This time, the Jews intuitively knew that the singing of *Shirah* was an appropriate and imperative response.

The same is true of Devorah's *Shirah*. She and Barack were able to participate in a miraculous war with the full cognition that their victory was solely G-d's doing. There too, their *Shirah* underscored that their military efforts were only G-d's method of manifesting His salvation through the appropriate measures of *hishtadlus*. Indeed, *Chazal* tell us that when Devorah was in the midst of her *Shirah*, she had a lapse of *Ruach HaKodesh* due to a fleeting thought of self-importance. *Shirah* can only be sung when the Divine victory is appropriately recognized.

We can now better understand both Chizkiyahu's silence as well as the criticism leveled against him. Chizkiyahu felt himself unworthy of waging battle against the Assyrians. He was afraid that if he would raise his sword and lift his spear, he would consign some measure of the victory to his own efforts. He, therefore, forced himself to remain idle while it would be clear beyond the shadow of a doubt that victory was wrought entirely and solely by G-d's doing. After the miracle had occurred, Chizkiyahu believed that just as he could not physically participate in the battle, singing *Shirah* would be construed as if he merited the miracle somehow. Thus, he remained silent.

Chazal criticize Chizkiyahu by saying that had he sang a *Shirah*, he could have been the Moshiach. How is this critique to be understood? It is entirely possible that on a personal level, Chizkiyahu was correct. Just as the Jews did not sing Shirah upon their Exodus when they were not involved in the miracle, so did Chizkiyahu remain silent. However, in his capacity as king, he ought to have made a different calculation. Chizkiyahu had wrought a revolution in the Land of Israel. The *bamos* had been eradicated, and the Torah level of the Jewish people, down to the youngest child, was unprecedented. These were changes of a Messianic proportion. Although Chizkiyahu was afraid that singing *Shirah* might be a haughty measure, he sent the wrong message to the Jewish people.

Pesach

They had, indeed, made great strides in their spirituality. While they may not have been on the level to wage war and appropriate all credit to G-d, their newfound devotion to G-d did make them worthy to sing Shirah. Chizkiyahu erred in his assessment of his people and lost the chance to become the Moshiach.

This distinction that is made between active participation and passive onlooking as a condition for public expression of praise to Hashem is most fascinating and is indeed, quite logical. There is a great deal more ebullience and joy following one's personal efforts and labors than after one's merely being a spectator to an historic event. Certainly, one who has sacrificed of his time, energy and person toward a specific goal is more apt to break out in song and share in the ecstatic moments of ultimate triumph than one who has just given moral or financial encouragement and aid to this ideal.

This increased celebration after one's active *hishtadlus* does not imply that one is taking credit in any way for the victory. Rather, as Ramchal teaches, one cannot truly enjoy even a heavenly reward if it comes without any personal effort.

With this thought in mind, we may perhaps offer a possible solution to a problem which has been puzzling me for quite some time. After the miraculous victory of the Israeli Defense Forces over the Arab states in the 1948 War of Independence, the Israeli Chief Rabbinate decreed that the Hallel be recited annually on Yom HaAtzmaut, celebrating the anniversary of their independence. The Israeli Rabbinate felt that the events surrounding the re-establishment of the first Jewish state in almost 2,000 years was truly miraculous – the weak defeating the strong, and the few smashing and vanquishing the many. They bestowed the highest praise and thanks upon He Who made it all possible. They wished to offer their gratitude to Hashem who took the Jewish people from the ashes of Treblinka and Auschwitz to the top of Mount Zion; from the nadir of Jewish history to its zenith in just three short years.

This opinion of reciting the Hallel on Yom HaAtzmaut has been widely accepted throughout the State of Israel. However, in many areas of the Diaspora, especially in the United States, this dictate has not been completely carried out. In many synagogues and yeshivos, the Hallel is not recited. The question is – why not? However, if we use the same distinction that we used between the Exodus from Egypt and the crossing of the Red Sea, the difference between passive observance and active participation, we may find a possible solution.

The Jews in the Diaspora gave moral support and financial aid to their Israeli brethren during the War for Independence. They were, however, more like bystanders and onlookers to that great and historic event. On the other hand, our fellow Jews in Israel exerted every effort and sacrificed their lives and the lives of their fathers, brothers, and sons to establish an everlasting home. Because of their sorrows, misfortunes, and hardships that they were forced to endure, the victory, the ecstasy and euphoria were all so much sweeter. It was because of their direct and active participation that the Israeli Rabbinate felt, as did our ancestors at the Red Sea, the need and desire to express their thanks to Hashem and recite the Hallel. However, because of our only passive and indirect participation, so many of the Rabbis in the Diaspora felt no need to do the same.

It should be noted that this is not the only reason that the Hallel is not universally recited on Yom HaAtzmaut both here in the United States and in many sections of Israel. Many scholars feel that a decision to add a prayer of this sort can only be rendered by the Sanhedrin, the highest Jewish court. However, the Sanhedrin will not be reestablished until the days of the Moshiach.

Others, even those whose love for Eretz Yisrael and for Medinat Yisrael is unquestionable, offer yet a third reason. In fact, this *psak* was posited by HaRav Ovadiah Yosef *zt"l*, the former Sephardic chief Rabbi of Israel and one of the great scholars of his day. He stated that Hallel is recited and chanted only on great historical events where Jews were saved from their enemy. The fifth day of Iyar, which is Israel's Independence Day, does not meet this criterion. That day, while certainly historic and most significant, nevertheless, does not fit this standard. Yes, we do commemorate that great Friday of ה' אייר תש"ח, May 14, 1948. However, it did not bring peace and tranquility. In fact, that very statement by David Ben Gurion, although it was the right thing to do at the right time, led to many Jewish deaths and countless injuries. It was on that day, 70 years ago, that the War for Independence began. Seven Arab armies joined forces and attacked the nascent state of Israel. The war lasted for almost a full year until the IDF were finally able to repel the attackers and achieve a very hard-fought victory. Therefore, many Rabbanim, both here in the United States and certainly in Israel feel that ה' אייר is not the right time to give שבח והודאה to Hashem for this great miracle.

This is in contradistinction, however, to Yom Yerushalayim. That day indeed commemorates and celebrates a monumental victory of miraculous and historic proportions. It celebrates the capture of East Jerusalem and the reunification of all of Yerushalayim into Jewish hands. Thus, the third argument given for not reciting Hallel on Yom HaAtzmaut falls away on the 28th day of Iyar, Yom Yerushalayim.

That was a day, for me and those of my generation, which we will never forget. We will, for the rest of our lives, remember and cherish that awesome day.

Today, as the great holiday of Pesach comes to a close, we are faced with a choice. Two roads lie before us – the path of active participation and the path of passive observance. The choice of where we go affects both our own private lives as well as our national affairs. We can, if we wish, passively sit by while others are involved in the events that can change the world. We can simply take a backseat and observe as our friends and relatives are actively involved in doing acts of chessed and kindness for our brethren the world over. However, if we internalize the message of this Seventh Day of Pesach, we can decide to take the plunge into the ferocious waters and join this great struggle. We can rise to the challenge of the day and make the world a little better and safer for all.

The day will soon come when the *Ribono shel Olam* will perform other great and monumental miracles for us. At that time, our people will be free and live in tranquility. Our brethren in Eretz Yisrael will finally reside in complete peace and harmony. They will no longer be threatened by enemies who desire their destruction and demise. At that time another שירה will be sung and the full and complete Hallel will be recited. There will be no disagreements. There will be no disharmony. All stripes and sections of Judaism will be able to join together in this great outpouring of love, affection, and appreciation of Hashem.

However, the level in which we participate then will be based on the path we have chosen today. As we say on Rosh HaShanah, "the righteous will rejoice and the upright will exult." However, only the greatest amongst us, the חסידים, those who do not merely avoid wrongdoing but actively pursue good, will "be mirthful with glad song," ברנה יגילו. Only those of us who have made the effort, only those of us who have stood up and helped our people will be able to chant the *Shirah* in joyous praise of Hashem. The question we must ask ourselves today is: will we be among them? Will we share in that great moment of ecstasy and ultimate triumph? That decision, my friends, is ours and ours alone. The future of our people depends in a great way on that decision. The message of Pesach, the message of freedom and redemption, reaches its climax today as we recall the events at the Red Sea. Then the Jews rose to the occasion, they stepped up to the plate. They played an important and significant role in their future and in the destiny of our entire nation.

Today, my friends, we are called upon to play such a role. If we do so, if we do not let this opportunity pass us by, then we too, like our ancestors before us, will then be able to sing praises to Hashem. Let us not miss the boat – for at the other side of the sea, a great and glorious *Shirah* and *Hallel* await us. Let us make the right choice.

I want to thank my dear son-in-law Rabbi Yaakov Kibel for his inspiration and assistance in the development and formulation of this Drasha.

39. Uncompleted Songs; Unfinished Tasks
Shevi'i shel Pesach

During the last six days of the holiday of Pesach, there is one aspect which stands out and sets these days apart, distinguishing them from all other festivals. In this respect, these last six days are different than the first two days of Pesach as well. The change being referred to is that in the recitation and chanting of the Hallel, we omit segments of Psalms 115 and 116. This is the only time during the major holidays of the year in which this change in the format of our prayers takes place. On all other festivals in which Hallel is recited, namely Sukkos, Shavuos, the eight days of Chanukah, and the first two days of Pesach, we do not exclude and pass over certain sections of this great praise to G-d.

Our rabbis have offered a number of reasons for this change of custom. They explain that it would be out of character to rejoice completely when our enemies were suffering. The Egyptian army, who had pursued our ancestors to the banks of the Red Sea, were subsequently drowned on the seventh day of Pesach. When the Angels in heaven wished to rejoice and show their appreciation, Hashem rebuked them. The Gemara tells us that G-d said

"מעשי ידי טובעין בים ואתם אומרים שירה!"

"The handiwork of My hands is drowning in the sea, and you want to sing praises to me?"

Similarly, in the book of *Mishlei* (24:17) we read:

בִּנְפֹל אוֹיִבְךָ אַל תִּשְׂמָח וּבִכָּשְׁלוֹ אַל יָגֵל לִבֶּךָ:

When your enemy falls, do not be happy, and when he stumbles, let your heart not rejoice.

Though the drowning of the Egyptians occurred on the seventh day of Passover, we nevertheless omit the complete Hallel during the intermediate days of the holiday as well. This is done in order that the days of Chol HaMoed not appear as more important than the last days of Yom Tov itself. We rejoice over our salvation and escape from danger, while, at the same time, we sympathize with the suffering of our enemies

However, we might humbly suggest a homiletic reason for the reciting of the half-Hallel on the last days of Pesach. It is a message of human feelings and personal experiences in the face of adversity. When our ancestors were in Egypt, they prayed and hoped for their emancipation and freedom. When they were finally redeemed from their servitude and oppression, they were filled with joy and exhilaration. They were finally free. They now could do and act as they wished. They no longer were under the yoke of their Egyptian taskmasters.

However, their joy was short-lived, for just seven days after their miraculous exodus from Egypt, they were confronted once again by the sight of the powerful Egyptian army pursuing them. With the sea in front of them and the enemy behind, they were filled with panic. Would they be able to survive yet another attempt at being subjugated? Their only salvation would be through a direct intervention by G-d.

Our forefathers lifted up their voices and cried out to G-d. Moshe allayed their fears and said:

יְקוָק יִלָּחֵם לָכֶם וְאַתֶּם תַּחֲרִשׁוּן:

"The L-rd will fight for you, and you just hold your peace."

Then the miracle occurred. The waters split apart and the children of Israel crossed on dry land. Their tormentors and pursuers were left behind them in the midst of the now onrushing waters which had subsequently come together again. Following this unique, historical occurrence, Moshe and the Jewish people joined together in the singing of the *Shirah,* a song of unparalleled thanksgiving to G-d for His divine intervention and for their salvation. This was the height of joy and appreciation, the zenith of the Jewish people's miraculous Exodus.

The Jews assumed that all their troubles were now over. Soon, they would reach the promised land in peace and happiness. Unfortunately, they journeyed for only three days and were then faced with yet another serious problem. They came to Marah and they were unable to drink the water. They were plagued by an unquenchable thirst and a new threat to their lives.

Instead of relying on prayer, petition, and supplication, instead of having the utmost faith in Hashem, they murmured against Moshe and against G-d. Their hoped-for dreams of being blessed with good fortune was short-lived. Once again, the Jews met with disappointment. They wondered, "Will we ever really be free from these hazards and from these threats to our survival? Will we be only given half a loaf of bread and never a complete one? Will our Hallel, our praise to G-d, ever be total and unqualified, or will it only be a half and an uncompleted prayer?

It is noteworthy that the Torah records the incident of the bitter waters immediately after the crossing of the Red Sea and the singing of the *Shirah* to Hashem. This is an indication that in life's experiences, one is never totally free of his cares, worries, and concerns. The final crossing of the "Red Sea" of life has not occurred in the past, but rather, it will be in the future. The opening words of the *Shirah* are "אז ישיר". Rashi cites the interpretation of our Sages who question the future tense of the word "ישיר" – "will sing" and interpret this as an allusion to a *Shirah* that will be sung in the future after the resurrection of the dead. Further on in the *Shirah* the verse states the need for future victories in the midst of this great victory:

עַד יַעֲבֹר עַמְּךָ יְקֹוָק עַד יַעֲבֹר עַם זוּ קָנִיתָ:

Until your nation crosses, G-d, until this nation whom You have acquired crosses.

Targum Onklus explains that this alludes to the future crossings of the Arnon and the Yardein. Even at this time of exultation, the Jews knew that they could not rest on their laurels; there would be future challenges to traverse.

This lesson is indeed most instructive. We are taught that if we succeed in one venture, if we can overcome one obstacle, that does not assure us of success or victory in all our future endeavors.

The celebration of Pesach does not just end with the crossing at the Red Sea and the unrestrained and uncontrolled elation and gaiety that followed. We do not rejoice with the singing of the complete Hallel. Our forebears were forced to weather many obstacles that were placed in their path before reaching the Land of Canaan. Great faith and courage were required in order to survive and fight the various enemies, warring nations, thirst and hunger, wild animals, and a hot, dusty, and parched desert. Before they would be able to reach their final destination, before they would be able to lead a peaceful and autonomous life of their own on the land of their own, much more was required. At a later time, they would be allowed to fully rejoice and celebrate. Until then, they were commanded to be joyful but discreet, optimistic but cautious and prudent. Until that time, they were commanded always to sing the Hallel, but not the entire prayer. We are only to chant and internalize the message of the *Chatzi Hallel*, the half Hallel.

As we look out on the Jewish scene today, there is indeed a great deal about which to celebrate. We observe with almost disbelief a state of our own, Israel, which has just celebrated its 70th birthday. She has, over the past seven decades, made remarkable progress in every area. In agriculture, industry, technology, education, and military preparedness, Israel has become a force with which to be reckoned and has made us all very proud. Most importantly, Israel has become a haven for the Jewish people, enabling us to thrive not only physically, but spiritually as well. The growth of the yeshivos and the renaissance of the Ba'al Teshuvah movement is something that could not have occurred in any other country in the world. Every once in a while, we should all sing our praise and thanks to Hashem for making this all possible.

However, we must also remember that our happiness must be tempered by the stark realization that Israel is continually, on a daily basis, pursued by the Pharaohs of today. They attempt to drive her into the sea. Thus, the prayer that we offer must, in essence, be a "Half Hallel," an uncompleted song. With Hashem's help, one day in the future, when there will be full and total peace, when we will have achieved our objective of becoming an עם קדוש לה', a holy and distinct nation onto G-d, we will be able to chant and sing the *Hallel Shalem,* the complete Hallel.

We eagerly look forward to that day. At that time, we will experience the complete אז ישיר. The total and undivided praise to Hashem will burst forth from our souls, the *Neshamos* of a people that has truly experienced the גאולה שלימה, a total and complete redemption and emancipation. May it come במהרה בימינו, Amen.

40. Igniting the Flame of Eternity

Yizkor- Acharon Shel Pesach

Pesach, the season of freedom and liberation, the holiday of redemption and emancipation, seems to suggest another opposing and divergent theme. In addition to the accounts of our liberty, we also recount instances of gloom. The question begs itself. If Pesach is such a joyous holiday on which the mitzvah of ושמחת בחגך applies, why do we even mention anything negative?

During the Seder, when we recite the עשר מכות, the 10 plagues which Hashem inflicted upon the Egyptians, we spill a little wine, signifying that we can indeed feel for and empathize even with the suffering of our enemies.

During the last six days of Passover, only half of the Hallel, the great praise to G-d, is recited. This is done to indicate that while we are forever grateful to Hashem for delivering and rescuing our forebears from the grips of their enemy, we are somewhat saddened. We are mindful of the fact that as a result of our redemption, the ancient Egyptians drowned in the Red Sea.

On Shabbos Chol HaMoed, we read in the Haftorah about the prophet Yechezkel's awesome dream of the Valley of Dry Bones. In his vision, the Navi finds himself in an area littered with bones. The Gemara in Sanhedrin (צב:) gives various possibilities as to the identity of the people whose bones these were.

Several opinions suggest that these were the bones of wicked men. Another opinion, however, explains that these bones consisted of members of the Tribe of Ephraim who left Egypt prematurely. They miscalculated the 400-year decree of exile that Hashem had relayed to Avraham Avinu and left Egypt 30 years prior to the Exodus. They were met by the Philistine army and were massacred.

Yechezkel's vision concludes, however, on a most optimistic and hopeful note. G-d gathers and knits together these dry bones and covers them with flesh and skin. He then breathes life into them, whereupon they arise and stand up as a great and mighty host. Thus, in a few paragraphs, the Navi foretells the future and the eventual revival of Israel as a nation and as a sovereign entity. The theme of this Haftorah conforms with the idea of depicting a scent of gloom and destruction followed by a glorious salvation.

This concept of beginning with darkness, melancholy, and pessimism and ending with brightness, encouragement, and hope is carried over time and time again throughout the holiday of Pesach. We are commanded: וְהִגַּדְתָּ לְבִנְךָ – we are to tell over to our children and to our family the story of our history. We first begin with the negative and conclude with the positive and our praiseworthy acts: מתחיל בגנות ומסיים בשבח. We say: מתחילה עובדי עבודה זרה היו אבותינו. "In the beginning, our fathers were idol worshipers," ועכשיו קרבנו המקום ברוך הוא לעבודתו – "but now, G-d has brought us near to serve Him."

We continue with more examples along this theme in the Haggadah:

אֲרַמִּי אֹבֵד אָבִי וַיֵּרֶד מִצְרַיְמָה וַיָּגָר שָׁם בִּמְתֵי מְעָט.
Laban the Armenian sought to destroy my father, and he went down to Egypt and he sojourned there, few in number.

This verse marks the ebb of early Jewish history. However, the verse concludes with an opposing high:

וַיְהִי שָׁם לְגוֹי גָּדוֹל עָצוּם וָרָב:
But there he became a great nation, mighty and populous.

However, just as our fortunes had begun to turn, we faced yet another decline:

עֲבָדִים הָיִינוּ לְפַרְעֹה בְּמִצְרָיִם.

We recount the bitter and torturous enslavement and bondage in Egypt, followed by the discussion of the glorious redemption and liberation, the Exodus.

Pesach

ויוציאנו ה' אלקינו משם ביד חזקה ובזרוע נטויה.

G-d brought us out of there with a strong hand and with an outstretched arm.

At a time when we rejoice, celebrate, and commemorate the liberation and freedom of our ancestors, why is it necessary to relate and recount the sad along with the good? Why must we place emphasis on the time when our forebears were enslaved and oppressed? Why must we describe how our ancestors originally were idolaters and led corrupt lives? Why do we not solely emphasize the שבח, the glory, the luster, and the splendor of our people? Why do we not restrict our discussion to their purely wholesome lives and their ethical and moral behavior?

The message of the Haggadah and Pesach in general is that we cannot appreciate the good and the beautiful without either an analysis or an experience of the bad and the unpleasant. Hashem created darkness and then brought light into being:

וַיְהִי עֶרֶב וַיְהִי בֹקֶר יוֹם אֶחָד.

He did this so that the contrast would be so much more beautiful, pronounced, and meaningful. A rose develops and grows surrounded in a bed of prickly thorns. This is so as to make its appearance so much more attractive and lovelier. Thus, without some knowledge or experience of the contrasting elements, one could never fully and totally value happiness, well-being, and the finer things in life.

Throughout our history, in every era and age, we have always experienced this twofold approach – night and day, gloom and happiness, sadness and cheerfulness. Always, before we experienced the beauty of the dawn of day, we underwent the travails and the difficulties in the blackness of night.

Before *Rashi HaKadosh* was able to enlighten the Jewish world in the 11th century, the great Jewish communities of Worms and Mainz were destroyed and its population murdered during the Second Crusade.

Before the first Jews began to settle and help develop America into the most welcome haven for Jews in all of our Diaspora, Spanish Jewry was forced to endure the horrible and catastrophic effects of the Inquisition and forced exile.

Before we rejoiced and celebrated the birth and the establishment of the State of Israel, before we reached the summit of our independence, we were forced to endure the ghastly and monstrous events of the Shoah. However, out of the ashes of Treblinka and Auschwitz, from the depths and the nadir of Jewish history, we experienced a glorious and illuminating light at the end of the tunnel. Three years after the liberation of the last concentration camps in Poland and in Germany, we reached one of the great heights of Jewish history, the beginning of the third Jewish Commonwealth and the first Jewish politically autonomous state in almost 2,000 years.

Before our ancestors in Egypt beheld and witnessed the Hand of G-d performing miracles and wonders, before their experiencing the sunshine of the Exodus, they suffered through more than 200 years of dusky and blinding servitude.

This pattern holds true with our generation as well. Although the future may appear bleak and foreboding in many areas of world Jewry, we will manage to survive. We will, in the not-too-distant future, truly experience the luster, brilliance, and splendor of Hashem intervening on our behalf.

We will eventually understand why, on this day of *Yizkor*, when we recall the souls of our dear departed loved ones, we also read the hopeful prophecy in the *Haftorah* from the book of Yeshayahu. The *Navi* delivered his message at a time of doom and pessimism in the Jewish community. מלכות ישראל was already

Pesach

destroyed. מלכות יהודה was rotting and decaying. The situation at that time was grievous and depressing.

Yet, Yeshayahu had faith that G-d will again gather the Jewish people from the lands of their present dispersion. He also talked of our future dispersion of which he prophesied that Hashem will then return us to our homeland. It was a great vision of messianism. It tells of a time when peace and harmony will reign supreme among men as well as among the beasts.

We read this *Haftorah* just before *Hazkaras Neshamos*, our remembrance of those who have passed on. We do so because when we remember our loved ones, initially we are very saddened and depressed by the thought that they are no longer with us. However, the purpose of *Yizkor* is not to evoke memories that will dishearten us. Rather, its goal is to uplift us and prod us into acting in a more positive and meaningful manner.

When we think of our parents and our other relatives who have passed on to their eternal rest, we miss them very much. We feel distraught that we can no longer feel their presence. We no longer have them around to help and assist us. However, we must see beyond the immediate and the present. We have to realize that our Rabbis designated these days as ימי זכרון in order for us to contemplate upon the lives that our loved ones led. We should recall their manifold contributions to Judaism and the impact that they made upon us. We are then asked to act upon that.

We recall the past and the difficult memories it evokes in order for us to go on positively toward the future. If we wish to make sure that our beloved relatives have not really died but merely passed on to another, holier, and totally spiritual plane, if we want to guarantee that they will live on through our lives, then we must elevate our spirits as they perfected their lives. That which was holy and sacred to them should be adopted by us – Jewish education, Jewish philanthropy, and the observance of all the Mitzvos and traditions of

Pesach

our faith. The Jewish family, its continuity, and all its ramifications must be prioritized and made a very important segment of our own personal lives.

My friends, if we remember that which we are called upon to recall, if we internalize the values of our loved ones and we adopt them as our own, then we will help guarantee that they never will have died at all. Our gloom and darkness will be transformed into happiness and sunshine.

If each of us does our share, we will help bring closer the prophecy of Yeshayahu that peace will indeed reign on earth. At that time –

וְגָר זְאֵב עִם כֶּבֶשׂ וְנָמֵר עִם גְּדִי יִרְבָּץ וְעֵגֶל וּכְפִיר וּמְרִיא יַחְדָּו וְנַעַר קָטֹן נֹהֵג בָּם:

And the wolf shall dwell with the lamb, and the leopard shall lie down with the kid, and the calf with the young lion and the fatling together, and a young child shall lead them.

We pray that this day will soon be here. Let us do what we can to hasten its arrival, במהרה בימינו אמן.

Yom HaShoah

41. Death Need Not be Final

Holocaust Memorial Day

Today, the 27th day of Nissan, is Yom HaShoah, Holocaust Remembrance and Memorial Day. In 1951, the Knesset, the Israeli Parliament, designated this day to be one of commemoration and observance. Even though we are still in the month of Nissan, where public mourning is frowned upon, even though we are less than one week past the end of Pesach – our celebration of emancipation and freedom, renewal and rebirth – today, we remember.

From 1948 to 1951, the Knesset debated and discussed which day should be designated as a memorial to the Six Million Jews. Some wanted it held earlier in Nissan to coincide with the start of the Warsaw ghetto uprising. Others, not wanting to mar the celebration and observance of the Yom Tov of Pesach, pushed to have this day set in Iyar. Eventually, a compromise was reached with the 27th of Nissan, the anniversary of the end of the Warsaw ghetto uprising. This day was deemed most appropriate because enough time would have lapsed after the celebration of Pesach. It was also one week prior to the observance of Yom HaAtzmaut, Israel's Independence Day. According to all, Yom HaAtzmaut is the fundamental response to the Holocaust.

The Jewish people responded to the total assault of death and destruction of European Jewry by an outpouring of life. Many survivors came to Israel and rebuilt their lives. They established new families and continued to build and add to the Jewish chain of destiny. Jewish life was made precious again. Nothing more could profoundly capture the relationship between the Holocaust and the State of Israel than the designation of this day as Yom HaShoah. The birth of Medinat Yisrael is not a reward or merely a product of the Holocaust. It is a response.

It is also most instructive that on Shabbos Chol Hamoed Pesach, just about 10 days ago, we read in the *Haftorah* about the prophet Yechezkel's awesome and mindboggling vision of the Valley of Dry Bones. While, on the surface, this *Haftorah* is apparently quite contrary to the mood of exhilaration and celebration of Pesach, in essence, it is indeed most fitting. It has, I believe, great significance and serves as a bridge between Pesach and Yom HaShoah.

We read in the *Haftorah* that Hashem said to Yechezkel (Ch. 37):

"Son of Man, can these bones live?"
And I said, "My L-rd, Hashem, You know."
And He said to me, "Prophesy over these bones and say to them, 'O dry bones, hear the word of Hashem. Thus says my L-rd Hashem to these bones: Behold, I am bringing breath unto you and you shall live. And I will put sinews upon you and bring flesh upon you and I will cover you with skin. And I will breathe into you and you shall live; and you shall know that I am the L-rd.'"

The prophet goes on to recount how the bones joined together and they became covered with flesh and skin. Yechezkel prophesied again and the spirit entered their bodies whereupon they stood upon their feet. The prophet continues:

And He said to me: "Son of Man, these bones, they are the whole family of Israel. Behold, they say, 'Our bones have cried, and our hope is lost. We are doomed.'
"Therefore, prophesy and say to them: 'Thus says my L-rd Hashem: Behold! I am opening your graves and I will raise you up

Yom HaShoah

from your graves, O my people, and I will bring you to the land of Israel. Then you shall know that I am the L-rd.'" ...

This seemingly, gloomy scene, which in essence became quite glorious, was Yechezkel's prophecy about the eventual revival of Judaism as a nation, as a people, and as a sovereign state.

We recall this נבואה on Pesach because this Yom Tov celebrates Israel's initial freedom from servitude and oppression. According to our tradition, our final redemption and the ultimate revival of the dead will also occur during this Yom Tov. Yechezkel's vision was offered to a nation that had become enslaved. They were bereft of their national sovereignty and independence following the destruction of the first Beis HaMikdash in 586 BCE. The vision revitalized the determination of the exiled Judeans to live as Jews.

This vision also imparted a most essential message of Jewish belief, the concept that death, the cessation of life, is not absolute or final. The placing of a body into an open grave does not necessarily terminate life from a Jewish perspective. There is hope in death. From a traditional Jewish vantage, there is even life in death – life in the sense of תחיית המתים, individual spiritual rebirth and also national physical resurrection.

We memorialize the victims of the Holocaust today because, as horrendous and devastating as this event was to the Jewish people and to the future of Judaism, as perplexing as it appears to the minds of mortal human beings, in the great plan of G-d, it was apparently a necessary component in the חבלי משיח, the birth pangs of Moshiach. It serves as the beginning of the Messianic era which will ultimately conclude with the תחיית המתים, the resurrection of the dead.

The Jewish ideals of standing up to our enemies, regardless of whether they outnumber us 2 to 1 or 50 to 1 or even 100 to 1, in terms of men and materiel, was not first demonstrated by our modern Israeli brethren. They have a Mesorah, a tradition. This was taught to them

Yom HaShoah

by the heroic Jewish men and women of Europe. In almost every ghetto and in several concentration camps such as Treblinka, Birkenau, Auschwitz, and others, forgetting about the fact that they were starving and were stricken with illness and disease, Jews by the thousands rebelled and revolted against their mighty Nazi tormentors.

And what about the millions who went to their deaths strong, erect, and brave? They did so without even begging or pleading to be spared. On the other hand, the millions of captured Russian soldiers begged for and groveled for clemency and mercy.

These wonderful and beautiful people are our real heroes. They smiled and looked up to heaven and said שמע ישראל and sang the famous אני מאמין. "I believe in G-d. I believe in the destiny of Israel. I believe in the very quick coming of the Messianic age. I go to my death willingly in order to sanctify and glorify the name of Hashem." This, my friends, was true bravery. This was death with dignity.

However, it was on Pesach, 1943, that the most remarkable event during the entire Holocaust occurred – the start of the Warsaw Ghetto Uprising. With homemade, crude, and quite primitive weapons, the Jews of this most famous ghetto battled the Nazi beasts and held them at bay for almost a month. A new respect filled the world for these Jews who wished only to prove that the Jew can fight valiantly and bravely if given the chance.

It was on Pesach, my friends, the holiday of freedom and independence, that these precious and pure people who did nothing to deserve their torture except to be born Jewish, began the modern-day recreation of the Exodus. They began putting sinews, flesh, and skin on these dry, old, and so very weak bones. To G-d's question to Yechezkel of "Will these bones live?" they responded with an unequivocal "Yes, we will survive. Whether we live or die, our

Yom HaShoah

ideals, our aspirations, our religion and our hope in the very future of our people will live and will never die."

Unfortunately, the insurrection began when only a very small segment of the Jewish community remained in the Warsaw ghetto. These Jews discovered that their precious brethren who were taken from the ghetto were not "resettled" to another area as the Nazis claimed. They were instead all systematically and ruthlessly murdered in Treblinka and some other camps. The surviving Jews concluded that they must take action. They knew that doing nothing would certainly lead to their deaths. They hoped that by their uprising, they would inflict a great price on the Nazis. They were optimistic that by their revolt, the deportations would perhaps cease, or, at the very least, slow down in pace. In any event, they knew that by their actions they would encourage Jews in other ghettos and concentration camps to begin their own insurrections.

While their heroic actions did not prevent the liquidation of the Warsaw ghetto, it did indeed inflict a significant military and psychological price on the "mighty German war machine." It also made a very strong impression upon the remaining European Jews as well as Jews throughout the world. In that sense, their sacrifice could be viewed as a monumental success.

It is no accident, my friends, that just three years after the last concentration camps were liberated, the next step towards the final redemption, the אתחלתא דגאולה, occurred. The prophecy of Yechezkel (37:12) came true:

לָכֵן הִנָּבֵא וְאָמַרְתָּ אֲלֵיהֶם כֹּה אָמַר ה' אלקים הִנֵּה אֲנִי פֹתֵחַ אֶת קִבְרוֹתֵיכֶם וְהַעֲלֵיתִי אֶתְכֶם מִקִּבְרוֹתֵיכֶם עַמִּי וְהֵבֵאתִי אֶתְכֶם אֶל אַדְמַת יִשְׂרָאֵל:

Behold, I am opening your graves and I will rise you up. I will bring you into the land of Israel.

In so short a span of time, this prophecy of the creation of the State of Israel came true. The spirit of these heroes of the Holocaust

Yom HaShoah

lived on and continues to live on in the lives of our brethren in Medinat Yisrael.

Last week, on אחרון של פסח, as we do on three other occasions during the year, we memorialized the souls of our departed relatives by the recitation of the Yizkor service. We said, as did the prophet Yechezkel, that we will put our spirits in them. We can by our positive actions and our Mitzvos fuse life into their dry bones. We can cause them to live again through our lives. By dedicating our lives to Torah and Mitzvos, we will assure them that they never will have completely died. They will live on through our deeds and actions.

On this day of memorial and observance, on this very special day of Yom HaShoah, we can do the same for our Six Million brothers and sisters who were so barbarically and systematically murdered.

If we can alter our lives just a bit, if we can become better Jews and better human beings, if we never forget our holy and precious martyrs, then they too can spiritually remain alive. We can make sure that their deaths were only in body but that their spirit will continue to invigorate us until the time of תחיית המתים.

Through our deeds of צדקה and מעשים טובים, through our constant devotion and dedication to the Torah and to *HaKadosh Baruch Hu,* we will guarantee that עם ישראל, ארץ ישראל, and תורת ישראל will continue to live, grow and thrive. The Six Million will remain alive in our hearts and in our souls and we will never ever forget them. Amen.

Yom Yerushalayim
42. G-d's Gifts and Israel's Responsibility

This week, on the 28th day of Iyar, we will be observing Yom Yerushalayim, the day which commemorates the capture of the old city of Jerusalem by the Israeli Defense forces in the Six Day War of 1967. With acts of heroism and dedication, the עיר דוד, the City of David, was reunited and placed in Jewish hands and control for the first time in almost 2,000 years. That event, I believe, more than anything else since the establishment of the State of Israel, provided our people with the optimism, determination, and the wherewithal to withstand all our enemies and face the future squarely and bravely. For Jerusalem, my friends, is not just another piece of land. It is not merely another chunk of territory which is here today and gone tomorrow. It is not an area which either we control or our enemies have dominion over. Rather, it is the cornerstone, the focal point of Jewish life.

Yerushalayim represents all that is sacred and precious to us. It was and remains one of the basic factors which has kept us alive as a nation and as a people. Twice a year, on Yom Kippur and Pesach, the holidays which represent, respectively, the spiritual and physical redemption of the Jewish people, we boldly and proudly recite the words:

"לשנה הבאה בירושלים"

"Next year in Jerusalem!"

After every meal, we mourn along with the Judean captives, who chanted the immortal words along the banks of Babylon:

שָׁם יָשַׁבְנוּ גַּם בָּכִינוּ בְּזָכְרֵנוּ אֶת צִיּוֹן.

"There we sat and cried as we remembered Zion."

We recite along with the psalmist:

אִם אֶשְׁכָּחֵךְ יְרוּשָׁלָם תִּשְׁכַּח יְמִינִי:

"If I forget thee, O Jerusalem, may my right hand forget it's cunning."

Wherever we were, whatever continent or country of oppression we found ourselves in, we cried along with Rav Yehudah Halevi:

לִבִּי בַמִּזְרָח וַאֲנִי בְּסוֹף מַעֲרָב.

"I may be in the West, but my soul is in the East."

And finally, we continually remember that *Am Yisrael, Toras Yisrael,* and *Eretz Yisrael* are one. The future of the Jewish people is linked to these great spiritual ideals. For without Torah, we are a nation of heathens. Without the sanctity of the land of Israel, we are not a people. Thus, we recite at least four times a week:

כִּי מִצִּיּוֹן תֵּצֵא תוֹרָה וּדְבַר ה' מִירוּשָׁלָיִם:

"For out of Zion shall go forth the Torah and the word of G-d from Jerusalem."

I ask you, my friends: can a non-Jew truly understand what Israel, and especially the sacred city of Yerushalayim, means to a Jew? Can he conceptualize that for almost 2,000 years, the Jew has constantly longed to return to the land which G-d promised to his forefathers? No substitute was ever good enough. Argentina was unacceptable. Uganda was rejected. Russia was never even considered. Every nation and every people must be in the land of their own in order to remain alive, vibrant, and strong. If this be the case with all other people whose ties with their country are purely nationalistic, this is certainly true with our people. Jerusalem was never meant to be solely the seat of the government of Israel. Rather, it is the home of G-d, the spiritual center of our people.

Would Catholics survive without the city of Rome? Could the Moslems exist without Mecca? Would anyone ever think of denying them their religious centers? Of course not. Only the Jews are denied control of and access to their spiritual capital. This concept of the *Kedusha,* the spiritual and moral uplifting of Yerushalayim for the

Yom Yerushalayim

Jewish nation, is an idea which the average non-Jew cannot even conceive of. Thus, he is not convinced of Israel's need to control her capital.

Can a non-Jew understand the Gemara in Taanis (5a) in which Hashem declared that He will not enter the heavenly Jerusalem, the ירושלים של מעלה, until He has entered the Jerusalem on earth, the ירושלים של מטה? Unless G-d is welcomed into Jerusalem on earth by the world political powers as well as by our actions, G-d will not enter the heavenly Yerushalayim. G-d's refusal to enter the Yerushalayim of above is a painful indication of the absence of His presence and influence over world affairs. This idea cannot be truly understood by one who is not Jewish. It cannot be internalized by one who has not immersed himself in the richness of Jewish tradition and Jewish values. However, it can be understood by Jews. At the present time, my concern is not so much with the non-Jewish world and their hypocrisy and warped sense of morality but with our fellow Jews and their lack of gratitude to Hashem.

For 2,000 years, we wept and cried bitterly until our tear ducts were dried up. We beseeched G-d to grant us our ancient homeland. We prayed to Hashem to bring us back to the land of our fathers. On every Yom Tov Mussaf, we repeatedly bemoan to G-d that as observant, faithful, and committed as we have been, we were only able to partially fulfill the duties of our faith. If only we could see Zion, if only we could possess Yerushalayim, how much more faithfully and completely would we be able to abide by all the laws of the Torah that are applicable only in the land of Israel. Now G-d has wrought miracles for us. He has delivered our people from the clutches of the enemy. He has provided us with our ancient homeland and given us complete control and jurisdiction over our most holy and sacred city. We now must ask ourselves one basic and elementary question. Have we lived up to our part of the agreement?

Yom Yerushalayim

In the Hallel which we recite on all the Yom Tovim and which many say on Yom Yerushalayim, we read (Tehillim 116):

מָה אָשִׁיב לַה' כָּל תַּגְמוּלוֹהִי עָלָי:

"What can I tender to G-d for all His kind acts towards me?"

כּוֹס יְשׁוּעוֹת אֶשָּׂא וּבְשֵׁם ה' אֶקְרָא:

"A cup of salvations shall I raise, and I will call upon the name of the L-rd."

נְדָרַי לַה' אֲשַׁלֵּם נֶגְדָה נָּא לְכָל עַמּוֹ:

"My vows to G-d will I now pay before His entire nation."

After observing the great miracles wrought for our people by *HaKadosh Baruch Hu* in 1967, we of course celebrated. We rejoiced. We paraded. We lifted up our cup of deliverance for the entire world to see. There never was as much *simcha,* real and genuine joy and happiness in the Jewish community as there was during those first weeks and months following the reunification of Jerusalem. We sang and danced and pointed with pride to our great military victory.

We also called upon the name of G-d by offering our thanks and appreciation. We went to our respective shuls and davened. We praised G-d for being with us and for providing us with this miraculous gift. Hundreds of thousands of Jews from all walks of life throughout the world made their way to the Kotel, the Western Wall, the last remnant of the second Beis HaMikdash, our holiest possession. During the first weeks after the war, there was a great upsurge of religious fervor. People who had been brought up on atheistic Kibbutzim wished to put on Tefillin and pray at the Kotel.

There was a feeling that we were about to witness the coming of Moshiach. There was love between Jews. Religious observance was about to be practiced by all. Israel, the people and the state, was strong and powerful. However, this was not to be.

Somehow, after only a little less than a year after Israel's glorious victory, the zeal, the fervor, and the complete allegiance to

Yom Yerushalayim

Hashem waned. Instead of continuing to acknowledge and thank God for His intervention, instead of ישראל בטח בה', *"Israel trusts and believes in Hashem,"* the new mantra became, ישראל בטח בצה"ל, *"The people of Israel put complete faith and trust in the Israeli Defense Forces."* When faith and religious belief in God's providence is replaced by man's belief in his own power and strength, כחי ועוצם ידי, then all progress and growth is completely lost. When that occurs, the happiness and joy which accompanied the aftereffects of the מלחמת ששת הימים is transformed into the cries, bitterness, and sadness of the מלחמת יום הכיפורים.

Indeed, the question is much deeper and even more profound. Has the religious commitment and spiritual deeds of our Israeli brethren who had not previously been observant increased because of our receiving the gift of Jerusalem? Are they still forever making excuses as to why they cannot be Shomer Shabbos and why real, genuine, and authentic Judaism is archaic and outdated? The answer, my friends, is quite obvious. Instead of increasing their religiosity and commitment, it has slowly dwindled to almost where it was previously. Some even dare question the omnipotence of G-d, exclaiming, "Where is G-d when we need him?" "Why did G-d let us down?" The non-Jew may not understand the Aggadah in the Gemara in Taanis, but we should. The fact is that because of the immoral, unethical, and spiritual deterioration of our society, G-d is unwelcome in the earthly Jerusalem. Because Jerusalem has not really become Yerushalayim, because the kind of Jewish behavior that Jerusalem merits is not there, G-d will not enter the heavenly Yerushalayim. And His not entering into the Yerushalayim of above is clearly indicated by the absence of His overt presence and influence over the affairs of the world.

The Torah in Devarim (31) says:

וְאָנֹכִי הַסְתֵּר אַסְתִּיר פָּנַי בַּיּוֹם הַהוּא...

"On that day, I will surely hide My face."

Yom Yerushalayim

Thus, our fate, and even the fate of Hashem, if you wish, is determined by man's actions. This idea is described in very powerful terms in the Torah portion of Bechukosai. The Torah there describes the rewards that Israel will receive for observing the Mitzvos. In a rather lengthy chapter, it then details the horrors and catastrophes which will occur if Israel disregards G-d's laws. The Sedra begins:

אִם בְּחֻקֹּתַי תֵּלֵכוּ וְאֶת מִצְוֹתַי תִּשְׁמְרוּ וַעֲשִׂיתֶם אֹתָם:

"If you will walk in My ordinances and keep My commandments, and do them."

The Sedra continues with a promise that by doing so, the Jewish people will be greatly rewarded – economically, physically, and politically. There will be sufficient wealth for all, Israel will achieve great military success, and we will live in peace externally as well as internally.

Rashi, commenting on the words "אם בחוקתי תלכו" quotes the Sifri: שתהיו עמלים בתורה. This is an admonition that we should study Torah with great zeal and intensity.

The key and most important element in serving Hashem is through the study of Torah and all the Mitzvos contained therein. It is only at that time when we all faithfully follow the word of Hashem in all areas of life, that *HaKadosh Baruch Hu* will be happy and content with us. This hopefully will help bring about our salvation and our complete redemption.

The *Mincha Belulah* explains the opening word of the Sedra, "אם". He points out that each redemption of Israel was led by two individuals whose names began with the letters 'א and 'מ. In *Golus Mitzrayim*, the Exodus from Egypt was led by Moshe (מֹשֶׁה) and Aharon (אַהֲרֹן). The redemption from the Golus of Paras and Madai, the Persian exile, was led by Esther (אֶסְתֵּר) and Mordechai (מָרְדְּכַי). In the future, the ultimate redemption will come about through Eliyahu (אֵלִיָּהוּ) and Moshiach (מָשִׁיחַ). Thus, the word "אם" is included in the sentence to inform us that real, true, and authentic redemption

Yom Yerushalayim

and salvation will occur only if Israel will observe the Torah and its numerous *Mitzvos, Mishpatim,* and *Chukim.*

Thus, we clearly see that in order for Hashem to complete His promise of providing us with an era of peace and prosperity, brotherhood and tranquility, we must first complete our end of the agreement. We must pay our debt by observing all that we have pledged to Him. It is our responsibility to double our efforts and make a greater attempt at observing the precepts of our faith.

My friends, the future of Judaism, the ushering in of the messianic era of brotherhood and unity in Israel, and, of course, peace and prosperity, will only come about when we begin to fulfill our responsibility and pay our debt to G-d. When we make Yerushalayim, the עיר שלם, the city that is whole and complete not only geographically speaking, but also in deed and observance.

Only then will we succeed. Only then, when this thought will spread far and wide throughout the Jewish world, will we be able to prove to the non-Jewish community that Israel, Jerusalem, and the Jewish people are indeed one. It is not only important to us strategically and nostalgically, but also religiously and spiritually. Only then will we have no difficulty in retaining Jerusalem and the other territories which are religiously important to us. For at that time we will have witnessed the coming of the Moshiach. The Almighty will then have entered into ירושלים של מעלה, the heavenly Jerusalem. The precipitating element is Israel's total observance of the Torah and the Mitzvos. Let us hope that day will be here soon. Amen.

43. The Most Beautiful Wakeup Call
Reflections on the Six Day War and its 50th Year Commemoration and Celebration
Yom Yerushalayim 5777 (2017)

On Wednesday, June 7, 1967, I was a college junior at Yeshiva University in New York. At about 6:00 AM, I was awakened to a loudspeaker radio transmission of the famous words by Lieutenant General Mota Gur: "הר הבית בידינו!"– "The Temple Mount is in our hands! The Kotel is in our hands!" Subsequently, I heard the magnificent sounds of the Shofar blown by then chief Rabbi of the Israeli Defense forces, Rabbi Shlomo Goren.

The entire yeshiva went onto Amsterdam Avenue. We sang and danced with much joy and thanksgiving. Our festivities lasted for about 1 ½ hours until it was time to daven Shacharis. That glorious, most beautiful and unforgettable morning, the wake-up call I received was truly transformative. It changed my life. I have remembered that morning every day since with reverence, pride and joy.

However, the story does not begin or end there. For about three weeks before the onset of hostilities, we were all very concerned. We had great trepidation. We feared for the future, for the very survival of our brothers and sisters in Eretz Yisrael.

On Monday morning, June 5, at around 3:00 AM, someone was frantically knocking on my dorm room. He informed me that war had just begun. Just two weeks before that, I had been installed as the president of the student body of Yeshiva College. We immediately began waking up all the students in the dormitory. We all went to the Beis HaMidrash where, for the next two hours, we recited Tehillim. The fervor, the intensity, the emotion of those Tefillos were such that I had never experienced either before or since.

Yom Yerushalayim

We did not know any of the details, for Israel had imposed a news blackout.

After our Tefillos, a few of the student leaders met privately. We unanimously concluded that due to this most dangerous situation which our brethren were facing, we could not complete our final exams that were scheduled for that day. We informed the administration of our decision and we then galvanized the student body. We ordered dozens of buses for the entire college. We made plans to transport all of the students to the United States mission of the United Nations. Our goal was to plead with our government to come to the aid and assistance of the State of Israel.

Later that morning, two of my colleagues and I flew to Washington, D.C. There we met with about 10 different congressmen. We implored them to pressure and to lobby the Johnson administration to come to the aid of a beleaguered and vulnerable Israel (or so we thought). It was only during our meetings in Washington that we discovered the great miracle of that morning. When the news blackout was lifted, we learned that Israel, during the first few hours of the war, had successfully destroyed almost the entire air forces of Egypt, Syria, and Jordan. For all practical purposes, the war was over.

The נסים ונפלאות associated with this war were monumental and incredible. The יד ה', the Hand of G-d, was quite apparent throughout those glorious days.

I recently read a story that occurred at West Point Military Academy. An officer was teaching a course to the cadets on great military battles and war strategies. A student asked the instructor why he did not include in his curriculum the battles of the Six-Day War. The instructor responded, "Here at West Point we teach about great strategies and great military victories; we do not teach about miracles."

Yom Yerushalayim

The entire Six-Day War was a *neis*. Some will say it was a נס גלוי, an open miracle. Others will say that it was a נס נסתר, a hidden miracle. Whichever way is correct, there is one thing that is very clear. The יד ה', the Hand of G-d, played a huge and pivotal role. The question which we must ask ourselves is – why did Hashem smile down on us at that very time? Why did He shine His countenance upon us? I think that we can, perhaps, answer this question with an understanding of an idea in Parshas Bamidbar and the *mefarshim* there.

Our rabbis tell us that Parshas Bamidbar is almost always read on the Shabbos preceding Chag HaShavuos. According to the Slonimer Rebbe and other *gedolim*, this occurs because the Parshah details the counting of Bnei Yisrael as one unit. This demonstrates in no uncertain terms the *achdus*, the unity, of *Klal Yisrael*. The only way that the Torah could be given to our people is for all of us to be together. We need to be standing completely as one with each other. There can be no arguments, no *machlokes*, no finger pointing.

Rabbeinu Efraim ben Shimon, the 13th century French commentator, gives a complementary insight. He says that the גימטריא, the numerical equivalent of the words "במדבר סיני" is 378. That is equal to the גימטריא of the word "בשלום", "with peace," which also equals 378. This, he says, teaches us that as Bnei Yisrael approached Har Sinai, they were unified. They acted as one, and they were at peace with each other

Rashi says the same idea in his comment on the *posuk* in Parshas Yisro:

וַיִּחַן שָׁם יִשְׂרָאֵל נֶגֶד הָהָר:

And they (literally "he") *camped opposite the mountain.*

Rashi says:

כאיש אחד בלב אחד.

Yom Yerushalayim

"As one man and with one heart." The *achdus,* the unity, the joining together of one mind was a prerequisite for Bnei Yisrael to be *zoche* to receive the holy Torah and the open manifestation of G-d's presence which accompanied it.

The second idea is found in the Gemara Bava Basra (דף קכג:) (quite ironically, it falls out this year as the *daf yomi* for the day after Yom Yerushalayim). The Gemara recounts that in Parshas Vayeitzei, Yaakov Avinu was about to leave the home of his father-in-law Lavan after 20 years. Yaakov felt ready to leave then because Yosef was born and he was now prepared to face and confront his brother Eisav, his antagonist and potential enemy.

The Gemara says:

ראה יעקב אבינו שאין זרעו של עשו נמסר אלא ביד זרעו של יוסף.

Yaakov saw through prophecy that the descendants of Eisav [Amalek] will only be given over to the descendants of Yosef. The Gemara explains that throughout Tanach, when the Jewish people confronted and battled against Amalek and other enemies, they were successful mostly whenever their leaders or their generals descended from Shevet Yosef.

In Bereishis Rabbah (Vayeitzei Parshah 73) however, *Chazal* change the nuance of this lesson ever so slightly:

דא"ר פנחס בשם ר"ש בר נחמן מסורת היא שאין עשו נופל אלא ביד בניה של רחל.

R' Pinchas says in the name of R' Shimon: We have a tradition that Eisav will only fall by the hands of the children of Rachel.

There are two questions one can ask on the Gemara and the Midrash. Firstly, what is unique about Yosef that he is the one who brings about the downfall of Eisav and his descendants? Secondly, what is the meaning of the apparent conflict between the Gemara and the Midrash? Perhaps the answer to the first question will

Yom Yerushalayim

demonstrate that there is indeed no conflict between these two statements of Chazal.

Let us look at the first question. What was unique about Yosef that gives him the merit to defeat Amalek? I would humbly suggest that it is because Yosef represented the epitome of אחדות ורעות, unity and brotherhood, on the highest level. We observe that at the end of Sefer Bereishis where the *tzidkus* and righteousness of Yosef is quite apparent. He could have easily repaid his brothers for the hatred and evil that they caused him. However, when he had the chance to take revenge, he did the very opposite. He showed love and respect, unity and solidarity.

However, this answer requires some clarification. At first glance, it might appear that Yosef represented the opposite of *achdus*. After all, did he not arouse the brothers' jealousy by conveying his dreams of lordship to them? Secondly, even if we can demonstrate that Yosef represented *achdus*, why is this the specific Midah that enables us to overcome Eisav?

Although it is true that Yosef incited his brothers' jealousy by revealing his dreams, and Yaakov indeed rebuked Yosef for sharing them, we have to ask what Yosef's motivation was. Was he really trying to act in a haughty and boastful manner over his brothers? The Sefas Emes (סוכות תרמ"ח) states that the very opposite was the case. Yosef described himself as being in the center of his brothers not in order to divide them but rather, to unite them. The brothers misinterpreted his attempt at *achdus* and sold him as a slave. Yosef's intentions towards *achdus* can indeed be seen in his attempt at drawing the children of Bilhah and Zilpah close, whereas the children of Leah treated them as second-class citizens.

At the critical juncture when Yosef reveals himself to his brothers, he tells them: "Come close to me." When the doors were closed and his brothers were completely vulnerable, Yosef chooses *achdus* over separation. The next action of Yosef is very telling.

Yom Yerushalayim

Yosef embraced Binyamin and they cried on each other's shoulders. Rashi says that Binyamin cried over the Mishkan which would be situated in Yosef's territory and would subsequently be destroyed. Yosef, on the other hand, wept over the two Batei Mikdash that would be built in Binyamin's *cheilek* and would also subsequently be destroyed. One observation from this Rashi is that they did not cry for their own plight; each cried over the plight of his brother. The second observation is that Yosef chose this exact moment to cry over the destruction of the Beis HaMikdash. Why did he see it fit to do so precisely at this time? One explanation can be that Yosef was bemoaning the divisiveness that had brought about his separation from his family. He understood that it would be this divisiveness in the future that would once again cause the destruction of the Beis HaMikdash.

While we see that Yosef represented total and complete *achdus*, how does that Midah enable him to defeat Eisav? In addition, how do we resolve the Midrash that states that it is not just Yosef, but "the children of Rachel," i.e. Binyamin as well, who can defeat Eisav?

The conflict between Yaakov and Eisav represents the greatest battle between two brothers in history. Even before they were born, the prophet predicted that there will be a constant struggle between the two, with one being successful and the other defeated. However, while these two siblings represent the epitome of sibling rivalry and dissension – albeit Yaakov representing the side of goodness and Eisav that of evil and wickedness – we can look at another two siblings who personified the very opposite. These siblings could have engaged in a similar controversy yet chose a different and very noble path. They were Leah and Rachel, two sisters who were also co-wives, a situation which *Chazal* term "צרות." Before Lavan deceived Yaakov into marrying both sisters, there was a real fear that the elder sister, Leah, would marry Eisav, Rivkah's oldest son. Indeed, even after Rachel married Yaakov, she feared that due to her barren state, Yaakov would divorce her and Eisav would marry her.

Despite the fear that that these two sisters had, this did not prevent Rachel from making the ultimate sacrifice. She relinquished her position as Yaakov's wife in order to save her sister from embarrassment. Rachel had no way of knowing that Yaakov would agree to marry her as a second wife – after all, this was a violation of the prohibition of marrying two sisters. As such, Rachel willingly put herself in the potential position of becoming Eisav's wife due to her love and loyalty towards her sister.

This adoration and devotion was reciprocated by Leah. When Leah became pregnant for the seventh time, she knew through prophecy that the fetus that she was carrying was a male, while Rachel was pregnant with a female. She realized that if Rachel would have less Shevatim than even the maidservants, Bilhah and Zilpah, her sister would be devastated. Although we know how much Leah yearned to have more Shevatim, she forsook having a seventh Shevet for Rachel's sake. As such, she davened to Hashem that their fetuses be switched. The relationship between Rachel and Leah is the epitome of *achdus*. The great love that existed between these sisters should be the model for all siblings in the future.

Yosef is chosen as the arch-enemy of Eisav, for in order to defeat the greatest sibling rival, he had to imbibe the lesson of the greatest sibling love. Yosef learned from his mother Rachel how to sacrifice everything for the sake of a sibling. Moreover, Yosef's very existence was only due to the love that Leah had for her sister. Although both Rachel and Leah displayed this ultimate *achdus*, Rachel's sacrifice is considered greater due to the potential outcome of her act. While Leah deprived herself from having another Shevet, Rachel knowingly put herself at risk of becoming Eisav's wife.

Yom Yerushalayim

We can now understand how the discrepancy between the Midrash and Gemara is actually complementary. Eisav is given over to the children of Rachel because they have inherited the values of sibling love and *achdus* carried out in a way that could have caused Rachel much pain and suffering. Because of Rachel's heroic act, she is rewarded in that Eisav will be given over into *her* hands. Yosef is mentioned specifically by the Gemara because on top of his being Rachel's son, his existence calls to mind Leah's act of sibling-love. This is especially appropriate according to those commentaries, such as the Yonason ben Uziel, who say that Yosef was actually conceived in Leah's womb and was switched into Rachel's womb as a result of Leah's prayer. Thus, Yosef was, in a sense, also a son of Leah, enabling him to carry the dual *zechus* of these two great *Imahos*, and making him the Shevet in whose hands Eisav's descendants will fall and be defeated and vanquished.

This teaching, that we achieve victory over our enemies only through *achdus,* was the lesson of the Six Day War. It was only when Premier Levi Eshkol formed a unity government that the mood of the country began to change. It was only when every party in the Knesset joined the government, when Menachem Begin was able to sit with Moshe Dayan, when the religious parties were able to join together with the irreligious parties, that they achieved the critical status of כאיש אחד בלב אחד. It was only at that moment of unity, harmony, and caring for each other that *HaKadosh Baruch Hu* performed נסים ונפלאות, great miracles and wonders.

The war and its aftermath brought tremendous respect and awe for Israel and its people throughout the world. From America to Russia, from Australia to South Africa, Torah institutions sprung up. The number of yeshivos and *batei midrashim* that began were almost as incredible as the miracles of the war itself. The problem, my friends, is that the *achdus*, the unity, friendship, and harmony did not last too long. Instead of it being a harbinger of the Moshiach, it all

Yom Yerushalayim

fell apart. Instead of it leading to greater commitment to Yiddishkeit and all that it represents, it lost its luster and its charm. We are and have been for so many years back to where we were before the war. We are bickering and name calling and fighting among ourselves. As such, there is no genuine *Shalom* among the Israelis themselves. There certainly is no longer any feeling of goodwill throughout the world towards the Jewish state.

If we would only take the lessons from Midbar Sinai, from Rachel and Leah, and from Yosef HaTzadik, things would definitely change. If we take it upon ourselves to think of and love others like ourselves, we would be much more successful. If we could once again act כאיש אחד בלב אחד, as one man with one heart, we will have made Hashem very happy. He will then once again shine His countenance upon us. At that time, no one will ever question the sovereignty of Yerushalayim, the city of peace. The world will finally acknowledge that the עיר דוד, the city which Dovid HaMelech designated as our capital almost 3,000 years ago, is unquestionably Jewish. We will once again, G-d willing, wake up one morning to the sound of the Shofar Gadol, the most beautiful wake up call. We will hear the words broadcast throughout the world – "הבית המקדש בידינו!"– "The Beis HaMikdash is in our hands!" As our *Chazal* have said, the Third Beis HaMikdash will come down from *Shamayim* completely built when we are worthy. We will hear the joyous words, "The Moshiach is here!" We will all experience peace and shalom, brotherhood and unity. Let us hope that this day will soon be here, Amen.

Shavuos

44. Our Ultimate Freedom
Shavuos 5736 (1976)
זמן מתן תורתינו

 The goal of each person and every nation is freedom and independence, the ability to make one's decisions based solely on whether it is beneficial or harmful to that specific individual or nation. Freedom, however, comes in all forms and fashions. A person can be physically let out of imprisonment and incarceration. An individual can do and act as he wishes. A nation may have the opportunity to choose its own leaders, pass its own legislation and govern and decide on its internal and external policies. In this context, the Jewish people are no different than any other nation. We love and respect liberty and equality. We have always been at the forefront of every movement whose goals were the elimination of oppression, servitude, and subjugation of the individual or the masses.

 However, in this universal quest, the Jewish road to freedom diverged from that of our non-Jewish neighbors, and we "took the one less traveled by." We maintain that physical freedom by itself is not sufficient. It is merely the first step in a long and difficult process toward the final goal and destination – spiritual freedom and holiness. In fact, the holiday of Pesach, which was observed seven weeks ago, has not, in our understanding, ended. Pesach represents the Exodus from Egypt of our forefathers three thousand years ago. They were physically freed from their long and arduous oppression and servitude. We commemorate that event with song, prayer, and a host of other symbols. But we do not end there. Our celebration and commemoration of the physical freeing of our people is continued fifty days later with the holiday of Shavuos. This is indicated by the

Mishnah and Talmud where Shavuos is called "*Atzeres*," which can mean not only "solemn assembly" but also "closing festival." This is so because in a great sense it concludes the festival of Pesach.

The Jew realizes that physical freedom is not in any way an end in itself. The physical Exodus from Egypt only gave our forebears the opportunity to proceed to Mt. Sinai and prepare themselves for the theophany, the great revelation by the Almighty. It was only when the Jews were presented with the holy Torah and became the chosen people of the L-rd that they experienced total freedom and independence. For only he who is bound to the commandments of the Torah is truly free.

In fact, our sages in *Pirkei Avos*, Ethics of the Fathers, taught:
והלוחות מעשה אלקים המה והמכתב מכתב אלקים הוא חרות על הלוחות אל תקרא חרות אלא חירות שאין לך בן חורין אלא מי שעוסק בתלמוד תורה
'And the Tablets were the handiwork of G-d, and the writing was the writing of G-d, engraved on the Tablets.' Do not read "engraved," but rather, "freedom," for there is no free man except one who is engaged in the study of Torah.

The purpose then of the Jew's performing the Mitzvos, the divine commandments, in every capacity is to assure his own future and guarantee the survival of the world. Shavuos is the festival which commemorates the Jews receiving the Torah. Our most spiritual holiday is thus considered the end, the closing period of Pesach, our most physical celebration.

Chazal designate Shavuos as "*Zeman Matan Toraseinu*," the season of the giving of the law. Even though Hashem revealed Himself only once in history, when the Torah was given at Mt. Sinai, it did not end there. It is as if Hashem constantly gives the Torah over to each and every generation. Each subsequent *dor* has the responsibility of making the *Matan Toraseinu* an ongoing process by giving over their understanding of Torah to the succeeding generation. It is as if Hashem appears *b'chol dor v'dor*, in each era, and gives the Torah anew to that generation.

Perhaps that is what the famous Midrash means when it says that at the time of *Matan Torah*, at that very moment in history, every Jewish *neshamah* was in attendance. Each of us, no matter when we were born, stood as one at the foot of Mt. Sinai. Together, we heard the words of Hashem reverberate to us. That is why each era of Jews must reaffirm its acceptance and commitment to the totality of the Torah. We do not rely upon the willingness of that first group of Jews thousands of years ago to adapt themselves and transform their lifestyles into one acceptable and desirable to Hashem. We must renew the solemn declaration that all that is contained within the Torah will be adhered to and observed unquestionably and unconditionally.

The Midrash in *Yalkut Shimoni* expands on this theme. It quotes a sentence in *Sefer Mishlei* (6:1) which says:

בְּנִי אִם עָרַבְתָּ לְרֵעֶךָ ...

"My son, if you have guaranteed for your friend."

This verse, according to the Midrash, indicates that at the time of the Revelation of the Torah at Mt. Sinai all Israel guaranteed for each other. The Almighty said to the Jewish people: "Give guarantors that you will observe the Torah." The children of Israel offered the *Avos*, Avraham, Yitzchak, and Yaakov as their insurers. Yet Hashem refused them, saying that they were still indebted to Him and cannot stand for themselves, let alone underwrite the future of the Jewish people. "Give Me sureties who are not indebted to Me, your children," said the Almighty. The children were immediately brought to *HaKadosh Baruch Hu*, and He said to them: "Do you stand as guarantors and certify that if I present your parents with the Torah they will observe it, and if not, you will be responsible for them?" They agreed whole-heartedly. After reciting the Ten Commandments and hearing them respond affirmatively to each one,

Shavuos

Hashem said: "Through your mouths I give the Torah to My people," as it is written in Tehillim (8:3):

מִפִּי עוֹלְלִים וְיֹנְקִים יִסַּדְתָּ עֹז

"From the mouth of babes and sucklings You have founded strength."

The Jews at Har Sinai faithfully promised to study the Torah and teach it to their children and to their children's children so that there would never be a time when this most important link in Judaism would be broken.

Thus, my friends, each of us, both you and I, not only have a great heritage and tradition from which to draw strength and sustenance, we also have a most difficult challenge. Each generation before us has fulfilled its commitment to G-d. They have served as the proud and dedicated guarantors of the survival of Torah.

In every capacity and in every area of life, the Jew served as a *Kiddush Hashem,* a sanctification of the Holy Name of G-d. He served his G-d faithfully and totally. He rendered great service to his fellowmen. Most importantly, he made the Torah his existence. The Bible, the Talmud, the Codes were all brought to life. They were certainly an עץ חיים היא למחזיקים בה: "A Tree of life for those that clung to it." Now, we are the next link in this great chain of history. Whether the Torah will continue to survive and whether the world will endure tomorrow is dependent solely upon our generation and how we conduct ourselves today.

If we follow in the right path set for us by our ancestors, if we lead a life dedicated to Torah and Mitzvos, then we, the Torah, and our entire civilization, will endure, grow, and develop. What then must we do to demonstrate the unique quality of our Jewishness? We must first decide once and for all that we are not like other people or other nations. While we must out of necessity live in a world which is not uniquely Jewish, we cannot, nor dare not, be influenced by the corrupt, immoral, and dishonest society around us.

Instead of influencing our non-Jewish friends and neighbors to accept and practice the Jewish concepts of brotherly love, tolerance of our fellow man, belief in G-d, and the distribution of charity, we seem to be relinquishing our value system and accepting in toto that of our secular associates. We are taking the words of the great Jewish convert Rus – the former Moabite princess who became the Jewish ancestress of Dovid HaMelech – and turning them around to suit our own purposes. We appear to be saying to the non-Jewish world: "Entreat us not to leave you and return from following after you; for where you go, we will go, and where you live, we will live; your people are our people, and your G-d will be our G-d. Where you die, we will die, and there will we be buried." In order to survive as Jews, we must very quickly abandon this self-defeating course.

Second, and most important, we must begin to have a thorough understanding of what is required of us as Jews. Being Jewish does not merely mean being born to a Jewish mother or converted properly into the Jewish fold. To be a Jew is indeed an art. It requires knowledge and information. In order to be a good and a committed Jew, one who can serve as a shining example to the rest of his people, and, indeed, to the non-Jewish world as well, it is crucial that we be aware of who we are and why we are. We must get back to basics. We must study our history, our laws and customs, our constitution and our entire legal system. In a word, my friends, we must become well-versed in the Torah and all its many commentaries.

Only he who knows the essence of Judaism will be able to properly and effectively practice his faith. We have been called the *"Am HaSefer,"* the People of the Book. The Book that is referred to is not the great American novel, nor is it historical or science fiction collections. The *Sefer* that we belong to is the holy Torah which we long ago made a commitment to learn, study and practice. *Avos D'R' Nasan* tells us that the teachings of the Torah are hard to acquire but easy to lose. It is high-time that the People of the Book begin to know and understand their Book.

The Jewish position in the world has become so precarious and so unpredictable that it is impossible for even the least religious among us not to realize that the time has come for Jews to change their objectives and perspectives. Instead of spending all our time and energy in wooing, placating and courting those who are bent upon destroying us, it would do us well to turn to the only One Who has our interest at heart. If Jews the world over would begin to have בטחון בה', complete and total faith in the Almighty and study the Torah and practice His commandments, we would then be in a most favorable position. For at that time we would need fear no human being. When we demonstrate in no uncertain terms that we are the children of G-d and the people of the Almighty, Hashem will certify that He is our G-d, our Father, and protector.

Let us then on this Shavuos demonstrate our true freedom through the reacceptance of the Torah. On this Yom Tov, which commemorates Israel's pledge to G-d of *Na'aseh V'Nishma*, we once again proclaim, "We will perform and pay strict attention to all that you demand of us." We will thereby fulfill the promise made by our ancestors and the oath that we, their children, took upon ourselves. And by so doing, we will in no unmistaken terms demonstrate, for the entire world to see, the art of being a Jew. Amen.

45. Who is a Jew?
Shavuos-Yizkor
מגילת רות

During the past number of years, one of the major religious ideological questions to appear on the Jewish scene was not a novel one. It was merely a repeat, a re-run of a question long-since asked and answered. It nevertheless, crops up time and time again. The question was asked 3500 years ago by the pharaohs of Egypt. It was asked by Torquemada, the vengeful and sadistic head of the Spanish Inquisition. It was asked by Hitler ימח שמו 80 years ago, and it was also asked by every despot and dictator whose goal was to eliminate and exterminate the Jewish people. Most importantly, להבדיל אלף הבדלות, it was asked by Hashem at Mount Sinai. The question is: "Who is a Jew?"

On the surface, this query is rather simple and elementary. Its response need not be profound nor exhaustive. Who is a Jew? A Jew is one who is either born of a Jewish mother or who converts to Judaism according to Halachic requirements.

The Conservative and Reform movements have tried over the past few generations to change this definition and make it easier for an individual wishing to enter the Jewish fold. In fact, the Conservative movement, this past year, has made a most radical change. They have decided to accept as members of their congregations the non-Jewish spouses of intermarried couples.

It is however, unnecessary to comment on this anti-Halachic approach. Rather, I believe that this question on a deeper level has a great deal of relevance for us today. "Who is a Jew?" can be understood to mean, "What is a Jew?" What does it mean to be Jewish? The question is not, "What is required of one who wishes to become a Jew?" That has already been made clear by our sages from

Maimonides to Rabbi Yosef Cairo to Rabbi Moshe Feinstein. What it means is, "What obligations and commitments must I make to demonstrate my Jewishness and my allegiance to my people and my G-d?

This question is, I believe, quite relevant now when we celebrate and commemorate the great event of the revelation of the Torah by G-d to the Jewish people.

There are two questions that I wish to pose. With a comprehensive analysis of both, I believe that we will understand what it means to be a Jew. First, the Torah, that great Divine invention, was given to the Jewish people in the most unlikely surroundings, a desert. Why was this so? Second, one of the most beautiful customs of the Shavuos holiday is the reading of the Book of Ruth. What significance does the Book of Ruth have with the Festival of Shavuos?

At first glance, it would appear that the Torah was given in an altogether strange environment. Perhaps it would have been more dramatic if Hashem would have brought all the Jews to Jerusalem, gather them on the Temple Mount, and there present them with the Torah. This would have certainly been very powerful. This would have made a greater impression upon the Jews than in a parched, sun-bleached empty desert. However, the fact of the matter is that this was not the case.

The Torah was given in the desert for a specific reason. It was to teach the Jewish nation that in order to follow and observe the precepts of the Torah, in order to be an authentic and good Jew, one need not live in Jerusalem, in Poland, or in Russia. To be a good Jew is something which is not dependent upon geographic location. You can be as good a Jew in Anchorage, Alaska, as you can be in Tel Aviv. You can be as good a Jew in New Jersey as you can be in B'nai Brak.

Shavuos

There was a time when Jews did not nor could not believe that this was true. Years ago, it was said that only in specific Jewish havens such as the great Jewish centers of Europe could one authentically remain true to his faith and heritage. America, that *Goyishe Medinah;* there, even the stones in the streets are *treife*. To be a complete and total Jew in America is impossible. Forty and fifty years ago, eulogies were being written about Orthodox Jewry in this country. We were being consigned to obsolescence.

Some Jewish thinkers today continue to maintain that Judaism in America, and especially Orthodox Judaism, is reaching the threshold of disappearance. This, my friends, is not the case. Instead of being relics of the past, traditional, legitimate, authentic Judaism today is the wave of the future. There is no longer a question of whether Judaism in America will survive. The only question is what kind of Judaism will survive. We believe that only those Jews who are prepared to make a commitment to the totality of Jewish life can thrive in the climate of this society. Only those Jews who are prepared to stand up and be counted will survive. It is those Jews who assert their independence and freedom, rather than being slaves to their desires and fancies, who will be able to transmit these values to the next generation. The greatest freedom, whether it was at Sinai 3,500 years ago or today, is the Jew's willingness to accept, observe, and practice the limitations on his physical freedom. In this manner, the Jew thereby liberates one's soul to become its true, spiritual self. The true עם חפשי are those who are prepared to make sacrifices, who are prepared to endure suffering and afflictions, who are ready to accept the yoke of Hashem like a Rus.

Some of our Rabbis tell us that the Book of Rus is read on Shavuos at the time of the Giving of the Torah so that we might be aware of the genealogy of Dovid HaMelech, the ancestor of Moshiach, from Rus the Moabite. This is done on Shavuos because the end of the Megillah recounts Dovid's ancestry and Dovid was born on Shavuos and also died on this holiday.

The Gaon of Vilna says that from the time of her birth, Rus was worthy of accepting the yoke of Mitzvos. In fact, the very letters of her name bear witness to this fact. The letters of רות add up to 606, which, taken together with the seven Noachide laws, add up to 613 Commandments.

We are told in *Yalkut Shimoni* on Rus that by reading this Megillah on Shavuos we are taught that the Torah is given only through suffering and affliction. Rus' entry into the Jewish fold did not come easily. This Moabite princess, daughter of the King of Moav, expressed her deep personal and empathetic feelings for the Jews not only in good and affluent times. Rather, she was loyal and helpful when the situation of the Jews appeared most bleak and the future was in doubt.

During a famine, when she experienced the loss of her husband, her brother-in-law, and her father in law, her unswerving support never for one moment diminished. Rus expressed her friendship and love for Israel at a time of national catastrophe when the future of the Jewish people was in grave jeopardy. She became a *ger Tzedek*, the epitome and ideal of the righteous and authentic convert to Judaism.

There is no doubt my friends that whether one is becoming Jewish or one is being reawakened to Judaism, the traits of authenticity, genuineness, and commitment are necessary. Being Jewish is not easy. The old saying, *"Is ez shver tzu zein a Yid,"* "It is difficult to be a Jew," should really be amended to read, *"Is ez shverer tzu zein an erlicher Yid,"* "It is even harder to be and remain a practicing and observant Jew." If you were born a Jew, you weren't born into ease. You were born into a life which is controlled by the Mitzvos, a life lived according to the commandments of G-d. This requires stamina, endurance, conviction, and conscientiousness.

Shavuos

While observant Judaism may appear hard and difficult, there is certainly a light at the end of the tunnel. Even though Rus lived through traumatic times, even though she could have turned her back on Judaism, she persevered and remained true to our faith. She was subsequently rewarded with seeing her great-grandson Dovid and his son Shlomo achieve the highest of honors. They were chosen as the kings of Israel. They began the dynasty which will eventually bring the Moshiach.

Who is a Jew? A Jew is one whose heart cries out when he observes his coreligionists throughout the world being subjected to anti-Semitic attacks. A Jew is one who will actively work for candidates who will help, assist, and support Jewish causes and try to defeat the enemies of our people. A Jew is one who davens and is concerned about the welfare of the citizens of Eretz Yisrael. A Jew is one who attempts to help his coreligionists when they are impoverished. A Jew is one who gives aid, comfort, and sage-advice to the widows, the orphans, and those stricken with illness. A Jew is thus one who was not merely born a Jew, but one who knows, understands, and observes Jewish laws and principles.

Who then is a Jew? A Jew is one who lives his life from the cradle to the grave, from birth to death, living, breathing, and practicing Judaism as it should be. A Jew is one who knows that he is the bearer of a great and ancient tradition which must be transmitted and passed on to another generation.

It does not matter where we are. We can reside in the most imperfect surroundings and environment. We can transform a wilderness into a blooming and vegetative Garden of Eden. We can change deserts into paradises if we just act as real and true Jews. A world without Torah, though on the surface may appear to be a paradise, will quickly become a wasteland. A world with Torah, where the L-rd reigns supreme, though on the surface may appear

Shavuos

vast and foreboding like a desert, can indeed become an enduring and perpetual paradise. The challenge is ours.

The Ohr HaChaim said that the name of Shavuos is to be pronounced Shevuos. The reason is that the term "Shevuos" comprises the idea of oaths in addition to weeks. One oath was taken by Hashem Who promised that He would not exchange us for another people. And the second oath we took unto G-d that we would not exchange Him for another. G-d, my friends, has fulfilled His oath. The task is for us to fulfill our part of the agreement.

In the next few moments we will recite the Yizkor service. At that time, we memorialize our loved ones who have passed away. It would do us well to recall their faith and devotion to their heritage and tradition. Life was often not very sweet or pleasant for them. They lived in rather difficult and arduous times, when being Jewish was no easy matter. Their commitment to Jewish principles and Torah often cost them their jobs, their financial support, and their very pride.

Our ancestors did not waver. They did not give up. They did not abandon their people even when to do so would have been quite logical, simple, and materialistically rewarding. No, they drew closer and closer to the Almighty and His way of life. They transmitted this love, this concern, and this affection for our religion to you, their children, as an everlasting and enduring inheritance.

Let us this morning, as we remember our real Yiddishe mothers and fathers, try to emulate their lives. Let us vow to become more dedicated Jews. In that way, in a very short time, the question, "Who is a Jew," no matter what the interpretation, will no longer be germane or applicable. At that time, the entire world will know that each of us is a living and breathing example of what the true and genuine Jew is. We will bring about the universal glorification of G-d's name amongst all mankind, thereby creating the ultimate *Kiddush Hashem.* May this day come very soon, Amen.

46. Yizkor: Our Unique Memorial Day
Shavuos
חג הביכורים

This past Monday, we joined with our fellow citizens of the United States and commemorated Memorial Day. This day was originally set aside to keep alive the memory of the hundreds of thousands of Americans who served in the Armed Forces and who sacrificed their lives in defense of our country. In recent years, however, this day has lost its significance. It has become just the end of a three-day holiday in which businesses are closed and people spend their time leisurely and in comfort. What a contrast this is to our own Yom HaZikaron, the Jewish Memorial Day, our Yizkor.

Today, the second day of Shavuos, is one of the four times during the Jewish year that we pause for a few moments from our hustle and bustle and take a break from our very hectic schedule to reflect upon our loved ones who have departed this world. Unlike the secular Memorial Day, we recall all Jews who have passed away. We sincerely believe that every Jew who ever lived was a soldier in the Armed Forces of the Almighty. Every Jewish mother and father, every Jewish son and daughter made a manifold and significant contribution to the development and growth of the Jewish people.

Unlike the American celebration of Memorial Day, the Jewish observance has not diminished with the passage of time. If anything, many Rabbis lament the fact that while many people often neglect the other areas of Jewish observance and practice, the Yom HaZikaron, the four-time-a-year-Yizkor is the most well attended service in the synagogue.

What is it that we are to remember today? Are we to recall the manner in which our loved ones amassed their fortunes? Are we to reflect on the good times and fun experiences that we had with our dearly departed? This certainly is not what Yizkor service is all about. Our Chazal would never have designated these days as times to reminisce and be reminded of the past if they would not impart a message of great moral significance for the future.

We are to focus on the ideas and thoughts which were so precious to our elders. We are to recall how they sacrificed unselfishly, how they gave up a future of prosperity and ease in order to remain loyal and devoted to their G-d and to their religion. That, in essence, is the goal of Yizkor.

If we think of our parents and remember how they observed Shabbos and Yom Tov, how they never partook of food except in places that were strictly kosher, then we have fulfilled the requirements of this day. If we recall our departed sitting in front of their *Sifrei Kodesh,* the holy books of our tradition, learning, studying, and teaching us the laws and regulations of our faith, we have done them a great service indeed. If we call to mind the time that our parents often donated their last nickels and dimes to charity so that one less fortunate than they could enjoy his Shabbos meal, we are then treasuring and cherishing their memory.

When we think back to the times of how they stood up and made their voices heard when it came to Jewish causes and issues, we are certainly making sure that they never be erased from our minds. Yizkor therefore is more than a time for nostalgia. It is much more than taking time off and remembering those of our beloved who are no longer with us. Yizkor, should serve as a period when we think of and remember the past while at the same time giving us inspiration, encouragement and the ability to face the future.

Judaism, my friends, is a religion with very deep and strong roots in the past. In all our *Tefillos* and texts, we fondly recall the good old days of yesteryear when we were firmly entrenched in our own land, without serious problems or difficulties. However, while we must show reverence for the days that are no more, we must certainly not ignore or pay scant attention to the present or the future. While we gather our motivation and stimulation from the days of antiquity, our creative thoughts and prudent policies for tomorrow are all planned and decided upon today.

Our religion thus encompasses the best of the past and the present but in essence is ultimately most concerned with the future. We are to utilize the lifestyles of our loved ones and have them serve as our examples and guides for the future. Thus today, on Yizkor, on the Jewish Memorial Day, we are to do a great deal more than reminisce and look back to the past and think of our long-departed relatives. We are to attempt to perpetuate and keep alive their memory and the ideals and goals that were so important to them.

Shavuos is a festival in which this idea can be readily applied. The Torah (Devarim 26:3-10) tells us that this holiday was a time for bringing the Bikurim, the first fruits from one's field and vineyards, to the House of G-d in Jerusalem. Whoever went up to the Beis HaMikdash for the Yom Tov of Shavuos brought his Bikurim with him in order to fulfill the Biblical decree (Devarim 26:2):

וְלָקַחְתָּ מֵרֵאשִׁית כָּל פְּרִי הָאֲדָמָה אֲשֶׁר תָּבִיא מֵאַרְצְךָ אֲשֶׁר ה' אֱלֹקֶיךָ נֹתֵן לָךְ וְשַׂמְתָּ בַטֶּנֶא וְהָלַכְתָּ אֶל הַמָּקוֹם אֲשֶׁר יִבְחַר ה' אֱלֹקֶיךָ לְשַׁכֵּן שְׁמוֹ שָׁם:

And you shall take from the first of all the fruit of the land which you shall bring from your land which the L-rd your G-d has given you; and you shall place it in a basket, and you shall go to the place which the L-rd your G-d will choose to rest His name there.

Harvesting season in ancient Israel began at Pesach time. Then, the barley crops began to be harvested and the Omer was brought to the Temple as a thanksgiving offering. The Bikurim, the offering of the first ripe fruits, were not brought before Shavuos. This Mitzvah contained within it a testimony of great significance. Each Jew who brought these first fruits thereby testified that he was not ungrateful or haughty, that he had not forgotten that it was only because of G-d's lovingkindness that he had become materially successful. The Mishnah in the Tractate Bikurim explains how these first fruits were to be set apart. When a person went down to his field and saw a ripe fig, a ripe cluster of grapes, or a ripe pomegranate, he then tied a piece of string upon it and declared: "These are Bikurim."

Today, when we no longer have the Beis HaMikdash in Jerusalem, the Mitzvah of Bikurim is no longer applicable. However, the commandments of contributing part of our hard-earned resources to the House of G-d did not cease with the destruction of the Beis HaMikdash. The sanctity of the one Temple in Jerusalem was divided throughout the world and transformed into the *Mikdashei Me'at*, the smaller sanctuaries, the houses of worship in each Jewish community around the world. Our parents and loved ones thoroughly observed this Mitzvah. They were most instrumental in making certain that the shuls and Batei Midrash were well supported and financed. If we today would only learn from their deeds and follow in their footsteps and help maintain our shuls, our yeshivos, and our educational centers, then we would help guarantee the survival of Judaism throughout the world.

Our loved ones were also greatly concerned for the spiritual survival of Judaism. They devoted their lives to observe the Mitzvos. If we wish to keep their memory and their acts alive, it would do us well to emulate their lifestyles and their commitment to the furtherance of Jewish knowledge. Let us learn all that we can about our tradition and our faith and let us try to practice every law and principle of Judaism.

Although many of our departed have not been with us for quite some time, we can indeed perpetuate their memory. We can make them come to life again by following their example and by patterning our lives after theirs. No matter where they lived, in the hovels of Poland and Russia, in the ghettos of Germany and Italy, in Spain during its golden era, or on the free shores of the United States, our relatives were always concerned for other Jews besides themselves. They were determined to keep Judaism physically alive at all costs, no matter what the sacrifice. When one Jew bled, when one Jew was in pain, when one Jew was despondent, they too felt his anguish, his torment, and his suffering. They would not rest until they could, with their limited ability and resources, help alleviate and sooth his wounds. This was true Jewish theology. This was sincere Jewish living.

If we would act on behalf of our fellow Jews throughout the world whenever and wherever the situation requires it and do so because of our heritage and because of our upbringing, then the lives of our loved ones would not have been in vain. They would have taught us a lesson by which we can survive and help guarantee the future of our people. If our voices cry out for the rights and liberties of our brethren throughout the world, we will certainly help them overcome their difficulties. If we are constantly vigilant on behalf of our brothers and sisters in the State of Israel, then we will do our share to help their continued growth and development. We will then have done our part in guaranteeing that Israel survives, thrives, and becomes a beacon of light to the nations of the world.

If we become actively involved in the affairs of the American Jewish community, if we act as Jews first and then as Americans, if we put our own interests before those of the general American community, we will have acted in a most noble manner. We will have guaranteed that Jewish life on this continent will continue to grow and flourish. By so doing, we will gain the respect and admiration of our non-Jewish neighbors. Together, we will help make America become a stronger and more humane country. Our society will become one based on ethics and morality. Eventually, we will export our values to the rest of the world. We will then all be able to live in peace, harmony, and tranquility.

If we wish to utilize this Yom HaZikaron, our Jewish Memorial Day, properly and effectively, then we must decide once and for all to devote ourselves body and soul to the ideals, concepts, and principles espoused, taught, and exemplified by our dearly departed loved ones. Their prayers will become our prayers, their laws and customs will be observed by us. Their never-ending fight for Jewish survival and development will become our battle. Their contributions to the synagogues, their modern-day reenactment of the Shavuos Bikurim, will be readily adopted by us. Let us make Yizkor day not a time in which we remember the dead. Rather, let us make it a day when we assure our loved ones that they have not really died at all. They live and will continue to live on eternally through our actions and our deeds. Amen.

47. Transforming a Desert into a Paradise
Shavuos 5734 (1974)
פרשת במדבר וחג השבועות

Each year on the Shabbos just preceding Shavuos, the Torah portion which is read is the first section of the book of Bamidbar, the fourth book of the Chumash. The fact that this section is read just prior to the Yom Tov of Shavuos is no accident. It was planned by our *Chachamim*, and we often double up on some of the preceding Torah portions in order to get to Parshas Bamidbar just before this holiday.

Many of our rabbis are puzzled by this. What is the connection between the fourth book of the Torah and the holiday of Shavuos? In fact, if we were to analyze the meaning of *bamidbar* and Shavuos, our difficulty would be compounded. *Bamidbar* means "in the desert," a wasteland in which nothing can grow or bring forth life. Shavuos is also known as *Chag HaBikurim,* the Festival of first fruits. It is in the season of early summer, a time of blossoming and growth. Thus, these two concepts – Shavuos and Midbar – seem not only dissimilar in nature but even contradictory. Why then are we instructed to link these two together?

Through closer observation we can readily discern the intention of our rabbis. A world without Torah, they say, is a barren wasteland. It is a place where man cannot grow spiritually in stature and in knowledge. However, if Torah is introduced into the world, then the *midbar* of this world can be transformed into *Bikurim*, a paradise, where man can grow to the loftiest of spiritual heights.

The first man, Adam, was placed by G-d in a paradise, the Garden of Eden. This was to be his permanent domain. His surroundings were superb and most conducive to great achievements and advancements. However, without Torah and by not carrying out his responsibilities, man's setting was changed from a paradise to a barren wilderness. Man was no longer able to live in peace and tranquility but was forced to survive through hard work and the sweat of his brow. In the ensuing generations, centuries, and millennia, Adam's descendants lived in a most corrupted and evil manner. They brought the world to the verge of destruction and annihilation.

Out of the midst of this global depravity, on a small mountain amidst the wasteland of the Sinai desert, the Torah was given by G-d to the Jewish people. The world was now given another opportunity to cultivate their wilderness and transform it into a paradise.

The holiday of Shavuos does not only commemorate the giving of the Torah; it is also the re-creation of the world. *Chazal* saw the giving of the Torah as the completion of creation, the filling in of the empty physical structure created years before. In fact, our rabbis say that G-d made the entire creation dependent upon the acceptance of the Torah by the Jewish people, for without Torah, the world is incomplete and worthless. With Torah, however, the world is complete and extremely valuable.

Today, on this anniversary of the giving of the Torah, we should strive to learn all aspects of Torah and internalize its teachings. We should study both the written Torah as well as the oral Torah – the Talmud, its commentaries, and all other aspects of Jewish law. We should impart this rich heritage, its great values and traditions, to our children, our families, and our friends. Only in this way will we be assured that the world will continue to grow and develop and be transformed from a *midbar* to *bikurim*, from a parched wasteland to a blooming, blossoming, and growing area. In this way, we will certainly guarantee that Torah will continue to be of paramount importance in our lives and in our hearts. The world then will never again be on the brink of destruction and annihilation. We will assure that the Gan Eden of old will once again spring forth.

And we will, with the help of *HaKadosh Baruch Hu,* once again live in the beautiful and wonderful Paradise.

Today, my friends, we are celebrating and commemorating a most illustrious and glorious chapter in the history of our shul. After much hard work and many months of learning and studying about the true essentials of the sanctity of the synagogue, קדושת בית הכנסת, we are very proud to dedicate the installation of our new, kosher *Mechitzah*.

Many people have been responsible for this great event. From the bottom of my heart, I want to thank each and every one of you for all your efforts and your contributions to this great project. By your actions, you have placed a great deal of faith and trust in me, and for that I am most appreciative. I hope, with the help of G-d, never to let you down.

Today we begin embarking together on a new and historic journey. Because of your help and assistance, we have truly transformed our shul. We have taken a virtual מדבר, an empty and parched desert, and made it into a most glorious paradise.

By our combined actions, we have, today, become very true to our name. From this point on we can say, "From Sinai came real, authentic, and genuine Torah." From this day forward, we can truly represent our synagogue's name, "Sinai Torath Chaim."

May we go מחיל אל חיל, from strength to strength. May we continue together to do G-d's work for many more wonderful and glorious years. Mazel Tov to each of us. Amen.

Postscript: Before accepting the rabbinate at Sinai Torath Chaim in September, 1973, I was faced with a major dilemma. Because the shul did not have a Mechitzah, I was uncertain as to whether I should accept their offer. The shul always adhered to the separation of men and women during davening. The congregation was strictly Orthodox in every way. However, they never installed a Mechitzah, a physical barrier between the sexes.

I posed this question to my Rosh HaYeshivah, HaRav Yosef Dov Soloveitchik zt"l and to Rav Moshe Feinstein zt"l. In addition, I discussed the matter at length with Rabbi Dr. Norman Lamm, a dear family friend who later became the President of Yeshiva University, my alma matter. They each enthusiastically encouraged me to accept the position. However, they added one caveat. They said that if I am unsuccessful in convincing the shul to change its policy during the term of my first contract, which was for two years, I must resign my position.

During my first year at the shul, I taught classes, gave shiurim, and met privately with many members on the topic of קדושת בית הכנסת, *the sanctity of the synagogue. With the help and guidance of Hashem, within seven months of arriving in Hillside, the members of the shul voted unanimously to install a Mechitzah in the main sanctuary.*

On the first day of Shavuos, 1974, on the very day that we commemorate Matan Torah, our receiving the Torah, the great theophany, our shul was able to be transformed from a veritable spiritual desert into a beautiful and glorious Paradise.

I shall never forget that magnificent and historic day. It is one which I look back to with much pride and satisfaction. I thank the Ribono shel Olam for giving me the opportunity to effect even a small change in the Halachic structure of my shul as well as the religious observance of my congregants. RHG.

Tisha B'Av

48. A Day to Mourn; a Time to Hope

Tisha b'Av, the ninth day of the month of Av, is undoubtedly the blackest day on the Jewish calendar. This day, sadly, commemorates numerous catastrophes which have befallen our people. Both Temples in Jerusalem were destroyed – the first by the Babylonians in 586 BCE; the second by the Romans in 70 CE. The Bar Kochba revolt against Rome was crushed on this day in 135 C.E., whereupon so many hundreds of thousands of our people were killed. The Golden age of Spanish Jewry that existed for hundreds of years ended on this day in 1492 as thousands upon thousands of Jews were expelled from the country which they called home. In the 20th century, Tisha b'Av marked the commencement of World War I. Thousands of Jews were killed and many hundreds of thousands more were displaced from their homes and suffered greatly during this so called "Great War."

Tisha b'Av was established as a mournful day very early in our history. When the 12 Tribal representatives returned to the Jewish people after spying on Eretz Canaan, 10 out of the 12 spies brought back a very negative report. They reported that there were giants living in the land and that they could not overcome or overtake them. They were worried that they would surely be slaughtered and annihilated. Unfortunately, the people sided with the spies rather than with Hashem and Moshe Rabbeinu. *HaKadosh Baruch Hu* had assured them that they would be able to get into the land and would be able to conquer any and all opponents. The Jews, instead, decided to go against G-d that night, and they cried bitter and mournful tears.

For this act of treason and insubordination, Hashem decreed that the Jews would be forced to wander in the desert for 40 years.

They were not able to enter into the Land of Israel immediately as planned. In addition, Hashem designated that day, the ninth day of Av, as a day in which the Jewish people would in the future experience great consequential tragedies and tremendous loss. This would always occur on this "day of infamy."

For thousands of years, Jews the world over observed this day of mourning by fasting, gathering together for public prayer, and by asking G-d to restore Israel to its former majestic glory. However, for the last 200 years or so, this day has become perhaps the most neglected and most misunderstood of our major festivals and feasts. The special significance of Tisha b'Av has been especially diminished in the eyes of many by the establishment of the State of Israel in 1948. The question arises: why is it necessary to continue mourning catastrophes which occurred 2,000 years ago? These questioners maintain that since Israel has been reestablished as a Jewish national home, the observance of Tisha b'Av has become obsolete. Instead of prolonging our mourning, let this day's past catastrophes become part of our historical record. It belongs together with the many other events which have helped mold and develop Judaism and for which there is no longer any public observance.

This question has been compounded by the events that occurred during the Six Day War in 1967. With the Israelis' capture of the Kotel and the Old City of Yerushalayim, many new questions have arisen. Many Israeli rabbis, most notably, the late chief rabbi, Rabbi Shlomo Goren *zt"l*, have questioned the continued recitation of certain *Tefillos* on Tisha b'Av. These prayers speak of seeing Jerusalem in its squalor, devastation, and loss of grandeur. Today, these rabbis say, Yerushalayim has been restored to its beauty and elegance of yesteryear. Thus, these *Tefillos* should be either deleted or changed.

While the questions above may reflect sincere theological discussions by faithful Jews, the attitude towards Tisha b'Av by unaffiliated Jews is deeply concerning. While most Jews throughout the world observe most of the Yom Tovim in one form or another, it appears that this is not the case at all with Tisha b'Av. A Reform website has this to say regarding the current relevance of Tisha b'Av: "In contrast to traditional streams of Judaism, liberal Judaism never has assigned a central religious role to the ancient Temple. Therefore, mourning the destruction of the Temple may not be particularly meaningful to liberal Jews." This website goes on to dispute *Chazal's* assertion that both *Batei Mikdash* were destroyed on this day. It finally concedes that Tisha b'Av might be observed as a day to commemorate other tragedies that have befallen the Jewish people, although how they arrived at this specific date on the calendar must remain a mystery. It is most telling that the Reform house of worship is known as a "Temple" and not a synagogue. This change of name was intentional indeed. As confirmed by the above quoted statement, Reform Judaism has no need for a Temple in Jerusalem as they already have their Temple. If such is their attitude, it is no surprise that they have wiped away the mourning on this day.

Although this attitude gives us an additional reason to mourn on Tisha b'Av, we might have an easier time excusing those Jews who live in the diaspora for not appreciating the message of this day. However, it is most painful that even in Eretz Yisrael, there are record number of Israelis who do not care about this most special day. In fact, just this past Tisha b'Av, it was reported that in Tel Aviv, instead of recognizing and commemorating the loss that this צום represents, there was a colossal act of depravity. 60,000 Jewish Israelis took part in a march standing up for the rights and protection of gays and lesbians throughout the State of Israel.

This act in itself is abominable and horrific. However, this *chilul Hashem* was compounded even more because of the day that they chose to march. One of the reasons the first Beis HaMikdash was destroyed was precisely because of immorality. Now, on the very day that we remember and commemorate that צרה, they participated in a march for the very cause of our great calamity. Such an act in the Holy Land on Tisha b'Av itself could, G-d forbid, cause further devastation to our people.

Aside from the question of the relevance of Tisha b'Av in our current day and age, there is a second problem related to the Halachic structure of Tisha b'Av. On this day, as opposed to other Jewish fast days, *Tachanun* and *Selichos*, the penitential *Tefillos* recited on all other fast days, are omitted. Our *Chachamim* tell us that in spite of its sadness, in spite of its gloom, Tisha b'Av is a Yom Tov, a festival, and it is described as such in the Shulchan Aruch, the Code of Jewish Law. How is it possible, they ask, that this, the most mournful and saddest of all Jewish days, is to be considered a holiday? This is compounded especially when we see that the lesser fast days which do not commemorate as much gloom and destruction as Tisha b'Av are not in themselves considered holidays.

These problems have plagued me for some time, but they have become more perplexing when Tisha b'Av took on an added dimension, one of deep personal meaning. For on Tisha b'Av in 1971, 47 years ago, my mentor and beloved uncle, Rabbi Hyman Tuchman ע"ה, passed away at the premature age of 49. My uncle was like a second father to me. Unfortunately, he never married. Thus, he viewed my sister and I like his children. We spent most Yom Tovim together, and he learned with me often and taught me many aspects of true Yiddishkeit.

He was a man of great intellect and great principle. He spent a short time as a pulpit rabbi. The rest of his brief but very productive life was in *chinuch*, the field of Jewish education. His innovations and contributions to the advancement of modern and progressive concepts in *chinuch* remain the model today for effective Jewish education.

He was the inspiration and, perhaps, the most important

impetus for my entering the Rabbinate. His untimely death on Tisha b'Av has made my mourning for the national tragedies of this day compounded with my personal mourning as I observe his yahrzeit and say kaddish for him on this, the saddest day on the Jewish calendar.

In regards to our first question, our Rabbanim feel that continued observance of Tisha b'Av is not only vitally important but absolutely mandatory. Unlike our non-religious brethren, we believe that Tisha b'Av is a most essential element of the Jewish past as well as that of the Jewish future. According to HaRav Shimon Schwab *zt"l*, HaRav Pinchas Teitz *zt"l*, and others, Tisha b'Av is the national day of mourning for all Jewish tragedies down through the years. This is especially so when we recite the *Kinos,* where we make mention of the horrors of the Crusades, the Spanish Inquisition, and the Shoah.

Thus, Tisha b'Av serves as a time for us to remember and commemorate all the tragedies that have befallen our people down through the ages. It began with the Bnei Yisrael crying for no reason on that first Tisha b'Av in the desert and continued with the destruction of both Temples. It remains a collective day of mourning even today for all of our צרות and tragedies.

The *Churban* of the Beis HaMikdash has become the model, the paradigm, for all future destructions. The book of Eichah, Lamentations, which Yirmiyahu wrote with divine inspiration is read on Tisha b'Av. Its poetry refers not only to the calamitous loss of the Beis HaMikdash; it contains within it the pain and the mourning of all areas of loss.

Rav Mordechai Gifter *zt"l*, the late Telzer Rosh HaYeshivah, explains that the words of the Navi Yirmiyahu, written over 2,500 years ago, are still quite relevant today. *Chazal* interpret Yirmiyahu's outcry of על אלה אני בוכיה – *"For these do I cry"* as referring to the events that occurred during the destruction of the

Second Beis HaMikdash, even though the prophet lived at the time of the First Beis HaMikdash. His words are the vehicle for us to view and understand the events of our time in the broad historical continuum through an *Emunah* perspective. In the words of Rav Gifter:

> When referring to Tisha B'Av, the Prophet Yirmiyahu calls this day a מועד, a word that usually refers to a festival. The Telshe Rav, HaRav Avraham Yitzchok Bloch, explains that the word מועד is derived from word ועד, appointment. It is a time when Hashem meets with the world, when His greatness is manifested. This greatness can be seen from two angles: through the miracles of redemption, joy and happiness, as with the Exodus from Egypt, or through destruction so great that it could have only been administered by divine plan. From the time the Second Temple was destroyed through the present, and on until the final redemption, we are caught in one long moment of "going out of Jerusalem," punctuated by especially harrowing experiences such as the Holocaust.

Therefore, the observance and commemoration of Tisha b'Av as a major fast day is not only very relevant today, it is absolutely necessary. Thus, many Rabbanim, including the Rav, HaRav Joseph Soloveitchik *zt"l,* maintain that the age-old *Tefillos* which we recite over the *Churban Beis HaMikdash* must remain intact. The Rav said that until the coming of the Moshiach and the building of the Third Beis HaMikdash, these prayers cannot nor should not be deleted or changed in any form.

We may address our second question, the issue of why Tisha b'Av is viewed as a *Moed,* a holiday, by examining an episode in the life of our patriarch, Yaakov Avinu. In Sefer Beraishis, we are told about the jealousies and hatreds which developed between Yaakov's older sons and Yosef, his most beloved. We read how the brothers, in a moment of rage, seized the young man, sold him as a slave, and then dipped his coat of many colors in animal blood. They then told their father Yaakov that Yosef was devoured by a wild animal.

Yaakov was shocked and grieved by the news. He tore his garments and mourned for many days. In fact, he refused to be consoled or comforted. Why, ask our *Chachamim*, did Yaakov not accept the inevitable? Why didn't he accept the will of G-d in whom he had a profound faith and end this period of mourning? In fact, the Halacha sets a definite period of time for one to mourn, after which one must begin to reconstruct his life. For all relatives, save for parents, the *aveilus*, the mourning period, only lasts for 30 days. And even for parents, the limit of *aveilus* is one year.

The Midrash in Beraishis Rabbah provides an answer. It says that a person does not accept consolation for the living whom he thought dead. Upon the dead it is decreed that after a certain period, they will be forgotten. The living, however, will always be remembered. When Yaakov Avinu was confronted with the evidence of Yosef's death, he continuously mourned for his beloved son. In fact, even after the prescribed period of *aveilus*, Yaakov refused to be consoled. He never ever forgot about Yosef. Even after the passage of two decades since his disappearance, Yaakov's grief was never mitigated. Although Yaakov believed Yosef to be dead, his memory of his son did not abate one iota due to the fact that he was, in truth, still alive.

This my friends, in essence, is the message of Tisha b'Av and in fact all of Jewish history. When the first Beis HaMikdash was destroyed and the Jewish political community was decimated, the Jews were sent into exile. These poor, impoverished individuals were led in chains to Babylon past the ruins of Yerushalayim. Their response to this tragedy was not one of despair but one of hope and optimism in the future. They exclaimed: אם אשכחך ירושלים תשכח ימיני,

Tisha B'Av

"If I forget thee, O Jerusalem, may my right hand forget it's cunning." To these exiles, Jerusalem and Judea may have been physically destroyed; it may have been reduced to rubble; Jewish sovereignty may have temporarily ceased; but the hope for the future was very much alive. "Israel will be rebuilt," they said. "Jerusalem will be restored to its former majestic glory. Jewish self-rule and government will one day be reestablished by Hashem." The exiled Jews knew that so long as they remained inconsolable over the loss of the Beis HaMikdash, its future construction was guaranteed. Just as Yaakov's endless mourning was a proof to Yosef's survival, our commitment to continually mourn the Beis HaMikdash is the true evidence that it will one day be rebuilt. Therefore, on Tisha b'Av, we mourn for the loss which is in our hearts, but we also look into the future.

The prayers of *Tachanun* and *Selichos* are omitted to indicate the optimism, the hope for the future of the Jew. We believe that this day of mourning will eventually become a Yom Tov, a festival and a day of rejoicing. We believe that on this very day, the saddest day presently in the Jewish calendar, the Moshiach was born. One day, from out of the depths of despair and destruction, the Jew will rise once again. He will do so with renewed faith and determined purpose. This day will be transformed into a happy and glorious day; one of abundant joy and elation.

The hope of the Jew, thus, is to have his dreams fulfilled, as did our father Yaakov. For as he lived to see his beloved son, Yosef, alive again, we too shall see our homeland completely and totally rebuilt amidst peace and tranquility. One day, we will see the Beis HaMikdash of old restored in all of its glory. Tisha b'Av, thus, is not only a day of sorrow and mourning; it is also a day in which we gain determination and begin to hope for the future. It is a day when we are spiritually strengthened. The prophetic message is that the day will soon come when iniquity will be wiped from the earth and when the world, united in peace, will acknowledge the one true G-d as the L-rd of all mankind. We pray that this day shall soon arrive. Amen.

Index

A

American Judaism 48
Anti-Semitism 205, 210, 241
Assimilation 180, 211, 284

C

Conservative Judaism 177, 276, 337

E

Entebbe 34

F

Fink, Rebbetzin Fruma 194

G

Genauer, Rabbi Heshy 136

H

Holocaust 50, 68, 73, 86, 140, 199, 229, 257, 264

I

Intermarriage 82, 121

J

Jewish Pride 126

L

Levin, Rabbi Yaakov 259

M

Menachem Begin 28

Missionaries 206
Modernity 168

O

Open Orthodoxy 277

R

Reform Judaism 174, 276

S

Salanter, Rabbi Yisrael 249
Six Day War 137
Soviet Jewry 115, 131
Spanish Inquisition 77, 82, 108
State of Israel 222
Supporting Israel 135

T

Tuchman, Rabbi Hyman 356

W

Warsaw Ghetto Uprising 312
Women in Judaism 255

Y

Yerushalayim, the Jewish claim 22
Yom HaAtzmaut 293
Yom Kippur War 90, 137

Z

Zionism 275

Made in the USA
Middletown, DE
01 September 2021